Gaut Gurley
Or, the Trappers of Umbagog
A Tale of Border Life

Daniel P. Thompson

Alpha Editions

This edition published in 2021

ISBN : 9789355391940

Design and Setting By
Alpha Editions
www.alphaedis.com
Email - info@alphaedis.com

As per information held with us this book is in Public Domain. This book is a reproduction of an important historical work. Alpha Editions uses the best technology to reproduce historical work in the same manner it was first published to preserve its original nature. Any marks or number seen are left intentionally to preserve its true form.

Contents

CHAPTER I.	- 1 -
CHAPTER II.	- 11 -
CHAPTER III.	- 19 -
CHAPTER IV.	- 27 -
CHAPTER V.	- 36 -
CHAPTER VI.	- 42 -
CHAPTER VII.	- 54 -
CHAPTER VIII.	- 62 -
CHAPTER IX	- 77 -
CHAPTER X.	- 89 -
CHAPTER XI.	- 99 -
CHAPTER XII.	- 111 -
CHAPTER XIII.	- 127 -
CHAPTER XIV.	- 144 -
CHAPTER XV.	- 152 -
CHAPTER XVI.	- 169 -
CHAPTER XVII.	- 177 -
CHAPTER XVIII.	- 187 -
CHAPTER XIX.	- 198 -

CHAPTER XX.	- 215 -
CHAPTER XXI.	- 232 -
SEQUEL.	- 250 -

CHAPTER I.

"God made the country and man made the town."

So wrote the charming Cowper, giving us to understand, by the drift of the context, that he intended the remark as having a moral as well as a physical application; since, as he there intimates, in "gain-devoted cities," whither naturally flow "the dregs and feculence of every land," and where "foul example in most minds begets its likeness," the vices will ever find their favorite haunts; while the virtues, on the contrary, will always most abound in the country. So far as regards the virtues, if we are to take them untested, this is doubtless true. And so far, also, as regards the mere *vices*, or actual transgressions of morality, we need, perhaps, to have no hesitation in yielding our assent to the position of the poet. But, if he intends to include in the category those flagrant crimes which stand first in the gradation of human offences, we must be permitted to dissent from that part of the view; and not only dissent, but claim that truth will generally require the very reversal of the picture, for of such crimes we believe it will be found, on examination, that the country ever furnishes the greatest proportion. In cities, the frequent intercourse of men with their fellow-men, the constant interchange of the ordinary civilities of life, and the thousand amusements and calls on their attention that are daily occurring, have almost necessarily a tendency to soften or turn away the edge of malice and hatred, to divert the mind from the dark workings of revenge, and prevent it from settling into any of those fatal purposes which result in the wilful destruction of life, or some other gross outrage on humanity. But in the country, where, it will be remembered, the first blood ever spilled by the hand of a murderer cried up to Heaven from the ground, and where the meliorating circumstances we have named as incident to congregated life are almost wholly wanting, man is left to brood in solitude over his real or fancied wrongs, till all the fierce and stormy passions of his nature become aroused, and hurry him unchecked along to the fatal outbreak. In the city, the strong and bad passions of hate, envy, jealousy, and revenge, softened in action, as we have said, on finding a readier vent in some of the conditions of urban society, generally prove comparatively harmless. In the country, finding no such softening influences, and no such vent, and left to their own workings, they often become dangerously concentrated, and, growing more and more intensified as their self-fed fires are permitted to burn on, at length burst through every barrier of restraint, and set all law and reason alike at defiance.

And if this view, as we believe, is correct in regard to the operation of this class of passions, why not in regard to the operation of those of an opposite character? Why should not the same principle apply to the operation of love as well as hate? It should, and does, though not in an equal degree, perhaps, apply to them both. It has been shown to be so in the experience of the past. It is illustrated in many a sad drama of real life, but never more strikingly than in the true and darkly romantic incidents which form the groundwork of the tale upon which we are about to enter.

It was on a raw and gusty evening in the month of November, a few years subsequent to our last war with Great Britain, and the cold and vapor-laden winds, which form such a drawback to the coast-clime of New England, were fitfully wailing over the drear and frost-blackened landscape, and the wayfarers, as if keenly alive to the discomforts of all without, were seen everywhere hurrying forward to reach those comforts within which were heralded in the cheerful gleams that shot from many a window, when a showy and conspicuous mansion, in the environs of Boston, was observed to be lighted up to an extent, and with a brilliancy, that betokened the advent of some ambitious display on the part of the bustling inmates. Carriages from different parts of the city were successively arriving, discharging their loads of gaily-dressed ladies and gentlemen at the door, and rattling off again at the crack of the whips of the pert and jauntily equipped drivers. Others on foot, and from the more immediate neighborhood, were, in couples and singly, for some time constantly dropping in to swell the crowd, witness, and perhaps add to, the attractions of the occasion, which was obviously one of those social gatherings that have been sometimes, in conventional phrase, not inaptly denominated a *jam*; where people go to be in the fashion, to see, be seen, and try as hard as they can to be happy; but where the aggregate of happiness enjoyed is probably far less, as a general rule, than would be enjoyed by the same company at home in the pursuit of their ordinary avocations.

Meanwhile, as the guests were assembling and being conducted to the withdrawing rooms, through the cash-bought and obsequious politeness of some of the troop of waiters hired for the occasion, the master of the mansion had taken his station in the nook of a window commanding the common entrance, and was there stealthily noting, as the company, severally or one group after another, mounted the doorsteps, who had honored his cards of invitation whom he wished to see there, and who had come whom he wished to have stayed away. He was a well-favored man, somewhat past the middle age of life, with regular features, and a good general appearance, but with one of those unsettled, fluctuating countenances which are usually found in men who, while affecting, perhaps, a show of independence, lack self-reliance, fixed principles, or some other of the essential elements of character. And such indeed was Mark Elwood, the reputedly wealthy merchant whom we have thus introduced as one of the leading personages of our story. Though often moved with kind and generous impulses, he yet was governed by no settled principles of benevolence; though often shrewd and sagacious, he yet possessed no true wisdom; and, though often bold and resolute in action, he yet lacked the faith and firmness of true courage. In short, he might be regarded as a fair representative of the numerous class we are daily meeting with in life,—men who do many good things, but more questionable ones; who undertake much, accomplish little; bustle, agitate, and thus contrive to occupy the largest space in public attention; but who, when sifted, are found, as Pope maliciously says of women, to

"have no character at all."

After pursuing his observations a while, with an air of disappointment or indifference, Elwood was about to turn away, when his eye caught a glimpse of an approaching group of guests, whose appearance at once lighted up his countenance with a smile of satisfaction, and he half-ejaculated: "There they come!—the solid men of Boston. The presence of these, with the others who will all serve as trumpeters of the affair, will quell every suspicion of my credit till some new strike shall place me beyond danger. Yes, just as I calculated, the money spent will be the cunningest investment I have made these six months. But who is that tagging along alone after the rest?" he added, his countenance suddenly changing to a troubled look, and slowly, and with a strange emphasis, pronouncing the name, "GAUT GURLEY!" he hurried away from his post of observation.

The person whose obviously unexpected appearance among the arriving guests had so much disturbed our host, having leisurely brought up the rear, now paused a few paces from the door, and took a deliberate survey of all that was visible through the windows of the scene passing within. He was a man of a personal appearance not likely to be forgotten. His strong, upright, well-proportioned frame, full, rounded head, and unexceptionable features, were unusually well calculated to arrest the attention, and, at a little distance especially, to secure the favorable impressions of others; but those impressions faded away, or gave place to opposite emotions, on a nearer approach, for then the beholder read something in the countenance that met his, which made him pause,—something which he could not fathom, but which at once disinclined him to any acquaintance with the man to whom that countenance belonged.

Perhaps it should be viewed as one of the kindest provisions of Providence, made in aid of our rights and instincts of self-preservation, that man should not be able wholly to hide the secrets of his heart from his fellow-men,—that the human countenance should be so formed that no schooling, however severe, can prevent it from betraying the evil thoughts and purposes which may be lurking within. It is said that God alone can read the secrets of the heart; but we have often thought that He has imparted to us more of this attribute of His omniscience than that which is vouchsafed us in any one of our other faculties; or, in other words, that, to the skill we may acquire by practice in reading the countenance, He has added something of the light of intuition, to enable us to pierce into the otherwise impenetrable recesses of the bosom, and thus guard ourselves against the designs which may there be disclosed, and which, but for that, the deceptions of the tongue might forever conceal. All this, we are aware, may pass as a mere supposition; yet we think its correctness will be very generally attested by officers of justice, policemen, jailers, and all those who have had much experience in the detection of crime.

But, whether the doctrine is applicable or not in the generality of cases, it was certainly so in that of the unbidden guest whose appearance we have attempted to describe. Unlike Elwood, he had character, but all those who closely noted him were made to feel that his character was a dark and dangerous one.

After Gaut, for such he was called among his acquaintance, had leisurely run his eye from window to window of the many lighted apartments of the house, and scanned, as he did, with many a sneering smile, the appearances within, as long as suited his pleasure, he boldly walked in, and, with all the assurance of the most favored, proceeded to mingle with the company.

On quitting his lookout, Elwood repaired to the reception-room, where Mrs. Elwood, the mistress of the mansion, was already in waiting, nerving herself to perform, as acceptably as she could, her part of the stereotyped ceremony of receiving the guests, and exchanging with them the salutations and commonplaces of the evening. Mrs. Elwood, though not beautiful, nor even handsome, was yet every way a comely woman; and the quiet dignity and the unpretending simplicity of her manner, together with a certain intelligent and appreciating cast of countenance, which always rested on her placid, features, seldom failed to impress those who approached her with feelings of kindness and respect. She looked pale and fatigued, from the labors and anxieties she had gone through in the preparations for the present occasion; and, in addition to this, which is ever the penalty to the mistress of the house in getting up a large party, there was an air of sadness in her looks that told of secret sorrows which were not much mitigated by all the show of wealth that surrounded her.

By this time the company, having mostly arrived and divested themselves of hats, gloves, bonnets, shawls, together with all other of the loose etceteras of dress then in vogue, and carefully consulted the confidential mirrors to secure that adjustment of collars, curls, smirks, and smiles which are deemed most favorable for effect in public, were now shown into the suit of apartments where the host and hostess were waiting to receive them.

But it is far from our purpose to attempt a detailed description of the thousand little nothings which go to make up the character of one of these great fashionable parties. Who ever came from one the wiser? Not one guest in ten, probably, is found engaged in a conversation in which the ordinary powers of the speaker are exercised. A forced glee and smartness seem everywhere to prevail among the company, who are continually sacrificing their common sense in their eager attempts to appear gay and witty. Who was ever made really happier by being in such an assemblage? Although the participants may exhibit to casual observation the semblance of enjoyment, yet a close inspection will show that they are only *acting*, and that, as we have already intimated, their apparent enjoyment is no more deserving the name of social happiness than that which is often represented as enjoyed by a company of stage actors, in the harassing performance of the fictitious scenes of some genteel comedy. Who was ever made any better? Any rational discussion tending to exalt or purify the mind would be deemed out of place; and any moral teachings would be ridiculed or find no listeners. And, finally, who was ever made healthier? In the bad air generated among so many breaths in confined apartments, the high nervous excitement that usually prevails among the company, and the exposure to cold or dampness to which their unprepared systems are often subjected in returning home, Death has marked many a victim for his own; while, at the best, lassitude and depression are sure to follow, from which it will require days to recover.

In these strictures on overgrown parties, we would not, of course, be understood as intending to include the smaller social gatherings, where men and women do not, as they are prone to do in crowds, lose their sense of personal responsibility, in deporting themselves like rational beings; for such doubtless often lead to pleasing and instructive interchange of thought, and the cultivation of those little amenities of life which are scarcely less essential than the virtues themselves in the structure of good society.

But it is time we had returned from this digression to the characters and incidents immediately connected with the action of our tale.

A short time after the frosts of formality, which usually attend the introductory scenes of such assemblages, had melted away and given place to the noisy frivolities of the evening, and while the bustling host, and pale, anxious-looking hostess, were together taking their rounds among their three hundred guests, bestowing their attentions on the more neglected, calling out the more modest, and exchanging civilities with all,—while this was passing, suddenly there arose from without a confused noise, as of quick movements and mingling voices, which, from its character and the direction whence it came, obviously indicated some altercation, or other disturbance, at the outer door. This attracting the quickened attention of Mr. and Mrs. Elwood, the former left his companion, and was threading his way through the throng, when he was met by a servant, who in a flurried under-tone said:

"There is out here at the door, Mr. Elwood, a sort of a countryfied, odd-looking old fellow, in rusty brown clothes, that has been insisting on coming in, without being invited here to-night, and without telling his business or even giving his name. And he pressed so hard that we had to drive him back off the steps; but he refused to go away, even then, and kept asking where Mark was."

"Mark! why, that is my given name: didn't you know it?" said Elwood, rebukingly.

"No, sir, I didn't," replied the fashionable *pro tempore* lackey. "And if I had, my orders has always been on sech occasions not to admit any but the invited, who won't send in their names, or tell their business. And I generally calculate to go by Gunter, and do the thing up genteel."

"Well, well," said Elwood, impatiently cutting short the other in the defence of his professional character, and leading the way to the door, "well, well, we had better see who he is, perhaps."

When they reached the front entrance, they caught, by means of the reflected light of the entry and chambers, an imperfect view of the object of their proposed scrutiny, walking up and down the bricked pathway leading to the house. But, not being able to identify the new-comer with any one of his acquaintances, at that distance, Elwood walked down and confronted him; when, after a momentary pause, he siezed the supposed intruder by the hand, and, in a surprised and agitated tone, exclaimed:

"My brother Arthur! How came you here?"

"By steam and stage."

"Not what I meant: but no matter. We were not expecting you; and I fear the waiters have made a sad mistake."

"As bad an one as I did, perhaps, in declining to be catechized at my brother's door."

"No, *you* were right enough; but the waiters, being only here for the extra occasion,—the bit of flare-up you see we have here to-night,—and not knowing you, thought they must do as others do at such times. So overlook the blunder, if you will, and walk in."

Mark Elwood, much chagrined and discomposed at the discovery of such an untoward first reception of his brother, now ushered him into the brilliantly-lighted hall, where the two stood in such singular contrast that no stranger would have ever taken them for brothers,—Mark being, as we have before described him, a good-sized, and, in the main, a good-looking man; while the other, whom we have introduced as Arthur Elwood, was of a diminutive size, with commonplace features, and a severe, forbidding countenance, made so, perhaps, by intense application to business, together with the unfavorable effect caused by a blemished and sightless eye.

"Well, brother," said Mark, after a hesitating and awkward pause, "shall I look you up a private room, or will you go in among the company,—that is, if you consider yourself in trim to join them?"

"Your rooms must all be in use, and I should make less trouble to go in and be lost in the crowd. My trim will not kill anybody, probably," was the dry reply to the indirect hint of the other.

In all this Mark's better judgment coincided; but he had no moral courage, and, fearing the cut and color of his somewhat outre-looking brother's garments might excite the remarks of his fashionable guests, he would have gladly disposed of him in some private manner till the company had departed. Finding him, however, totally insensible to all such considerations, he concluded to make the best of it, and accordingly at once led the way into the guest-crowded apartments.

Here, contrary to his doubting brother's expectation, Arthur Elwood, whose character appeared to be known to several of the wealthier guests, was soon treated with much respect, for, in addition to what a previous knowledge of him secured, Mrs. Elwood had promptly come forward to greet him, and be cordially greeted in return, and, unlike her husband, had not hesitated to bestow on him publicly the most marked attentions. As soon, however, as she had thus testified her sense of the superiority of worth over outward appearance, and thus, by her delicate tact, given him the consideration with the company which she thought belonged to the brother of her husband, she gracefully relinquished him to the latter; when the two, by tacit mutual consent, sought a secluded corner, and seated themselves for a private conversation.

"As I said, I did not expect you, Arthur," commenced Mark Elwood, in the unsteady and hesitating tone of one about to broach a matter in which he felt a deep interest. "I was not looking for you here at all, these days; but presumed, when I wrote you, that, if you concluded to grant the favor I asked, you would transact the business through the mail."

"Loans of money are not always favors, Mark," responded the other, thoughtfully; "and when I make them, I like to know whether they promise any real benefit. I could, as you say, have transacted the business through the mail, but I confess, Mark, I have lately had some misgivings and doubts whether your commercial fabric here in Boston was not too big and broad for the foundation; and I thought I would come, see, and judge for myself."

"But I only asked for the loan of a few thousands," said Mark, meekly. "The fact is, Arthur, that, owing to some bad luck and disappointments in money matters, I am, just now, a little embarrassed about meeting some of my engagements; and I trust you will not refuse to give me a lift. What say you, Arthur?"

"I don't say, but will see and decide," replied the other. "But, Mark," he added, after a pause, "Mark, what will this useless parade here to-night cost you?"

"O, a mere trifle,—a few hundreds, perhaps."

"And you think hundreds well spent, when you are wanting thousands to pay your debts, do you?"

"O, you know, Arthur, a man, to keep up his credit, must *display* a little once in a while."

"No, I did not know that, Mark. I did not know that the throwing away of hundreds would help a man's credit in thousands, especially with those whose opinion would be of any use to him. But go," added the speaker, rising, "go and see to your company: I can take care of myself."

The brothers, rising from an interview in which they had felt, perhaps, nearly an equal degree of secret embarrassment,—the one believing that his last hope hung on the result, and the other feeling conscious of entering on a most ungracious duty,—now separated, and mingled with the gay throng, who, swaying hither and thither, and, seemingly without end or aim, moving round and round their limited range of apartments, like the froth in the circling eddies of a whirlpool, continued to laugh, flirt, and chatter on, till the advent of the last act of the social farce,—the throwing open of a suit of hitherto sealed apartments, and the welcome disclosure of the varied and costly delicacies of the loaded refreshment tables, which the company, by their strong and simultaneous rush thitherward, the rattling of knives and forks, spoons and glasses, the rapid popping of champagne corks, and the low, eager hum of gratified voices that followed, evidently deemed the best, as well as the closing, act of the evening's entertainment.

While this scene was in progress, Gaut Gurley, who had been for some time in vain watching the opportunity, caught Mark Elwood unoccupied in one of the vacated apartments, and abruptly approached and confronted him.

"Well, what now, Gaut?" exclaimed Elwood, with an assumed air of pettishness, after finding there was no further chance of escaping an interview which he had evidently been trying to avoid; "what would you have now?"

"I would just know whether you intend to keep your engagement," replied Gurley, fixing his black, quivering eyes keenly on the other.

"What engagement?"

"To give me a chance to win back that money."

"Which you demand when you have taken from me an hundred to one!"

"And who had a better right? Through whose means did you make your fortune? Besides this, haven't I always given you a fair chance to win back all you could?"

"I want no more of such chances,"

"But you promised; and I want to know whether you mean to keep that promise or not."

"Supposing I do, you would not have me leave home to-night, would you?"

"Yes, to-night."

"But my brother, as you have already discovered, I presume, has just arrived on a visit; and you know I can't decently leave him."

"And what do *I* care for that? Say whether you will meet me at the old room, or not, as soon as your company have cleared out?"

"You are unreasonable, cruel, Gaut."

"Then say you will *not* go, and see what will come of it, Mark Elwood!"

"I must go—I *will* go, Gaut," replied Elwood, turning pale at the last intimation. "As soon as I get rid of the company, I will start directly for the place."

"Well, just as you can afford," said Gaut, doggedly, as he turned on his heel, and made his way out of the house.

Mark Elwood drew a long breath as he was thus relieved of the other's presence, and was leaving the room, when Mrs. Elwood, who had felt much disturbed at discovering among her guests one of whose questionable character and connection with her husband she was already apprised, and who, from an adjoining apartment, had caught a slight glimpse of the meeting just described, and enough of the conversation to enable her to guess at its import, hurriedly came forward, and, in a voice tremulous from suppressed emotion, said:

"You surely are not going out to-night, Mr. Elwood?"

"No—that is—only for a short time," he said, hesitating, and a little confused at the discovery of his design, which a second thought told him she had made; "only for a short time. But don't stop me to talk now; you see the company are retiring. I must see the gentlemen off."

"Mr. Elwood, I must be heard," persisted the troubled and anxious wife. "I cannot bear to have you go off, and leave your only brother, whom you have not seen for years, and for such company! O Mr. Elwood, how can you let that bad man—"

"Hush! don't get into such a stew. I shall soon be back," interrupted the other. "You can excuse my absence. There, I hear them inquiring for me. I must go," he added, abruptly breaking away, and leaving his grieved companion to hide her emotions as she best could from the guests who were now seen approaching for their parting salutations.

In a few minutes the company had dispersed for their respective homes, and with them, also, had unnoticed slipped away their infatuated host.

CHAPTER II.

"At first, he, busy, plodding poor,
Earned, saved, and daily swelled his store;
But soon Ambition's summits rose,
And Avarice dug his mine of woes."

For the better understanding of some of the allusions of the preceding chapter, and of others that may yet appear in different parts of our tale, as well, indeed, as for a better appreciation of the whole, we will here turn aside from the thread of the narrative just commenced, to take a brief retrospect of the leading events and circumstances with which the previous lives of the several personages we have introduced had been connected, and among which their characters had been shaped and their destinies determined.

Some twenty two or three years previous to the juncture we have been describing, Arthur and Mark Elwood, by the fruits of their unremitting industry as laborers on a farm in summers, and as pedlars of what they could best buy and sell in winters, added to the few hundred dollars patrimony they each inherited, were enabled, in a few years, to realize the object of their early ambition, in the opening of a small retail store, in one of the little outskirt villages of northern New-Hampshire.

Such, like that of hundreds of others among us who now count their wealth by half millions, was the slender beginning of these two brothers. And, although they were from the first, as we have seen them at the last, as different in their general characters as they were in their persons, they yet got on very well together; for, however they might disagree respecting the modes and means of acquisition, they were always as one in regard to the great result each alike had in view, and that was to make money and be rich. And, by a sort of tacit understanding, falling into the departments of business best suited to their different tastes and capacities, the quiet, cautious, calculating, and systematic Arthur confined himself to the store, kept the books, contrived the *ways and means*, and, in short, did the principal head-work of the establishment; while Mark, being of a more stirring turn, and, from his brisk *bon homme* manner and less scrupulous disposition, better calculated for drumming up customers and securing bargains for the store, did most of the outdoor business, riding about the country, contracting for produce, securing barter deal, and making himself, in all things, the runner and trumpeter of the company. At night they usually met together to compare notes and report progress; and they were never happier than when they sat down in their small store-room, hemmed in and surrounded by casks of nails, quintals of codfish, farming tools, etc., on one side, and narrow shelves of cheap calicos, India cottons, and flaunting ribbons, on the other, and recounted to each other the business and bargains of the day. Thus the two, working on, like the spring and balance-wheel of some piece of mechanism, in harmony together, soon placed themselves beyond all fears of failure, and seemed happy and contented with their situation and prospects.

This situation of affairs, however, was not destined to be of very long continuance. Not long after finding themselves safely on the highway to independence, they very naturally began to think of selecting, from among the fair young customers of their store, the ones who might make them eligible companions for life. And, as the wayward love-fates would have it, they both secretly fixed their affections on one and the same girl,—the pretty and sensible Alice Gregg, who, though a plain farmer's daughter, was, to the vexation and envy of her numerous rustic suitors, to be won by nothing short of one of the village merchants. Alice was not long in discovering her advantage, nor in deciding to avail herself of it, so far as to confine her election to one of these, her two undeclared lovers. And, after balancing a while in her mind the account between her judgment, which would have declared for the reserved but sterling Arthur, and her fancy, which clamored hard for the manly-looking and more social Mark, she finally yielded the reins to the latter, and took measures accordingly. After this, Arthur's taste in selecting a piece of goods did not, as before, seem to be appreciated. Her handkerchief was never dropped where he had any chance to pick it up; and she was never quite ready to go till Mark was nearest at hand to help her into her wagon or side-saddle. By this delicate system of female tactics, common with girls of more pretensions than Alice, she effectually repressed the advances of the one, and as effectually encouraged those of the other; and the result, as she had anticipated, was a declaration from Mark, an acceptance on her part, and a speedy marriage between them. Arthur's heart bled at the event; but it bled inwardly; and he had at least the consolation of believing that no one suspected the state of his feelings, except, perhaps, Alice, and he was not unwilling that *she* should know them. He therefore put the best face on the matter he could,—appeared wholly unconcerned,—attended the wedding, and with forced gayety *openly* wished the new married couple the happiness which he *secretly* wished was his own. The tender passion had been a new thing to the money-loving Arthur. By its elevating influences, he, who had looked for enjoyment only in wealth, had been enabled to raise his vision to a higher sphere of happiness. And thus to lose the bright glimpses, and be thrown back to earth again, was, in reality, however he might disguise the fact from others, a serious blow to his feelings, and one, indeed, which soon mainly led to a movement on his part that gave a new turn to his apparent destinies, and a no less one, probably, to those of his then almost envied brother Mark. For, finding it impossible to feel his former interest in business, in a place whose associations had become painful to him, he secretly resolved to leave it as soon as he believed he could do so without leading to any surmises respecting the true cause of the change he contemplated. Accordingly, in a few months, he began to suggest his own unfitness for making a profitable partner in country trade, and finally came out with a direct proposition to his brother to buy him out at a sum which he knew would be a temptingly low one. And the result was, that the proposition was accepted, "the partnership dissolved by mutual consent," and the released Arthur, with his portion, soon on his way to one of the eastern seaports, to set up business, as he soon did, for himself alone.

The withdrawal of Arthur Elwood deprived this little establishment of its only really valuable guidance, and left it to the chance fortunes of greater gains or greater losses than would have been likely to occur under the cautious and hazard-excluding system of business which he had adopted for its control. But, nothing for a year or two occurring to induce Mark Elwood to depart from the system under which the business had been conducted, and Arthur's prudent maxims of trade, to which he had been accustomed to defer, remaining fresh in his mind, he naturally kept on in the old routine, which he was the more willing to follow, as by it he found himself clearly on the advance. He was blessed in his family; for his wife, who had no undue aspirations for wealth or show, had not only proved an efficient helper by her economy and good counsels, but added still more to his gratification by bringing him a promising boy. Being the only trader of the village, or hamlet it might more properly be called, he was conscious of being the object of that peculiar kind of favor and respect which was then—more freely than at the present day, perhaps—accorded to the country merchant by the masses among whom he resided. And, finding his still comparatively moderate expectations thus every day fully realized, he was satisfied with his condition in the present, and hopeful and happy in the prospects it presented in the future; for the demon of unlawful gain had not then tempted him into forbidden paths by the lure of sudden riches.

But that demon at length came in the shape of Gaut Gurley. From what part of the country this singular and questionable personage originally came, was unknown, even in the neighboring village (which was within the borders of Maine) where he had recently located himself with a young wife and child. And, as he very rarely made any allusions to his own personal affairs, every thing relating to his origin, life, and employments, previous to his appearance in this region, was a matter of mere conjecture, and many a dark surmise, also, we should add, respecting his true character. For the last few years, however, he was known to have followed, at the appropriate seasons of the year, the business of trapping, or trading for furs with the Indians, around the northern lakes. He had several times passed through the village on his returns from his northern tours, and called on the Elwoods, whose contrasted characters he seemed soon to understand. But he pressed no bargains upon them for his peltries; for, disliking the close questionings and scrutinizing glances of Arthur, and finding he could make no final trade with Mark without the assent of the former, he gave up all attempts of the kind, and did not call again during the continuance of the partnership, nor till this time; when, finding that Mark was in trade alone, he announced his intention of spending some time in the village, to see what arrangements could be made, as he at first held out to Elwood, for establishing this as his place for the regular sales or deposit of his furs.

But the fur traffic, whatever it might have been formerly, was now not the main, if any part of the object he had in view. The times had changed, closing many of the old avenues of trade, but opening new ones to tempt the ever restless spirit of gain. And, although the fur trade was still profitable, there was yet another springing up, which, for those who, like him, had no scruples about engaging in it, promised to become far more so. The restrictions which it had been the policy of our government to throw around commerce, in the incipient stages of our last national quarrel with Great Britain, had caused an unprecedented rise in the prices of silks and other fine fabrics of foreign import. This had put whatever there was of the two alleged leading traits of Yankee character, acquisitiveness and ingenuity, on the *qui vive* to obtain those goods at the former prices, for the purpose of home speculation. And Canada, being separated by a land boundary only from the States, presented to the greedy eyes of hundreds of village mammonists, who, like Elwood, were plodding along at the slow jog of twenty per cent profits, opportunities of so purchasing as to quadruple their gains; which were quite too severe a test for their slender stock of patriotism to withstand. It was but a natural consequence, therefore, that all of them whose love of gain was not overcome by their fear of loss by detection and the forfeiture of their goods, should soon be found, in spite of all the vigilance and activity of the host of custom-house officers by whom the government had manned the Canadian lines, secretly engaged in that contraband traffic.

The history of smuggling as carried on between the Northern States and Canada, from the enactment of the embargo at the close of 1807, and especially from the enactment of the more stringent non-intercourse law of 1810, to the declaration of war in 1812, and even, to a greater or less extent, to the proclamation of peace in 1815, is a portion of our annals that yet remains almost wholly unwritten. Although the contraband trade in question was doubtless more or less followed along the entire extent of our northern boundaries, from east to west, yet along no portions of them half so extensively, probably, as those, of Vermont and New Hampshire, which, from their close contiguity to Montreal and Quebec, the only importing cities of the Canadas, afforded the most tempting facilities and the best chances for success. Along these borders, indeed, it was for years one almost continuous scene of wild warfare between the custom-house officers and their assistants, and the smugglers and their abettors, both parties carrying arms, and the smugglers, especially, going armed to the teeth. In these skirmishes many were, at different times, killed outright; many more were missing, even on the side of the officials, for whom dark fates were naturally conjectured; while hundreds, on both sides, were crippled or otherwise seriously wounded. Sometimes, when a double sleigh, or wagon, deeply laden with smuggled goods, in charge of three or four stout and resolute fellows aboard, who, with as many more, perhaps, of their confederates on horseback or in light teams, before and behind, were making their way, at full speed, with their prize, from the line to some secret and safe depository in the interior, was suddenly beset and brought to a stand by an equal or greater number of government officials, deeply intent on a seizure, a most furious conflict would ensue, in which the combatants, growing desperate for the seizure or defence of the prize, would ply their hard yeoman fists, clubs, loaded whipstocks, or whatever was at hand, with terrible effect, and often prolong the melee till the snow or ground was encrimsoned with blood, and scarcely an uninjured man remained on the ground. Sometimes the besetting officials were made prisoners, and marched off at the cocked pistol's mouth into the deep woods, and, after being led forward and backward through the labyrinths of the forest till bewildered and lost, were suddenly left to find their way out as they best could,—a feat which there was no danger of their accomplishing till long after both the smugglers and their goods were beyond the reach of pursuers. And sometimes the smugglers, when closely pressed and seeing no hope of rescue if taken, as their last resort, drew their dirks and pistols; and wo to the official who then persisted in attempting a seizure.

But the system of tactics more generally practiced by the smugglers was that of craft and concealment, carried out by some ingenious measure to prevent all suspicion of the times and places of their movements, by travelling in the night or in stormy weather, or in the most unfrequented routes, and, when pursued, by putting the pursuers on false scents, or by feints of running away with loads of empty boxes to mislead pursuit, till the goods, which had been previously taken to some place of temporary concealment, could be removed from the vicinity of the search and sent on their destination.

Such were the general features of the illicit traffic which characterized the period of which we are treating,—a traffic which laid the foundations of many a village fortune, whose dashing heirs would not probably be very willing to acknowledge the true source from which the wealth and position they may now be enjoying was derived,—and finally a traffic which, in its attending homicides and desperate affrays, its hot pursuits and marvellous escapes, its curious concealments and artful subterfuges, and, lastly, in the family and neighborhood feuds which it left behind, would furnish materials for a series of tales as wild and romantic, if not always as creditable to the actors, as any thing ever yet spread before the public.

It was this questionable business which was then occupying the thoughts of Gaut Gurley, and in which it was his aim to involve Mark Elwood, whom he had pitched on for the purpose, as not only a man of sufficient means, with no scruples which could not be overcome, but a man whom he believed he could make dependent on him, when once enlisted, and to whom he could dictate terms for his own services. And it is no wonder that a man of his dark cunning, working on one of the obtuse moral sense, the love of money, and the thoughtlessness of consequences, of Elwood, should, as he did, soon completely succeed in his objects. For, after having kindled Elwood's political prejudices against the embargo law, which was held up to be such an outrage on the commercial rights of the North that it were almost a merit to violate it, Gaut proceeded to show how enormous were the profits to be made in this trade, and how safely the goods might be smuggled in, through the back roads and forest routes with which he was familiar, by employing Frenchmen, as he could, at a cheap rate, to bring them in large panniers on the backs of their Canadian ponies, or by engaging Indians, who could be enlisted for even less wages, to bring them in knapsacks through the woods. And so clearly did he demonstrate all this to the mind of Elwood, that the latter, being unable any longer to resist the temptation of thus securing the gains of a traffic, by the side of which the small profits of his store at home dwindled into contempt, soon resolved to engage in it.

From this time Gaut was in high favor with Elwood. The two, indeed, seemed to have suddenly become inseparable. They were always found together, and always engaged in some closely private conversation, the purport of which no others were permitted to know, or were enabled to conjecture, except from the new business movement which was observed soon to follow the forming of their mysterious connection. And that movement was that Elwood put his store in charge of a clerk, and, giving out that he was about to engage more extensively in the fur trade, which would require him to be often absent, went off with a strong and fleet double team, in a northerly direction, with Gaut for his only companion.

With the advent of this new era in the life of Elwood, every thing became changed about his establishment. His bustling presence, with his bantering, off-hand, and communicative talk, no longer enlivened the store and neighborhood; and people, who before seemed to know every thing about his business and plans, now knew nothing. For he was now most of the time absent in conducting his operations at the north, or in his stealthy journeyings thence to the cities, to receive and dispose of the valuable packages which he had put on their passage. He generally came and departed in the night, and, even during his brief stays at home, he kept himself secluded, seeming to wish to be seen as little as possible. All this, of course, led to considerable talk and various speculations; but he so well shrouded his movements from the public, and kept afloat so many plausible stories to account for his change of business, that he prevented suspicions from taking any definite shape about home, or spreading abroad to any extent that endangered his operations, although those operations were constantly continued for years, and, from cautious and small beginnings, at length became more bold, extensive, and successful, perhaps, than any thing of the kind ever carried on in the interior of New England. But there was one whose suspicions of the true character of the business in which he was engaged, notwithstanding his denials and evasions, even to her, and whose fears and anxieties on account of the dangers she believed he was constantly incurring, not only from seizure of his property and the personal violence to which he was exposed in trying to defend it, but from his association of reckless confederates, especially Gaut Gurley, of whose dark character, as little as she had seen of him, she was already filled with an instinctive dread,—there was one whose suspicions, and consequent anxieties, he could never succeed in quieting; and that was his discreet and faithful wife. She had, during the first year or two of his new career, often expostulated with him on the doubtful character of his business; but he, by always making light of her fears, by telling her some truth and withholding more, and disclosing as great a part of his astonishing gains as he supposed would pass with her for honest acquisitions, generally silenced, if he did not convince, her; and she, finding him always light-hearted and satisfied with himself, when he came home, finally ceased her remonstrances, having concluded she would try to conquer her doubts and fears, or at least say no more on the subject.

At length, however, after a prolonged absence on a tour, in which he had a large venture at stake, he came home in a greatly altered mood. His usual buoyancy of spirits was gone; he appeared gloomy and abstracted; and, although, in reply to the anxious inquiries of his wife, he represented himself to have been entire successful,—even to a greater extent than ever before,— yet it was quite obvious that something very untoward, to say the least, must have happened to him. He would not leave his house after dark, he placed loaded pistols within the reach of his hand when he went to bed, and he would often start up wildly from his sleep. His whole conduct, indeed, was such as to excite the deeper concern of his perplexed wife, for she feared it betokened his connection with something very wrong,—something that had brought him into deadly peril,—something, perhaps, done to others, which made her tremble to think of, but something, at all events, which made her more than ever dread to have him go back again to the scene of his operations. But of the last-named of her fears she was shortly relieved; for, to her agreeable surprise, he soon assured her of his determination to break off entirely from the business he had been pursuing, and, as much to her gratification as to the evident vexation of Gaut Gurley, who had come on to look his employer up, he firmly persisted in carrying out his resolution. Nor was this all. He rapidly drew his business to a close, broke off his old associations, privately left the place, and, in a few weeks, sent for his family to join him in Boston, where it appeared he had been for some time secretly transferring his capital, and where he had now established himself in business, with all the means required, even there, of doing it to the best advantage. And for some years he *did* engage in business to advantage, the same strangely good luck attending him, and prospering wonderfully in all he undertook, till he gained the reputation of being among the wealthiest of the city. But the spoiler came in a second appearance of Gaut Gurley, who, having squandered in the country the bounteous sums of money which Elwood had paid him for his services, now followed the latter to the city. And, with the coming of that personage, together with the foolish ambition that had, about that time, seized Elwood, to outshine some of his city competitors in display and expensive living, commenced the wane of a fortune which, as large as it was, it had required but two short years to bring to the verge on which we represented its unhappy master as standing in the opening scene of our story.

Having now related all we designed in this retrospect of events, we will return from the somewhat long but necessary digression, and take up the thread of the narrative where we left it.

CHAPTER III.

"I strive in vain to set the evil forth.
The words that should sufficiently accurse
And execrate the thing, hath need
Come glowing from the lips of eldest hell.
Among the saddest in the den of woe,
Most sad; among the damn'd, most deeply damn'd."

Once on a time, before the dark catalogue of vices was made complete by the wicked inventions of men, or the evil made to counterbalance the good in the world, the Arch Enemy of mankind, deeply sensible of the vantage-ground occupied by the antagonistic Being, and anxiously casting about him for the means of securing an equilibrium of power, called around him a small company, consisting of those of his Infernal subjects whom he had previously noted for their excellence, in subtility and devilish invention, and, after fully explaining his wants and wishes to his keenly appreciating auditory, made proclamation among them, that the Demon who should invent a new vice, which, under the name and guise of Pastime, should be best calculated to seduce men from the paths of virtue, pervert their hearts, ruin them for earth and educate them for hell, should be awarded a crown of honor, with rank and prerogative second only to his own. He then, with many a gracious and encouraging word to incite in them a spirit of emulation, and nerve them for exertion in the important enterprise thus set before them, dismissed them, to go forth among men, observe, study, and come again before him on a designated time, to report the results of their respective doings, and submit them to his decision. Eager to do the will of their lord and Lucifer; as well as to gain the tempting distinctions involved in his award, the commissioned, fiend-group dispersed, and scattered themselves over the earth, which was understood to be their field of operations. And, after noting, as long as they chose, all the different phases of human society, the secret inclinations of those composing it, their follies, weaknesses, and points most vulnerable to temptation, they each returned to the dark dominions whence they came, to cogitate in retirement, concoct and reduce to form those schemes for securing the great object in view, which their observations and discoveries on earth had suggested.

At the time appointed for the hearing and decision, the demoniac competitors again assembled before their imperial arbiter; not this time in secret conclave, but in the presence of thousands of congregated fiends, who, having been apprised of the new plan about to be presented for peopling the Commonwealth of Hell with recruits from earth, had come up in all directions from their dismal abodes, to hear those plans reported, and witness the awarding of the prize for the one judged most worthy of adoption.

Lucifer then mounted his throne, commanded silence, and ordered the competitors to advance and present, in succession, such plans as they would lay before him for his consideration and decision. They did so; and one of them, a young and genteel-looking devil, to whom, from a suppose congeniality of tastes and feelings with the objects of his care, had been especially assigned the duty of supervising the fashionable walks of society, now stepped confidently forward and said:

"I present for your consideration, most honored Lucifer, I present FASHION as one of those social institutions of men which might the most easily become, with a little fostering at our hands, to us the most productive of vices, under a name least calculated to alarm. It already holds an almost omnipotent sway over the wealthier, or what they call the higher, classes of society, who hesitate at no sins that can be committed with its sanction; and the disposition is every day growing stronger and stronger, among all classes, to fall in with its behests. Encourage its progress, make its rule absolute with all, and the world's boasted morality would trouble us, devils, no more. This would be the direct and natural result among the most wealthy, who would leave no vice unpracticed, no sin uncommitted, provided they could excuse themselves under plea that it was fashionable. With those of more limited means the effect would be still better; for devotion to Fashion would beget extravagance—extravagance, poverty—poverty, desperation—desperation, crime; so with all classes, the result, for our purpose, would be equally favorable and *much the same*. The new vice I therefore propose is the one to be made out of, and go under the name of, FASHION."

"There may be something in this conception," said Lucifer, thoughtfully, after the speaker had closed; "but is it safe against all contingencies? What if the world should take it into their heads to make it fashionable to be good?"

"Not the least danger of that," rejoined the other, promptly. "That is a contingency about as likely to happen as that your highness should turn Christian," he added, with a sardonic grin.

"You are right," responded Lucifer; "and, as your scheme comes within the rule, on the score of originality, we will reserve it for consideration."

"My plan," said the next demon who spoke, "consists in inciting man to the general use of intoxicating drinks, under the plea of taking a social glass; for, let the use of these become general, and all men were devils ready made, and——"

"True, most true!" interrupted Lucifer; "but that is not new. That is a vice I invented myself, as long ago as the time Noah was floating about in the ark, and the first man I caught with it was the old patriarch himself. Since then it has been my most profitable agent in the earth, bringing more recruits to my kingdom than all the other vices put together. But our present movement was to insure something new. The plan, therefore, does not come within the rule, and must be set aside."

"The new vice which I propose," said the third demon who came forward, "is involved in the general cultivation of music, which I contend would render men effeminate, indolent, voluptuous, and finally vicious and corrupt, so that whole nations might eventually be kept out of heaven and secured for hell through its deteriorating influences."

"I am not a little dubious about trying to make a vice out of music, which would be all reliable for our purposes," remarked Lucifer, with a negative shake of the head. "I fear it might prove a sword which would cut both ways. It may, it is true, be doing a pretty fair business just now in some localities; but methinks I already see, in the dim vista of the earth's future, a cunning Wesley springing up, and exhorting his brethren 'Not to let the Devil have all the good tunes, but appropriate them to the service of the Lord.' Now if the religious world should have wit enough, as I greatly fear me they would, to follow the sagacious hint of such a leader, they might make music an agency which would enlist two followers for the white banner of Heaven where it would one for the red banner of Hell. The experiment would be one of too doubtful expediency to warrant the trial. The proposition, therefore, cannot be entertained."

Many other methods of creating an efficient new vice were then successively proposed by the different competitors; but they were all, for some deficiency, or want of originality, in turn, rejected, till one more only remained to be announced; when its author, an old, dark-eyed demon, who was much noted for his infernal cunning, and who, conscious perhaps of the superiority of his device, had contrived to defer its announcement till the last, now came forward, and said:

"The scheme I have devised for the accomplishment of the common object of the patriotic enterprise which your Highness has put afoot, proposes a new vice, which, passing under the guise of innocent pastime, will not only, by itself, be fully equal to any other of the many vices now known among men, for its certainty to lure them to its embrace, fascinate, infatuate, deprave, and destroy them, but will insure the exercise and combine the powers of them all. It addresses itself to the intellectual by the implied challenge it holds out to them to make a trial of their skill; it appears to the unfortunate in business as a welcome friend, which is rarely turned away; it presents to pride and vanity the means of gratification that are not to be rejected; it holds out to avarice an irresistible temptation; it begets habits of drunkenness; and thus insures all the fruits of that desolating vice; it engenders envy, hatred, and the spirit of revenge; in short, it brings into play every evil thought and passion that ever entered the head and heart of man, while it the most securely holds its victims, and most speedily hunts them down to ruin and death."

"The name? the name?" eagerly shouted an hundred voices from the excited fiend-throng around.

"The name," resumed the speaker, in reply, "the name by which I propose to christen this new and terrible device of mine, to counteract the power of virtue, and curtail the dominions of Heaven, is GAMBLING!"

"Gambling! Gambling!" responded all hell, in thunders of applause; "and Gambling let it be," shouted Lucifer, as the prize was thus awarded by acclamation to the distinguished inventor of Gambling.

From this supposable scene among the demons, we pass, by no unnatural transition, to a kindred one among men.

In a back, secluded room, in the third story of a public house in Boston, of questionable respectability, there might have been found, a few hours after the dispersion of the party before described, a small band of men sitting around a table, intently engaged in games of chance, in which money was at stake; while on a sideboard stood several bottles of different kinds of liquors, with a liberal supply of crackers and cigars. Of this company, two, who have been already introduced to the reader,—Mark Elwood and Gaut Gurley,— seemed to be especially pitted against each other in the game. It was now deep into the night, and Elwood said something about going home. But his remark being received only with jeers by the company, he sank into an abashed silence and played on. Another hour elapsed, and he spoke of it again, but less decidedly. Another passed, and he seemed wholly to have forgotten his purpose; for he, as well as all the rest of the company, had, by this time, become intensely absorbed in the play, allowing themselves no respite or intermission, except to snatch occasionally a glass of liquor from the sideboard, in the entrancing business before them. And, as the sport proceeded, deeper and deeper grew the excitement among the infatuated participants, till every sense and feeling seemed lost to every thing save the result of each rapidly succeeding game; and the heat of concentrated thought and passion gleamed fiercely from every eye, and found vent, in repeated exclamations of triumph or despair, from every tongue, according to the varying fortunes of the parties engaged. On one side was heard the loud and exultant shout of the winner at his success, and on the other, the low bitter curse of the loser at his disappointment; the countenance of the one, in his joy and exultation, assuming the self-satisfied and domineering air of the victor and master, and the countenance of the other, in his grief and envy, darkening into the mingled look of the demon and the slave.

And thus played on this desperate band of gamesters till morning light, which, now stealing through the shutters of their darkened room, came and joined its voiceless monitions with those which their consciences had long since given them, in warning them to break up and return to their families, made wretched by their absence. So completely, however, had they abandoned themselves to the fatal witcheries of the play, that they heeded not even this significant admonition; but, with uneasy glances towards the windows, to note the progress of the unwelcome intrusions of day, turned with the redoubled eagerness often shown by those who know their time is limited to their hellish engagement.

Through the whole night, Fortune seemed to have held nearly an even scale between Elwood and his special adversary, Gaut Gurley, contrary to the evident anticipations of the latter, and despite all his attempts to secure an advantage. Thus far, however, he had signally failed in his purpose; and, at the last game, Elwood had even won of him the largest sum that had as yet been put at stake between them. This seemed to drive him almost to madness; and in his desperation he loudly demanded that the stakes should be doubled for the next trial. It was done. The game was played, and Gurley was again the loser.

"I will now stay no longer," said Elwood, rising. "I was forced here tonight, as you well know, Gurley, against my will, and against all reason, to stop your clamor for a chance to win back what you absurdly called your money lost at our last sitting; though Heaven knows that what I then won was but a pitiful fraction of the amount you have taken from me, within the last two years, in the same or in a worse way. I have now given you your chance,—yes, chance upon chance, all night,—till your claim has been a dozen times cancelled; and, I repeat I will stay no longer."

"You shall!" fiercely cried Gurley, with an oath. "You shall stay to give me another chance, or I will brand you as a trickster and a sneak!"

"Gentlemen," said Elwood, turning to the company, in an expostulating tone, "gentlemen, I appeal to you all if I have not—"

"I will have no appeal," interrupted Gurley, in a voice trembling with rage. "I say I *will* have another chance, or—"

"Take it, then," hastily interposed Elwood, as if unwilling to let the other finish the sentence; "take it: what will you have the stakes?"

"Double the last."

"Double?"

"Yes, double!"

"Have your own way, then," said Elwood, with forced composure, taking up and shuffling the cards for the important game.

The stake was for a thousand; and the trembling antagonists played as if life and death hung on the event. And the whole company, indeed, forgetful of their own comparatively slight interest, in the momentous one thus put at stake, at once turned their eyes on the two players, and watched the result with breathless interest. That result was soon disclosed; when, to the surprise of all, and the dismay of Gaut Gurley, the victory once more strangely fell to the lot of Mark Elwood, who, gathering up the stakes with trembling eagerness, hastily rose from the table, as if to depart.

"What in the name of Tophet does all this mean?" fiercely exclaimed Gurley, throwing an angry and suspicious look round the table upon those who had doubtless been, at other sittings, his confederates in fleecing Elwood. "Yes, what is the meaning of this? I ask *you*, and *you*, sir?"

"Better ask your own partner," said one of the men addressed, with a defiant look.

"Elwood? Pooh!" exclaimed Gaut, with a bitter sneer.

"And why not?" responded the former. "He may have as good luck as the best of us, as it appears he has had. And hark ye, Gaut, you look things at us that it might not be safe for you to say in this room."

"Gentlemen, you will all bear me out in leaving, now," here interposed Elwood, beginning to make towards the door.

"Stop, sir!" thundered Gaut. "You are not a-going to sneak off with all that money in your pocket, by a d—d sight!"

"Why not, sir?" replied Elwood; "why not, for all you can say?"

"Because I have lost, sir!" shouted Gurley, hoarse with rage. "I have lost three games running,—lost all I have. I demand a fair chance to win it back; and that chance I will have, or I'll make you, Mark Elwood, curse the hour you refused it."

"Gaut Gurley, you insatiate fiend!" exclaimed Elwood, in a tone of mingled anger and distress; "you it was who first led me into this accursed habit of play, by which you have robbed me of untold thousands yourself, and been the means of my being robbed of thousands more by others. You have brought me to the door of ruin before, and would now take all I have to save me from absolute bankruptcy."

"Whining hypocrite!" cried Gurley, starting up in rage. "Do you tell that story when you have my last dollar in your pocket? But your pitiful whining shall not avail you. If you leave this room alive, you leave that money behind you."

"Stop, stop!" here interposed one of the company, who had noted what had inadvertently fallen from Elwood, in his warmth, respecting his apprehended bankruptcy; "stop, no such recriminations and threatenings here! I can show Elwood a way to dispose of a part of his money, at least, without bringing on *any* one the charge of robbing or being robbed. Here is a note of your signing, Mr. Elwood,—a debt of honor,—for a couple of hundreds, contracted in this very room, you will remember. You may as well pay it."

"I have a similar bit of paper," said another, coming forward and presenting a note for a still larger sum.

"And I, likewise," said a third, joining the group, with an additional piece of evidence of Elwood's folly, in the shape of a gambling note; "and I shall insist on payment with the rest, seeing the money cannot be disposed of between you and Gaut without a quarrel and danger of bloodshed."

With a perplexed and troubled air Elwood paced the room a moment, without uttering a word in reply to the different demands that had so unexpectedly been made upon him. He glanced furtively towards the door, as if calculating the chances of escaping through it before any one could interpose to prevent him. He then glanced inquiringly at the company for such indications of sympathy or forbearance as might warrant the attempt; but in their countenances he read only that which should deter him from resorting to any such means of escaping the dilemma in which he now found himself. And, suddenly stopping short and turning to the new claimants for his money, he said:

"Well, gentlemen, have your way, then. I had hoped to be permitted to carry away money enough to meet my bills and engagements of to-day,—at least, as much as I brought here. But, as I am not to be allowed that privilege, hand on your paper, every scrap of my signing, and you shall have your pay."

A half-dozen notes of hand were instantly produced and thrown upon the table, and the holder of each was paid off in turn; the last of whom drew from Elwood nearly every dollar he had in his possession.

"There, gentlemen," he exclaimed, with a sort of desperate calmness, "in this line of deal, at least, my accounts are all squared. I am quits with you all."

"Not with me, by a d——d sight!" exclaimed Gurley, no longer able to restrain his rage at being thus baulked in his desperate purpose of getting hold of Elwood's money, by fair means or foul, before permitting him to leave the room. "Not with me, sir, till the amount of that last stake, which was just enough to make me whole, is again in my pocket; and I'll follow you to the gates of hell, but I'll have it!"

Cowering and trembling beneath the threats and fiendish glances of the other, Elwood siezed his hat, and rushed from the room.

On escaping from this "den of thieves," and gaining the street below, Elwood's first thought was of home and his shamefully neglected family, and he turned his steps in that direction. But, before proceeding far, he began to hesitate and falter in his course. He became oppressed with the feelings of a criminal. He was ashamed to meet his family; for, fully conscious that his looks must be haggard, his eyes red and bloodshot, and his whole appearance disordered, he knew his return in such a plight, at that hour in the morning, would betray the wretched employments of the night, especially to his keen-sighted brother, on whose assistance he now doubly depended to save him from ruin. He therefore changed his course, and was proceeding towards his store, when he met his confidential clerk, who was out in search of him, and who, in great agitation, informed him that his drafts of yesterday had all been returned dishonored; that bills were pouring in, and the holders clamorous for their pay. Struck dumb by the startling announcement, it was some moments before Elwood could collect his thoughts sufficiently to bid his clerk return, and put off his creditors till the next day, when he would try to satisfy them all. And, having done this, he turned suddenly into another street, wound his way back to the inn he had just left, took a private room, locked himself in, and for a while gave way to alternate paroxysms of grief, remorse, and self-reproaches. After exhausting himself by the violence of his emotions, he threw himself upon a bed, and, thinking an hour's repose might mend his appearance, so as to enable him the better to disguise the cause of his absence, on his return to his family, which he now concluded to defer till towards dinner-time, he fell into a slumber so profound and absorbing, that he did not awake till the shadows of approaching night had begun to darken his room.

Leaping from his couch, in his surprise and vexation at having so overslept himself, he hastily made his toilet, and immediately set out for home,—a home which, for the first time in his life, he now dreaded to enter. To that wretched home we will now repair, preceding his arrival, to relate what had there occurred in his absence.

CHAPTER IV.

"Better is a poor and wise child than an old and foolish *father*, who will no more be admonished."—ECCL.

After the breaking up of the party, as described in the former chapter, Arthur Elwood, on joining the family circle, and not meeting his host and brother there, as he naturally expected, expressed his surprise at the circumstance, and inquired the cause of his absence. But, perceiving that the subject gave pain to Mrs. Elwood, who deemed it prudent but to repeat, as she hesitatingly did, what her husband had told her, that he had gone out, soon to be back, the former forbore any further inquiries or comments, and soon retired to rest, wishing her a good-night and pleasant slumbers.

"Good-night and pleasant slumbers!" slowly and murmuringly repeated the anxious and troubled wife, on whose ear the words, kindly meant as she knew them to be, fell as if in mockery to her feelings. "Pleasant slumbers for me! Heaven grant they may be made so by his speedy coming; but—" and, being now alone, and thus relieved of the restraining presence of others, she burst into tears, and wept long and bitterly.

Woman was not created to act independently. The sphere in which she is formed to move, though different, is yet so immediately connected—with that of man, that her destiny is inseparable from his. Her happiness and prosperity are not in her own keeping. The welfare of the husband is the welfare of the wife; and, if poverty and disgrace, the concomitants of vice, fall on him, she must participate equally in the physical evil, and drink as much deeper of the cup of moral misery as her unblunted sensibilities are more lively, and her sense of right and wrong are more acute, than those of him who has become dead to the one and lost to the other. What wonder, then, that she should so agonize and weep in secret over his moral deviations, and all the more bitterly, because, with the most intense desire to do so, she has no power to remedy the evil? But, for that sorrow and suffering, who before high Heaven will be held responsible? Who, but the doubly-guilty husband whose conduct has caused them?

Through the whole of that, to her, long and dreary night, Mrs. Elwood never once thought of retiring to rest, but kept up her vigils in waiting and watching for her husband: now listening pensively to the wind that seemed to moan round her solitary apartment in unison with her own feelings; now straining her senses to catch some sound of his approach; and now, perhaps, throwing herself upon a sofa, and falling, for a moment, into a troubled slumber, but only to start up at the first sound of the rattling windows, to listen again, and again to be disappointed. In this manner she wore away the lingering hours of the night, till the long prayed-for daylight, which she supposed, at the farthest, would bring back her truant husband, made its welcome appearance. But daylight came not this time to remove the cause of her anxieties. Elwood had several times before staid out nearly through the night, but the approach of daylight had always, till now, brought him home; and, not making his appearance, as she confidently expected, she became, as the morning advanced, really alarmed for his personal safety, and would have immediately sent out for him, but she knew not whom to send. She therefore concluded to put off the already long-delayed breakfast no longer; and, summoning her brother-in-law, who, with herself (her son, whom we have yet more particularly to introduce to the reader, being temporarily absent from town), now constituted all the family remaining to join in the repast. The two then sat down to the table, and partook the meal mostly in gloomy silence, one still hoping all might yet turn out well, and therefore repressing her twofold apprehensions; and the other, out of regard to her feelings, kindly forbearing to pain her with remarks and inquiries on a subject which they mutually felt conscious was oppressing the hearts of both.

After the meal was over, Arthur Elwood arose, and, briefly announcing his intention of going out to look up his brother, who, he said, would be likely soon to be found at his store, left the house. At the usual dinner hour, Arthur Elwood returned to the house, and was met at the door by his anxious hostess, whose countenance quickly fell as she perceived him to be alone.

"Have you not yet seen my husband?" she eagerly demanded.

"No, but have heard of him. He is somewhere in the city, I believe," replied the other.

"In the city and not return?" persisted the surprised and distressed wife. "How can this be?—what does it mean?"

"I do not know," replied Arthur, with a thoughtful and perplexed air.

Mrs. Elwood for a moment stood mute as a statue; for, but too well conjecturing what was passing in the mind of the other, she durst not ask his opinion. But, soon regaining her usual composure, she led the way to the dinner-table, where the meal that followed was partaken much as the one that preceded it,—in silence and mutual constraint, which was only relieved by an occasional forced, commonplace remark.

"I shall again go to Mark's store," said Arthur, with stern gravity, as he rose from the table, after he had finished his repast, "and I shall also take the liberty of looking into the condition of his affairs. After that, I may return here again, though to remain only for a short time, as I leave for home in the evening."

Towards night Arthur Elwood returned, and in his usual quiet way entered the room where Mrs. Elwood was sitting; when, shaking his head as if in reply to the question respecting her still absent husband, which he saw, by the painfully inquiring expression of her countenance, was rising to her lips, he took a seat by her side, and, with an air of concern and a slight tremor of voice, commenced:

"I have been debating with myself, sister Alice, whether it were a greater kindness to go away without seeing you, and of course without apprising you of what I may have discovered respecting your husband and his affairs, or come here and tell you truths which would be painful,—too painful, perhaps, for you to bear."

"'Tis better I should know all," rather gasped than uttered Mrs. Elwood. "You will tell me the truth,—*others* may not. Go on."

"Your husband," resumed the other, "wrote me for the help of a few thousands, which I would have freely loaned, but for my suspicions that all was not right with him; and, as I plainly told him, I came on to ascertain for myself whether such help would be thrown away, or really relieve him, as he represented, from a mere temporary embarrassment. I have now been into the painful investigation, and find matters, I grieve to say, tenfold worse than I suspected. He is, and must have been for a long time, the companion and the victim of blacklegs and cutthroats, and—"

"I suspected,—I knew it," interrupted the eager and trembling listener; "and O Arthur, how I have tried and wept and prayed to induce him to break off from them; for I felt they would eventually ruin him."

"*Eventually* ruin him! Why, Alice, with his own miscalculations in business, folly and extravagance in every thing, they have done so already."

"But the main part of his property," demanded the other, with a startled look, "you don't mean but what the main part of his property is still left?"

"Yes, I do, Alice,—but I see you are not prepared for this. Still, you may as well know it now as ever. Yes, Alice, your husband is irretrievably bankrupt!"

Mrs. Elwood was not *indeed* prepared for this development. She had foreseen, it was true, the coming evil; but she supposed it was yet in the distance. She knew her husband's property had been a large one; and the announcement, from one she could not disbelieve, that it was all gone, struck her dumb with surprise and consternation. She uttered not a word. She could not speak, but sat pale and trembling, the very picture of distress.

After pacing the room a few moments, with frequent commiserating glances at the face of the other, whose distress evidently deeply moved him, Arthur Elwood stopped short before her and said:

"Sister Alice, my time is about up,—I must go."

"Have you no word to leave for my husband when he comes?" asked Mrs. Elwood, with an effort to appear composed.

"No,—none whatever to *him*; but with you, Alice," he added, drawing out a small package of bank notes and dropping them into her lap, "with you, and for you alone, against a day of necessity, I leave that trifle—no hesitation—keep it—put it out of sight—there, that is right. Now only one thing more,—what of your son?"

"Claud?"

"Yes. You know it has happened that I have never seen him."

"I do know it, and have much regretted his absence; for I wished you to see him. But I am now looking for him every hour, and if you could delay—"

"No, no, I must go. Tell him to forget, at once, that he was ever a rich man's only son and heir, and learn to profit by a rich man's errors; for, till he does this, which, if he is like others, will require some time, he will make no real advance in life."

"Your impression may be natural, but it hardly does him justice. He is *not* like most others. Claud is a man now."

"So much the better, then, for you and himself. But you see with a mother's eyes, probably, and speak with a mother's heart. I will inquire about him, however, as indeed I will about you all. Good-by."

Thus did the unimpassioned Arthur Elwood, with a seeming business-like roughness and want of feeling, assume to hide the emotions which he really felt in the discovery of his brother's ruin, and in witnessing the distress he had just caused in communicating it, hurry through the painful interview, and abruptly depart, leaving Mrs. Elwood to struggle in secret with the chaos of thoughts and emotions which Arthur's unexpected revelation had brought over her. She was not left long, however, to struggle with her feelings alone. In a short time the sound of a familiar footstep hastily entering the front hall of the magnificent mansion,—alas! now no longer her own,—suddenly caught her ear; when, with the exclamation, "Claud, O Claud!" she rushed forward to her advancing son, and, to use the expressive language of Scripture, "fell on his neck and wept."

"I heard of father's failure," said the son, a fine looking youth of about twenty, with his mother's cleanly cut features and firm, thoughtful countenance, joined to his father's manly proportions. "I learned, as I came into the city, an hour ago, that father had just failed, his store been shut up, and all his property put into the hands of his creditors; and I hurried home to break the news to you. But I see you know it all."

"Yes, that the blow was impending, but not that it had already fallen, as you now report; but it may as well come to-day as to-morrow or next week. Half my nights, for months, Claud, have been made sleepless by the bodings and fears of the evil day, which, as things were going, I felt must eventually come; but never, till within this very hour, did I dream that our misfortunes were so near. But, though the storm has burst so much sooner than I expected, I could bravely face it, could we say that it was caused by no fault of our own; but to be brought upon us in this manner, my son, it is hard, hard to bear."

"But you have not been to blame, mother; and I did not suppose you thought enough of wealth to grieve so at its loss."

"I do not, Claud. It is not that; still, I could not help thinking of your disappointment, even in that view of the misfortune."

"Mine, mother? Why, I am no worse off than father was when he started in life; no worse off than thousands who begin with no other resources than what lie in clear heads and strong hearts. I can take care of myself; and, what is more, I can take care of you, dear mother. Surely, you won't doubt me?"

"No, Claud, no. You have *always* been my pride, latterly almost my only hope; and I know not now but that you must be my only staff, on which to lean as I pass down the decline of life."

"And I will be one to you, mother; but come, cheer up, and let us go in and talk over these matters more calmly."

The mother and son accordingly retired to her usual sitting-room; where, since her overcharged bosom had found relief in tears, and her sinking spirits had been raised by the kind and comforting words of her dutiful son, she told him all that had occurred during the two preceding days, which constituted the brief but eventful period of his absence. They then were beginning to counsel together on the prospects and probabilities of their gloomy future; but their conversation was suddenly cut short by the abrupt entrance of the wretched husband and father, who, on his way from the hotel where he had spent the day in sleeping off his debauch in concealment, having received an intimation of what was going on among his creditors, had hurried home, with a confidence and self-possession which he could not summon when he started; for, out of this movement among his creditors, which he still would not believe was any thing more than a sort of practical menace to enforce payment, he saw not only how he could frame a plausible excuse for his guilty absence, but make the circumstance an irresistible plea for forcing from his brother a loan sufficient to enable him to arrest his failure and continue business. On entering the room, therefore, after saluting his wife and son in a sort of brisk, unconcerned manner, and muttering that he "thought they would never let him get home again," he eagerly inquired for Arthur; and, on being informed that his brother had started for his home, without leaving any note or word for him, and especially on being told by his son—as he at length calmly and persistingly was, in despite of his multiplied prevarications and denials, what they all knew, and what he himself should have been the last to be ignorant of—that the question of his failure, for more than he could ever pay, had already been settled against him, he became frantic in the outpourings of his rage, disappointment, and chagrin; sometimes declaring that the world, grown envious of his prosperity, had all suddenly become his enemies, and grossly belied him; sometimes savagely charging his brother, wife, and son with conspiring together against him; and sometimes cursing his own blindness and folly. And thus he continued to rave, and walk the room for hours, till his wife and son, having partaken their evening meal before his unheeding eyes, and become sick and wearied in listening to his insane ravings,—to which they had wholly ceased making any reply,—retired to rest, leaving him to partake such food as was left on the table, to occupy, as he chose to do, the same sofa which his hapless wife had done the night before, to sleep down the wild commotion of his feelings, and awake a calmer and more humbled, but not yet a better or much wiser man.

But we do not propose to describe in detail the rapid descent from opulence and station to poverty and insignificance, which now transpired to mark this era in the singular fortunes of Elwood and his family. Their history, for the next three months, was but the usual painful one which awaits the failed merchant everywhere in the cities. The crushing sense of misfortune which, for the first few days after the unexpected blow has fallen, weighs down the self-deceived or otherwise unprepared victims; the succeeding weeks of dejection and mortified pride; then the painful trial of parting with the showy equipage, the costly furniture, and the cherished mementoes, which had required, perhaps, the care of half a life in gathering; then the compulsory abdication of the great and conspicuous mansion for the small, obscure, hired cottage; then the saddening bodings and deep concern felt in seeing the means of living daily diminishing, with no prospect of ever being replenished; and, finally, the humiliating resort of the wife and children to the needle or menial employments, for the actual necessaries of life,—these, all these, are but the usual graduated vicissitudes of sorrow and trial which are allotted to those whose folly and extravagance have suddenly thrown them on the downward track of fortune, and which the Elwoods, in common with others, were now doomed to experience, and, on the part of Mrs. Elwood, especially, with aggravations not necessarily incident to such reverses. She would have borne all the deprivations and evils incident to her husband's failure without a murmur, could she have seen in him any amendment in those habits and vicious inclinations which had led to his downfall. But she could not. The hopes she had confidently entertained, that his misfortunes would humble and reform him, were doomed to disappointment. He still madly clung to his old associates of the gambling-table; and all the money he could get was lost or squandered among them, till he became too poor and desperate even for them, and they drove him from their society to join another and a lower set, who in turn compelled him to seek other still lower and more degraded associations. And so descended, step by step, along the path of degradation, the once princely merchant, till, despised and shunned by all respectable men, he became the fit companion of the meanest thimble-riggers of the cellars, and the lounging tipplers of the streets.

His case, however, as hopeless as it might appear, was not permitted to become an irretrievable one. Through a seemingly accidental circumstance, a light one day broke on his beclouded and half-maddened brain, that led to a self-redemption as happy for himself and family as it was unexpected by all. A former friend, one morning, moved perhaps by his forlorn appearance, in passing him with a light carriage, invited him to ride a few miles into the country; where, being unexpectedly called off in another direction, he left Elwood to return on foot by a nearer route across the fields to his home. After travelling some distance, he reached an elevation which overlooked the city, and, feeling a little fatigued, he sat down on a mossy hillock to rest and enjoy the prospect. As he cast his eye over that busy haunt of men, with its numerous spires shooting upward, its long lines of princely dwellings, its encircling forest of masts, its lofty warehouses, and other evidences of wealth and business, his own former important participation in its busy scenes, and his present worse than insignificant position there, rose in vivid contrast in his awakening mind; and the thought of his past but squandered wealth came up only to add poignancy to the sense of his present poverty and humiliation, which thus, and for the first time, was brought home to his agitated bosom. Suddenly leaping from his seat, from the torturing force of the reflection, he exclaimed: "Must I bear this? Cannot I still be a man? I will! yes, before Heaven, I *will*!" And, resuming his seat, his mind became intently engaged in studying out ways and means for carrying the sudden but stern resolution into effect; when, after another hour thus employed, he again jumped up, and, with the air of one who has reached some unalterable conclusion, he rapidly made his way homeward.

While the besotted Elwood was undergoing, so unexpectedly, even to himself, such a moral transformation in the solitude of the fields, an event occurred to his sorrowful wife at home, which was equally unexpected to *her*, which, though of a wholly different character, produced an equally great revulsion in her feelings as the one happening to her husband, about the same hour, was to him, or was producing in *his* feelings, and which, by the singular coincidence, seemed to indicate that the angel of mercy was at length spreading his wings at the same time over both heads of this unfortunate family. She had been having one of her most disconsolate days, and was sitting alone in her little room, gloomily pondering over her disheartening trials, without being able to see one ray of light in the dark future, when she received a call from one of her husband's chief creditors; who announced that those creditors, at a recent meeting, having ascertained her meritorious conduct and needy situation, had voted her the sum of five hundred dollars, which, confiding in her discretion for a judicious outlay of the money, he now, he said, had the pleasure of presenting her. And, having placed the money in her hands, and taken the tear of gratitude—which, preventing the utterance of the word-thanks she attempted, had started to her cheek at the unexpected boon—as a sufficient acknowledgment, he kindly bade her adieu, and departed.

That evening the husband and wife met as they had not for months before: each at first surprised at seeing the unclouded brow and hopeful countenance of the other, but each soon instinctively feeling that something had occurred to both, which was not only of present moment, but the harbinger of happier days to come. When confidence and hope are springing up in doubtful or despairing bosoms, the tongue is soon loosened from the frosts of reserve, however closely they may have before imprisoned it. Elwood, with many expressions of regret at his past conduct, and of wonder at the blindness and folly which had permitted him so long to persevere in it, told his gratified companion all that had that day passed through his mind,—his sudden sense of shame and degradation; his bitter self-reproaches, and succeeding determination to reform; to atone for the past, as far as he could, by future good conduct; to begin, in fine, the world anew, and, after placing himself beyond the reach of those temptations to which he had so fatally yielded, devote the remainder of his days to honest industry. And she, anxious to encourage and strengthen him, and fearing his total want of means might defeat his good resolutions,—she, also, as she believed it would be true wisdom to do, informed him of *her* good fortune, and offered him a portion of her unexpected acquisition, to enable him to engage in such business as he should decide to follow. They then discussed, and soon mutually agreed on, the expediency of leaving the city, where, as they had once there enjoyed wealth and station, they must both ever be subjected to mortifying contrasts,—both constantly doomed

"To see profusion which they must not share,"—

and he be exposed to temptations which he might not always have the firmness to withstand.

"But I resolved," said Elwood, after a pause, "not only on going to the country, but on to a new lot of land in the very outskirts of civilization. You, however, should I succeed in getting up comfortable quarters, would not be content to make such a place your home?"

"Anywhere, Mark; and the farther from the dangerous influences of this wicked city, the better. Yes, to the very depths of the wilderness, and I will not complain."

"It is settled, then. I was once, in one of my early excursions, along the borders of the wild lakes lying on the northeastern line of New Hampshire, where a living may be obtained from the cultivation of the soil alone; but where more may be made, at particular seasons, in taking the valuable furs that there abound. There I will go, contract for a lot of land, and prepare a home, leaving you, and Claud, if he shall decide for a woodman's life, to come on and join me next summer."

"That Claud will do; for he often declares himself disgusted with the trickery of trade, and to be longing for the country life of his boyhood. But here he comes, and can speak for himself."

The son now joined in the family deliberations, and learning, with surprise and gratification, what had occurred during the eventful day, joyfully fell in with his father's proposition; when it was soon decided that the latter should take half the money that day given to Mrs. Elwood, to lay out in a lot of land and house, and immediately proceed on his journey.

Whatever Mark Elwood had once firmly decided on, he was always prompt and energetic in executing. Before nine o'clock that evening, his knapsack of clothing was made up for a journey on foot, which, contrary to the wishes of his wife and son, he decided should be his mode of travelling. He then went to bed, slept six hours, rose, dressed, bade his family good-by, turned his back on the now loathed city, and, by sunrise next morning, was far on his way towards his designated home among the distant wilds of the North.

CHAPTER V.

"There is a pleasure in the pathless woods,
There is a rapture in the lonely shore,
There is society where none intrudes,—
I love not man the less, but nature more."

Once more in the green wilderness! Welcome the wild scenes of our boyhood, which, as the checkered panorama of the past is unrolled at our bidding, rise on the mental vision in all their original freshness and beauty! It was here we first essayed to study the works of nature, and in them trace the Master-hand that moulded and perfected them. It was here we learned to recognize the voice of God in the rolling thunder, and his messengers in the swift-winged lightnings; to mark the forms of beauty and grandeur in every thing, from the humble lichen of the logs and rocks, to the high and towering pine of the plain and the mountain,—from the low murmurings of the quiet rivulet, to the loud thunderings of the headlong cataract,—and from the soft whisperings of the gentle breeze, to the angry roar of the desolating tornado; and, finally, it was here that our first and most enduring lessons of devotion were learned, here that our first and truest conceptions of the grand and beautiful were acquired, and here that the leading tone of our intellectual character, such as it may be, was generated and stamped on us for life.

The second part of our story, to which the preceding chapters should be taken, perhaps, as merely introductory, opens about midsummer, and among that remarkable group of sylvan lakes—nearly a dozen in number—which, commencing on the wild borders of northerly New Hampshire, and shooting off in an irregular line some fifty miles northeasterly into the dark and unbroken forests of Maine, appear on the map, in their strangely shapeless forms and scattered locations, as if they must have been hurled, by the hand of some Borean giant, down from the North Pole in a volley of huge ice-blocks, which fell and melted where they now lie, sparkling, like rough gems, on the shaggy bosom of the wilderness.

Near the centre of an opening of perhaps a dozen acres, about a mile from where the sinuous Androscoggin debouches full grown, like Minerva from the head of Jupiter, from its parent reservoir, the picturesque Umbagog, stood a newly rigged log house, of dimensions and finish which indicated more taste and enterprise than is usually exhibited in the rude habitations of the first settlers. It was a story and a half high, and the walls were built of solid pine timber, originally roughly hewed, but recently dressed down with broad axe over the whole outward and inner surfaces so smoothly that, at a little distance, they presented, with their still visible seams, more the appearance of the wainscoting of some costly cottage than the humble log cabin. The building had also been newly shingled, new doors supplied, the windows enlarged, the yard around leveled off, with other improvements, of a late date, betokening considerable ambition for appearance, and considerable outlay of means, for so new a place, to fit up a tidy and comfortable abode for the occupants. In the surrounding field were patches of growing maize, wheat, potatoes, and some of the common table vegetables; the hay crop for the winter sustenance of the only cow and yoke of oxen, the best friends of the new settler, having been just cut and stored in an adjoining log-building, as was evident from the fresh look of the stubble, and the stray straws hanging to the slivered stumps or bushes in the field, and from the fragrant and far-scenting locks protruding from the upper and lower windows of the well-crammed receptacle passing under the name of barn. Beyond this little opening, and bounding it on every side, stood the encircling wall of woods, through and over which gleamed the bright waters of the far-spreading Umbagog on the north; while all around, towering up in their green glories, rose, one above another, the amphitheatric hills, till their lessening individual forms were lost, or mingled in the vision with the lofty summits of the distant White Mountains in the south and west, and of the bold detached eminences which shot up from the dark wilderness and studded the horizon in all other directions.

Such, and in such a locality, was, as the reader probably has already inferred, the residence which Mark Elwood had pitched upon for beginning life anew. On leaving the city, as represented in the last chapter, he had, under the goading remembrance of follies left behind, and the incitements of hope-constructed prospects before, perseveringly pushed on, till he reached this lone and wild terminus of civilized life; when, finding, a mile beyond the last of the scattered settlements of the vicinity, a place on which an opening had been made and the walls and roof of a spacious log house erected, the year before, he had succeeded in purchasing it, for ready money, at a price which was much below its value, and which left him nearly half his little fund to be expended in more thoroughly clearing the land, getting in crops, making the house habitable, and felling an additional tract of forest. And with so much energy and resolution had he pursued his object of seeing himself and family once more united at a comfortable home, that, within three months from the time he commenced operations, which was in the first of the spring months, he had accomplished it all; for his wife and son, rejoicing in the knowledge of his success which he had communicated to them, and promptly responding to his invitation to join him, had come on, with their little all of goods and money, in teams hired for the purpose; and they were now all together fully installed in their new home, pleased with the novelty and freshness of every thing around them, proud and secure in their conscious independence and exemption from the dangers and trials they had recently passed through, and contented and happy in their situation.

The particular time we have taken for the reappearance of the family on this, their new stage of action, was a warm but breezy afternoon, on one of the last days of July. Elwood was engaged in his new-mown field, in cutting and grubbing up the bushes and sprouts which had sprung up during the season around the log-heaps and stumps, and could not easily or conveniently be cut by the common scythe while mowing the grass. He was no longer robed in the broadcloth and fine linen, in which, as the rich merchant, he might have been seen, perhaps, one year ago that day, sauntering about "on 'change" among the solid men of Boston. These had been mostly worn out or sold during the changing fortunes of the year, and their place was now wisely supplied by the long tow-frock and the other coarse garments in common use among the settlers. Nor had his physical appearance undergone a much less change. Instead of the pallid brow, leaden eye, fleshly look, and the red cheek of the wine-bibber and luxurist of the cities, he exhibited the embrowned, thin, but firm and healthy face, and the clear and cheerful complexion of the contented laborer of the country,—telltale looks both, which we always encounter with as much secret disgust in the former as we do with involuntary respect in the latter. He now paused in his labors, and stood for some time looking about the horizon, as if watching the signs of the weather; now noting the progress of the haze gathering in the south, and now turning his cheek first one way and then another, apparently to ascertain the doubtful direction of the wind, which, from a lively western breeze, had within the last hour lulled down into those small, fluctuating puffs usually observable when counter-currents are springing up, balancing, and beginning to strive for the mastery. After a while he moved slowly towards the house, continuing his observations as he went, till he came near the open window at which Mrs. Elwood was sitting at her needle-work, from which she occasionally lifted her eyes, and glanced somewhat anxiously along the path leading down through the woods to a landing-place on the lake; when, looking round and observing her husband standing near, giving token of being about to speak, she interposed and said:

"You have seen nothing of Claud, I suppose? What can be the reason why he does not return? He was to have been at home long before this, was he not?"

"Yes," carelessly replied Elwood, "unless he concluded to take a bout in the woods. He took his fowling-piece with him, to use in case the trout wouldn't bite, you know. Phillips, the old hunter, came into the field where we were last night, and said he was out of meat, and must skirt the lake to-day for a buck. I presume Claud may have joined him. There! hark! that sounded like Claud's piece," he added, as the distant report of a gun rose from the woods westward of the lake and died away in swelling echoes on the opposite shore. "And there, again!" he continued, as another and sharper report burst, the next moment, from the same locality,—"there goes another, but not his, as he could not have loaded so quick. That must have been Phillips' long rifle. They are doubtless together somewhere near the Magalloway,—some three miles distant, I should judge,—and are probably having fine sport with something."

"That may be the case, perhaps," responded Mrs. Elwood. "I wish, however, he would come; for I cannot yet quite divest myself of the idea that there may be danger in these wild scenes of the lakes and the woods. But what was you about to say when I first spoke? You were going to say something, I thought."

"O—yes—why, I was about to say that I had made up my mind to set fire to the *slash*. It is dry enough now to get a good burn; and it looks to me a good deal like rain. I wish to get the land cleared and ready to sow with winter wheat by the first of September; and I don't like to risk the chance of finding every thing in so good order again."

"There is no danger that the fire will spread, or be blown to the buildings, is there?"

"No, the wind is springing up in the south now, and will drive the fire only towards the lake in the direction of the landing."

"But Claud may be there."

"Well, if he should be, the fire won't burn up the lake, I think; and, if it besets the path in the woods, he can come round some other way," jocosely said Elwood, moving away to carry his purpose into execution.

Having procured a parcel of splinters split from the dry and resinous roots of some old pine stub,—that never-failing and by no means contemptible substitute for lamp or candle among the pioneers of a pine-growing country,—he proceeded rapidly to the edge of the *slash*, as a tract of felled forest is generally denominated by the first settlers, especially of the northern States. Here, pausing a moment to mark with his eye the most favorable places to communicate the fire, he picked his way along the southern end to the farthest side of the tangled mass of trees of every description composing the slash, which was a piece of some four or five acres, lying on the western border and extending north and south the whole length of the opening. And, having reached his destination, and kindled all his splinters into a blaze, he threw one of them into the thickest nest of pine or other evergreen boughs at hand, and darted back to his next marked station, where he threw in another of his blazing torches, and so on till he reached the cleared ground, which was not one moment too soon for his safety. For so dry and inflammable had every thing there become, under the scorching sun of the preceding fortnight, which had been relieved by neither rain nor cloud, that, the instant the fire touched the tinder-like leaves, it flashed up as from a parcel of scattered gunpowder; and, bursting with almost explosive quickness all around, and swiftly leaping from bough to bough and treetop to treetop, it spread with such astonishing celerity that he found it hard on his heels, or whirling in a hot cloud over his head, at every pause he made to throw in a new but now unnecessary torch, in his rapid and constantly quickened run through the slash. And when, after running some distance into the open field, to escape the stifling smoke and heat by which he was even there assailed, he turned round to note more fully the surprising progress that the terrible element he had thus let loose was making, he beheld all that part of the slash which he had a moment before passed through already enveloped, from side to side, in a continuous blaze, whose red, curling crest, mounting every instant higher and higher, was advancing with the seeming speed of a racehorse on its fiery destination. Half-appalled by the sight of such a sudden and unexpected outburst of the fire he had kindled, Elwood hurried on to his house, and joined his startled wife in the yard; when the two took station on an adjoining knoll, and looked down upon the conflagration in progress with increasing wonder and uneasiness,—so comparatively new was the scene to them both, and so far did it promise to exceed all their previous conceptions, in magnitude and grandeur, of any thing of the kind to be met with in the new settlements. And it was, indeed, a grand and fearful spectacle: For, with constantly increasing fury, and with the rapidity of the wind before which it was driving, still raged and rolled on the red tempest of fire. Now surging aloft, and streaking with its winding jets of flame the fiercely whirling clouds of smoke that marked its advance, and now dying away in hoarse murmurs, as if to gather strength for the new and more furious outburst that the next moment followed, it kept on its terrific march till it reached the central elevation, which embraced the most tangled, densely covered, and combustible part of the slash, and on which had been left standing an enormous dry pine, that towered so up high above the surrounding forest as to have long served as a landmark for the hunters and fishermen, in setting their courses through the woods or over the lake. Here the fiery billow, as if governed by the human tactics of a military assault, paused, parted, and swept by on either side, till it had inclosed the elevation; when suddenly it shot up from every side in an hundred converging tongues of flame, which, soon meeting and expanding into one, quickly enveloped the whole hill in one broad, unbroken robe of sheeted fire, encompassed and mounted the veteran pine, and around its colossal trunk formed a huge, whirling pyramid of mingling smoke and flame that rose to the mid-heavens, shedding, in place of the darkened sun, a lurid glare over the forest, and sending forth the stormy roar of a belching volcano. The next moment a shower of cinders and the burning fragments of twigs, bark, and boughs which had been carried high up by the force of the ascending currents, fell hot and hissing to the earth over every part of the adjoining fields, to and even far beyond the spot where Elwood and his wife were standing.

"Good Heavens!" exclaimed Elwood, aroused from the mute amazement with which he and his more terrified companion had been beholding the scene, as soon as these indications of danger were thus brought to his very feet. "Good Heavens! this is more than I bargained for. See,—the fire is catching on the stumps all over the field!"

"The house!" half-screamed Mrs. Elwood. "What is that rising from the shingles up there near the top of the roof?"

"Smoke, as I am alive!" cried the other, in serious alarm, as he glanced up to the roof, where several slender threads of smoke were beginning to steal along the shingles. "Run, Alice, run with the pails for the brook, while I throw up the ladder against the gable. We must be lively, or within one hour we shall be as houseless as beggars."

"O, where is Claud? where is Claud?" exclaimed the distressed wife and mother, as she flew to the house to do her husband's bidding.

Yes, where was Claud? At the risk of the charge of purposely tantalizing the reader, we must break off here, to follow the young man just named, in the unexpected adventures which he also had experienced during that eventful day. But for this we will take a new chapter.

CHAPTER VI.

"To sit on rocks, to muse o'er flood and fell,
To slowly trace the forest's shady scene,
Where things that own not man's dominion dwell,
And mortal foot hath ne'er, or rarely, been;
To climb the trackless mountain all unseen,
With the wild flock that never needs a fold;
Alone o'er steeps and foaming falls to lean,—
This is not Solitude: 't is but to hold
Converse with nature's charms, and view her stores unroll'd."

It was about the middle of the forenoon, on the day marked by the incidents narrated in the preceding chapter, when Claud Elwood, who had become pretty well initiated into the sports of the locality, entered his light canoe, with his fishing-tackle and fowling-piece, and pushed out upon the broad bosom of the forest-girt Umbagog. Having had the best success, when up on the lake the last time, on the western margin, he pulled away in that direction, and, after rowing a couple of miles up the lake, he laid down his oar, unrolled his elm-bark cable, and let down his stone anchor, at a station a furlong or so from the shore.

It was a beautiful spot, and a beautiful day to enjoy it in. From the water's edge rose, deeply enshrouded in their bright green, flowing, and furbelowed robes of thickly interwoven pines, the undulating hills, back to the summit level of that long, narrow tongue of forest land, which, for many miles, only separates the Umbagog from the parallel Magalloway, the noble stream that here comes rushing down from the British highlands, to join the scarcely larger Androscoggin, almost at the very outset of its "varied journey to the deep." Turning from this magnificent swell on the west, the eye, as it wandered to the right over the bright expanse of intervening waters, next rested on the long, crescent-shaped mountain ridge, behind which slept, in their still deeper and wilder seclusion, the broad Mooseeluk-maguntic and the Molechunk-a-munk, which, with the Umbagog, make up the three principal links in this remarkable chain of lakes. Still farther to the right lay the seemingly boundless, rolling forests, forming the eastern and southern rim of this basin of the lakes; whose gradually sloping sides, like some old pinnacled city, were everywhere bristling with the giant forms of the heaven-aspiring pine, and whose nearer recesses were pierced, in the midst, by the long, lessening line of the gleaming Umbagog; while around the whole circle of the horizon, scattered here and there far back into the blue distance, rose mountain after mountain in misty grandeur to the heavens.

After thus slowly sweeping the horizon, to note, for the tenth time, perhaps, the impressive character of the scenery, whose everywhere intermingling beauty and grandeur he was never tired of contemplating, Claud withdrew his gaze, and turned his attention to, the more immediate object of his excursion. After a few moments spent in regulating his hook and line, he strung his angle-rod, and threw out to see whether he could succeed in tempting, at that unfavorable hour, the fickle trout from their watery recesses. But all in vain the attempt. Not a trout was seen stirring the water at the surface, or manifesting his presence around the hook beneath; and all the endeavors which the tantalized angler made, by changing the bait, and throwing the line in different directions around him, proved, for the next hour, equally fruitless. While he was thus engaged, intently watching his line, each moment expecting that the next must bring him a bite, one of those peculiar, subdued, but far-reaching sounds, which are made by the grazing of the oar against the side of the boat in rowing, occasionally greeted his ear from some point to the south of him; though, for a while, nothing was to be seen to indicate by whom the sounds were produced. Soon, however, a man in a canoe, who had been coasting, unseen, along the indentures of the shore, and whom Claud instantly recognized as Phillips, the hunter already named, shot round a neighboring point, and, in a few minutes more, was at his side.

"Well, what luck?" cheerily exclaimed Phillips, a keen, hawk-eyed, self-possessed looking man, with a round, compact, and sinewy frame. "What luck to-day, young man?"

"None whatever," replied Claud, with an air of disappointment.

"I suppose so, unless you began before ten o'clock."

"But why did you suppose so?"

"O, I knew it from my knowledge of human nature," said the hunter, humorously. "Trout are very much like other folks, only a great deal more sensitive to heat. Now, you don't see men, who are well fixed under a cool shade in a sweltering hot day, very anxious to run out bare-headed in the sun, when there is no call for it; much less, then, the trout, that can't bear the sun and heat at all. Though there are, probably, a ton of them within a stone's throw of us, not one will come out with this bright sun; they are lying behind the rocks and old logs at the bottom, and won't begin to circulate these three hours."

"And are you not a-going to try them?"

"I? No; I would as soon think of fishing now on the top of these hills. Besides this, I have a different object. I am bound to carry home something that will pass for fresh meat, if it is nothing but a coon. I shall haul up my canoe somewhere about here; follow up the lake-shore a mile or so, with the idea of catching a deer in the edge of the water, come there to keep off the flies; then, perhaps, cross over to the Magalloway, down that, and over to this place; when, by way of topping off, I will show you, by that time, if you are about here so long, how trout are taken."

So saying, the hunter dipped his springy oar into the water, and, with a few vigorous strokes, sent his canoe to the shore, and, having moored it to a root, he glided into the thickets, and disappeared with a tread so noiseless as to leave Claud, for many minutes, wholly in doubt whether the man was standing still in the bushes or proceeding on his excursion.

It was now noon, and Claud, seeing no prospect of any immediate success in his piscatory employment, which had been made to appear to him, by the remarks of the hunter, more discouraging than ever, drew up his anchor, and rowed to a point of the shore which was embowered by a group of magnificent pines. Here, finding a cool spring, as well as a refreshing shade, he drew out his lunch, and very leisurely proceeded to discuss it, with the ice-cold water of the spring by which he had seated himself for the purpose. His fare was coarse; but it was partaken with a relish of which those who have never experienced the effects of the air and exercise, incident to a life in the woods, can have no just conception; and to which the palled appetite of the

"vain lords of luxury and ease, Whom slumber soothes not, pleasure cannot please,"

is poor in comparison, though all the king's banquets and metropolitan feasts in the world should vie together to make good the substitute. Claud's life had thus far been, in the main, a quiet and commonplace one; nothing having occurred to him to arouse those strong and over-mastering passions to which it is the lot of most of us, at some period of our lives, to become subjected. It had been checkered, however, by one bit of romance, which, to say the least, had greatly excited his imagination. About a year previous to the time of which we are now writing, and one day while he was walking the streets of Boston, a small, closely-enwrapped package was put in his hand by an unknown boy, who, with the simple announcement, "*For you, Sir*," turned quickly away, and made off with the air of one who has completed his mission, and would avoid being questioned. Glancing within the wrapper, and perceiving it inclosed a small encased picture, or likeness, of some female, which he thought must have been delivered to him through mistake, Claud looked hastily round for the messenger, and, not seeing him, he walked backward and forward along the street, and lingered some time in the vicinity, still expecting the boy would soon return to claim the package. But, being disappointed in this, he went home, and, retiring to his room, undid the wrapper, which he carefully but vainly examined for some name, mark, or other clue to the mystery; and then, with much interest, fell to inspecting the picture. It was, obviously, a well-painted miniature likeness of a fair, dark-eyed girl, but representing no remembered face, except in the peculiar expression of the strong and commanding countenance; which, he thought, either in man or woman, he must have somewhere before encountered. The whole likeness, indeed, together with the circumstances under which it came into his hands, made, at the time, a lively impression on his mind; and, keeping the affair wholly to himself, he often contemplated that fair face in private; and, for months afterwards, he never was in a public assembly, where the sex were present, without running his eye over it in search of the original. But, as he never found it, the impression gradually wore away, and, in the exciting changes that had occurred in the fortunes of his family, it had been nearly obliterated from his mind; when, that morning, while searching his trunk for some implement belonging to his gun, he came across the miniature, and put it in his pocket. And now, in the leisure that followed his repast, he bethought him of it; and, laying it before him on the bed of moss on which he was reclining, he contemplated it with renewed interest, and that sort of dreamy enthusiasm which the sudden revival of old associations in such solitudes is apt to awaken in the mind, especially when those associations are connected, as now, with a matter of mystery and romance.

After indulging in his reveries a while, he put up his miniature, aroused himself from his day-dream, and rose to his feet when, feeling inclined for some kind of action, he decided on a short excursion in the woods, in the direction of the Magalloway, where probably he would fall in with Phillips, and return with him to the lake. Accordingly, after loading his gun with ball and buckshot, so as to be prepared for any large wild animals he might chance to encounter, he leisurely took his way through the heavy, ascending forest that lay in his course; here pausing to note the last night's bed of some solitary bear, and there to trace the marks of the death-struggle of a victim deer, that, with all its vigilance and wondrous agility, had been surprised and brought down by the stealthy and far-leaping catamount. The ever-varying tenants of the forest, also, were constantly presenting as he passed on, some novelty to attract his unaccustomed eye; now in the smooth, tall shaft of the fusiform fir—the dandy of the forest—standing up with its beautiful cone-shaped top among its rougher neighbors, trim and straight as the bonneted cavalier of the old pictures, among the slouchy forms of his homelier but worthier opponents; now in the low and stocky birch standing on its broad, staunch pedestal of strongly-braced roots below, and throwing out widely above its giant arms, as if striving to shoulder and stay up the weight of the superincumbent forest; and now in the imperial pine, proudly lifting its tall form an hundred feet over the tops of the plebeian trees around, to revel in the upper currents of the air, or bathe its crowning plumes of living green in the clouds of heaven.

Proceeding in this manner, he at length found himself gradually descending the western slope of the hill; when he soon arrived in the vicinity of the river, a glimpse of which, together with a small clearing and a tidy-looking cottage on its banks, he now caught through the tops of the intervening trees. While still walking on, his attention was attracted to a comparatively open place in the woods, where, at some previous period, a severe fire had killed all the smaller trees, and consumed the underbrush, which had been replaced by scattering shrubs of the white poplar intermingled with a plentiful growth of the black-raspberry, whose luscious fruit—the first to reward the pioneer, and for which he has to contend sharply with the birds and bears to obtain his share—was now beginning to ripen. As he was entering this open space, which appeared to extend some distance round the point of a screening knoll, he was suddenly brought to a stand by a noise somewhere in the bushes or woods ahead, such as had never before saluted his ears. It was like nothing else, or *if any* thing else, like the wild snorting of a frightened horse prolonged into the dying note of the steam whistle. Claud recoiled a step before the unaccustomed sound, and involuntarily cocked and raised his gun to his shoulder. But he was allowed no time to speculate. The next instant, the loud and piercing shriek of a female, nearer but in the same direction, rose and rang through the forest. With a speed quickened at every step by the rapidly repeated cry of distress, he bounded towards the spot, when, turning the point of the knoll, he suddenly found himself in full view of the object of his solicitude,—a girl, in the full bloom of youthful beauty, who, with bonnet thrown back and her loosened hair streaming in wild disorder over her shoulders, instantly rushed forward for his protection. Claud stopped short, in mute surprise at the unexpected apparition; for the first glance at her face told him that the original of his mysterious miniature was before him,—before him, here in the woods! Breathless and speechless in her wild affright, she pointed, with a glance over her shoulder, to a thick, high tangle of large, strongly limbed, knotty, windfallen trees, a short distance behind her, and fled past him to the rear. Looking in the indicated direction, the startled and perplexed young man distinguished the outlines of a monstrous moose madly plunging at the woody barrier, and trying to force his enormous antlers through the unyielding limbs preparatory to leaping it in pursuit of his victim, who had eluded the infuriated animal, and barely escaped the fatal blows of his uplifted hoofs, by creeping under the providentially placed obstruction. Claud instantly raised his piece, when, feeling uncertain of his aim, he withheld his fire, and stood waiting for a fairer view. But, before he could obtain it, the moose, tired of vain attempts to force his passage through the bristling barricade of logs and limbs before him, disappeared for one moment, but the next came crashing round the nearest end of it, and, with renewed demonstrations of rage and hostility, made directly for the new opponent he beheld in his way. Still unalarmed for his own safety, Claud waited with levelled gun till his formidable assailant was within forty yards of him, when he took a quick aim and fired. Reeling under the discharge of his heavily loaded piece, and blinded by the smoke, he could not, at first, see the effect of his fire; but when he did so, the next instant, it was only to behold the monster brute, maddened, not stopped, by the flesh wounds inflicted, rushing on him with a force and fury which compelled him to leap suddenly aside, to avoid being beat into the earth by those terrible hoofs, which he saw lifted higher and higher, at each approaching step, for his destruction. Mindful, in his peril, of the precautions already learned from the hunters, Claude, while the moose, whose tremendous impetus was driving him straight ahead, could break up, so as to turn in the pursuit,—Claud made, with all the speed of which he was master, for a huge hemlock, luckily standing at no great distance on his right; a course which he thought would divert the monster from pursuit of the maiden, and, at the same time, best insure his own safety. But, so prodigious was the rushing speed of the foiled and now doubly exasperated moose, that the imperilled huntsman had barely time to reach the sheltering tree and dodge behind it, before the hotly pursuing foe was at his heels, rasping and tearing with his spiked antlers the rough bark of the tree, in his attempts to follow round it near and fast enough to overtake and strike down his intended victim. Round and round then sped both pursuer and pursued, as fast as the frantic rage of the one, and the keen instinct of self-preservation in the other, could impel them. Although the moose, from the great width of his interfering horns, was compelled to sweep round the tree in a circle requiring him to go over double the distance travelled by Claude, yet so much greater was his speed, that it called for the utmost exertions of the latter to keep clear of the battle-axe blows which he heard falling every instant with fatal force behind him. His gun had already been struck, shivered, and beat from his hand; and, as he glanced over his shoulder and saw the fierce and glaring eyes of his ruthless pursuer, and his uplifted and forward-thrown hoofs striking closer and closer to his heels at every bound, a sense of his deadly peril flashed over his mind with that strange and paralyzing effect which the first full conviction of impending death often produces on the stoutest hearts. He felt his strength giving way, his brain beginning to whirl, and he was on the point of yielding himself to his fate; when a stream of smoke and flame accompanied the startling report of a rifle, shot out from the edge of a neighboring thicket. The moose gave a convulsive start, floundered forward on his knees, swayed backward and forward an instant, then fell over broad-side into the bushes with a heavy crash, straightened out, gasped, and died.

"Dunno but you'll think I waited too long, young man," cried Phillips, now advancing with a quick, leaping step from his covert. "The fact was, I felt, on seeing you getting into such close quarters, that I had better be rather particular about my aim, so as to stop him at once; besides that, I was at first a little out of breath. I had heard the fellow blow when an hundred rods off,—then the woman scream,—then your gun; and, thinking like enough there would be trouble, I legged it for the spot, and got to my stand just as he treed you."

"I feel very grateful to you, Mr. Phillips, for this timely rescue," responded Claud, recovering his composure. "This, I suppose, is the far-famed moose?"

"Yes, and a bouncer at that," replied the hunter, going up and, placing his foot on the broad and still quivering flank of the huge animal. "Good twenty hands high, and weighs, well, not much short of fifteen hundred, I should say."

"But are they often thus dangerous?" asked Claud.

"Not very often, perhaps," rejoined the hunter. "But still the bull moose, at this season of the year, is sometimes, when wounded, about as ugly a customer as you meet with in the woods. This fellow I judge to have been *oncommon* vicious, as he begun his tantrums before he was touched at all, it seems. I dunno but 'twas the woman put the devil into him, as women do into two-legged animals sometimes,—don't they, young man?"

"The woman? O yes, the young lady," said Claud, reminded of his duty as a gallant by the remark, though unwilling to appropriate to himself the prophetic joke with which it was coupled. "Where is she? I must go and see to her."

"She has already seen to herself, I guess," said the hunter. "As I was coming up, I glimpsed her cutting round and running, like a wild turkey, for the clearing, to which the moose had cut off her retreat. She has reached the house by this time, doubtless; for it is hard by, down on the river here, a hundred rods or such a matter."

"Who is she? Do you know the family?" eagerly inquired the young man.

"No," answered the hunter. "They are new-comers in these parts."

"What could have brought her here so far into the woods?" persisted Claud.

"The raspberries, very likely," said the other, indifferently, while taking out and examining the edge of his knife. "But come, we must get this moose into some condition, so that he will keep; then be off to let the settlers know of our luck. And early to-morrow morning, we will, all hands, come up the river in boats, and distribute him. He will make fresh meat enough to supply the whole settlement."

The hunter now, with the assistance of his new pupil in the craft, proceeded to dressing the moose, the process of which, bleeding, disemboweling, and partially skinning, was soon completed; when, cutting some stout green skids with the hatchet he ever carried in his belt, and inserting the ends under the bulky carcass, the two contrived to raise it, by means of old logs rolled up for the purpose, several feet from the ground, so as to insure a free circulation of air beneath it. This being done, the hunter kindled two log fires, one on each side, to keep off, he said, the wolves and other carnivorous animals. They then, after cutting out the tongue and lip, which are esteemed the tidbits of this animal, took up their line of march for the lake, which, with the long, rapid lope of the woodsman, measured off, as usual, in Indian file, and with little or no interrupting conversation, they reached in a short time, and without further adventure.

"Now," said the hunter, as he reached the spot where his canoe was tied, and turned round towards his lagging companion,—"now, sir, what say you to taking a five-pound trout?"

"Perfectly willing," replied Claud, smiling; "and I would even take up with a smaller one."

"Well, I won't,—that is, not much smaller; and I think I'll have one of at least the size I named."

"What makes you so confident?"

"Because, it being a hot, shiny morning, they took to their coverts early, and must be sharp-set, by this time. Besides that, it is just about the best time for them that could be got up: a deep cloud, as you see, is coming over the sun, and this wind is moving the water to the bottom. All sizes will now be coming out, and the big ones, like big folks, will make all the little ones stand back till their betters are served."

Each now taking to his canoe, they pushed out some twenty or thirty rods into the lake, cast anchor, and threw out their lines. Claud, who baited with grubs, soon had drawn in two, weighing as many pounds a piece, and began to feel disposed to banter the hunter, who had baited with a flap of moose-skin, which he had brought along with him, and which, to Claud, seemed little likely to attract the fishes to his hook. But he soon found himself mistaken; for, turning to give utterance to what was passing in his mind, he beheld the other dallying with a trout, which he had hooked, and now held flapping on the surface of the water, evidently much larger than either of his own.

"That is a fine one!" cried Claud. "Why don't you pull him in?"

"Not big enough," said the hunter, in reply to the question; while he turned to the fish with an impatient "Pshaw! what work the cretur makes of it! Hop off, hop off, you fool! There," he added, as the trout at length broke away and disappeared, "there, that is right. Now be off with yourself till you grow bigger, and give me a chance at the fine fellow whose tail I saw swashing up round here just now."

The hunter then carefully adjusted his bait, and threw out the whole lingth of his line. After alternately sinking his hook, and then drawing it to the surface, for two or three throws, the line suddenly straightened, moved slowly backward at first, then swept rapidly round and round, or darted off in sharp short angles, with downward and forward plunges so quick and powerful as to make the stout sapling pole sway and bend, like a whipstock, in the steadying hands of the hunter. For four or five minutes he made no attempt to draw in his prize, but let the fish have full play to the length of its tether, till its efforts had become comparatively feeble; when, slowly bringing it alongside, he took the line in his hand, and, with a quick jerk, landed the noble fellow safely on the bottom of the canoe.

"There, sir!" exclaimed the hunter, seizing the trout by the gills, and triumphantly holding it up to view, "there is about what I bargained for: two feet long, not an inch shorter,—seven pounds weight, and not an ounce lighter! Now, being satisfied, I am done."

"What, leave off with such luck?" asked Claud in surprise.

"Yes, young man," said the other, "I hold it all but a downright sin to draw from God's storehouse a single pound more than is really needed. This will last my family as long as it will keep, this warm weather, with the plenty of moose-meat we shall have. Any thing more is a waste, which *I* will not commit. And *you*, sir, who have just hauled in your third and largest one, I perceive, and have now nearly as many pounds as I have,—what can *you* want of more? Come, let us pull up and off for our homes. It is nearly time, any way."

Although loth to break off his sport, yet inwardly acknowledging the justness of the hunter's philosophy, Claud reluctantly drew in and wound up his line, hauled in his anchor, and, handling his oar, shot out abreast of the other, who had already got under way, into the heaving waters of the now agitated lake. Side by side, with the quick and easy dip of their elastic single oars, the rowers now sent their light, sharp canoes, dug out to the thinness of a board from the straight-grained dry pine, rapidly ahead over the broken and subdued waves of the cove, in which they had been stationed, till they rounded the intervening woody point which had cut off the view of the lower end of the lake.

"Good Heavens!" exclaimed Claud, starting back, with suspended oar, as now, coming out in view of the lake, his eye fell on the huge pillar of smoke, which, deeply enshrouding that part of the distant forest lying east of the outlet of the lake with its expanded base, was rolling upward its thousand dark, doubling folds; "good Heavens, Phillips, look yonder! Where and what is it? It looks like a burning city."

"It is a fire, of course, and no small one, either; but where, I can't exactly make out," slowly responded the hunter, intently fixing his keen eyes on the magnificent spectacle which had thus unexpectedly burst on their view in the distance. "Let me see," he continued, running his eye along the border of the lake in search of his old landmarks: "there is the tall stub that stands half a mile down on the west bank of the river, and is now just visible in the edge of the smoke; but where is the king pine, that stands nearly against it, over in your slash? Young man," he added, with a startled air, "was your father calculating to burn that slash to-day?"

"No, unless it looked likely to rain."

"Well it *does* look likely to rain, in the shape of a shower gathering yonder, which has already given out one or two grumbles of distant thunder, if my ears served me as well as usual."

"Yes; but such a smoke and fire can't come from our slash. It must be a larger and more distant one."

"So I thought at first; but I begin to think different. Do you see that perpendicular, broken line of light, occasionally flashing out from the smoke, and extending upward to a height that no ground fire ever reached? That is your king pine in a blaze from bottom to top. Hark! why, I can hear it roaring clear here, like a distant hurricane. It must be a prodigious hot fire to make all that show and noise."

"Can it endanger our buildings?" asked Claud, in alarm.

"I am afraid so," replied the other, with a dubious shake of the head. "But hark again! 'tis your father's horn blowing for help."

"Let us row, then, as for our lives!" cried the now thoroughly aroused and agitated young man. "If any thing happens before I get there, I shall never forgive myself for my prolonged absence, to the last day of my life. You will join me in going there, will you not?"

"Yes, and outstrip you by half a mile. But that won't be the best way. Throw your anchor into the stern of my canoe, and fall in behind. There; now keep the anchor-line slack between us, if you can," rapidly said the hunter, bending his sinewy form to the work, with a power that sent his canoe half out of the water at every stroke of his swiftly-falling oar.

Leaving them to bound over the billowy waters of the lake towards their destination, with all the speed which strong arms and nerves made tense with excitement could impart, let us anticipate their arrival, to note what befell the objects of their anxieties, whom we so abruptly left in their perils from the fire, to bring up the other incidents of the day having an equal bearing on the story, with which we have thus far occupied the present somewhat extended chapter.

The immediate danger to their house from the fire, with which we left the alarmed Elwood and his wife contending, was, indeed, easily overcome by dashing pails of water over the roof. But scarcely had they achieved this temporary triumph in one place over an element proverbially terrible when it becomes master, before it was seen kindling into flickering blazes on the roof of the barn and the locks of hay protruding from its windows and the crevices between the logs of which it was built. Here, also, they soon succeeded in extinguishing the fire in the same manner. They were not, however, allowed a moment's respite from either their labors or alarms. The fences were by this time on fire in numerous places; and the chips and wood in the door-yard were seen to be igniting from the sparks and cinders which, every instant, fell thicker and hotter around their seemingly devoted domicil. The fences, after a few vain attempts to save them, were given up a prey to the devouring element, and the whole exertions of the panting and exhausted sufferers were turned to saving their buildings; and even at that they had no time to spare; for, so hot had the air become from the burning slash, which, through its whole length, was now glowing with the red heat of a furnace, that every vestige of moisture had soon disappeared from the drenched roofs, and they were again on fire.

"Is there no way of raising help?" exclaimed Mrs. Elwood, in her extremity, as she witnessed these increasing manifestations of danger.

"I never thought of that," said Elwood. "Hand me the dinner-horn. If there are any within hearing, they will understand, with the appearance of this fire, that we are calling for assistance."

With a few sharp, loud blasts, Elwood threw aside the horn, and again flew to the work of extinguishing the fires where they became most threatening. And thus, for nearly another hour, the distressed settler and his heroic wife, suffering deeply from heat and exhaustion, toiled on, without gaining the least on the fearful enemy by which they were so closely encompassed. And they were on the point of giving up in despair, when the welcome shout of "Help at hand!" from the ringing voice of the hunter, then just entering the opening, revived hope in their sinking hearts. The next moment that help was on the spot; but it was unnecessary. A mightier Hand was about to interpose. From the bold, black van of the hurrying and deeply-charged rack of cloud, that had now unheeded gained the zenith, a stream of fire, before which all other fires paled into nothing, at that instant descended on the top of the burning pine, and, rending it from top to bottom by the single explosion, sent its wide-flying fragments in blazing circles to the ground. A sharp, rattling sound, terminating in a cannon-like report, followed, shaking the rent and crashing heavens above, and the bounding earth beneath, in the awful concussion. Before the stunned and blinded settlers had recovered from the shock, or the deep roll of the echoing thunder had died away among the distant mountains, another and more welcome roar saluted their ears. It was that of the rapidly-approaching rain striking the foliage of the neighboring forest; and, scarcely had they time to gain the cover of the house, before the deluging torrents poured over it with a force and fury beneath which the quelled fires speedily sunk, hissing, into darkness and death.

CHAPTER VII.

"Wo is the youth whom Fancy gains,
Winning from Reason's hands the reins."

The morning of the next day, serene and beautiful as a bride decked in her fresh robes and redolent in her forest perfumery, came smiling over the wilderness hills of the east, to greet our little pioneer family on their deliverance from the perils of yesterday. The war of the elements, that had raged so fearfully round their seemingly devoted domicile, had all passed away; and, after sleeping off the fatigue and excitement of the previous day, they rose to look around them, to find themselves safe, and call themselves satisfied. Their buildings had been, after all, but very slightly injured, and their green crops but little damaged; their fences, indeed, were mostly consumed; but these could be replaced from the timber of the burnt slash, with little more labor than would be required to pile up and burn that timber where it lay. But, whatever such additional labor might be, it was more than compensated by the very intensity of the fire which caused it, and which, at the same time, had so utterly consumed all the underbrush, limbs of the trees, and even the smaller trees themselves, that weeks less than with ordinary burns would be required in the clearing. Elwood, therefore, came in from his morning survey happily disappointed in the supposed extent of his losses; and, joining his wife and son in the house, whom he found busily engaged in cutting up, mealing, and placing in the hissing pan over the fire the broad, red, and rich-looking pieces of trout, the fruit of yesterday's excursion on the lake, he told them, with a gratified air, the result of his observation, which, on a merchant-like calculation of loss and gain from the conflagration, he made out to show even a balance in his favor. Mrs. Elwood rejoiced with her husband on the happy turn of affairs, and wondered why her son did not manifest the same flow of spirits. But the latter, for some reason or other, appeared unusually abstracted during the whole morning; and, when asked to relate the particulars of his perilous adventure with the moose, which he had the evening before but briefly mentioned, he exhibited a hesitation, and a sort of shying of the question, in that part of the adventure relating to the rescued girl, which did not escape the quick eye of the mother. It was evident to her that something was kept back. But what that something was she was wholly unable to conjecture. It was so unusual for her son to show any lack of frankness that the circumstance disturbed her, and, though she knew not exactly why, sent a boding chill over her heart, which caused her also to become thoughtful and silent. And Mr. Elwood, who possessed none of those mental sympathies which, in some, will often be found unconsciously mingling with the thoughts of others, so far, at least, as to apprise them of the general character and drift of those thoughts, now, in his turn, wondered why his wife, as well as son, should all at once become so unsocial and taciturn.

It will doubtless be generally said that this mental sympathy, or the intuitive perception of the main drift of what is passing in the minds of others, has an existence only in the fancy of fictionists. We, however, after years of close observation, have wholly ceased to doubt its reality. Scores of times have we been affected by thoughts and intentions which we knew must have a source other than in our own mind. Scores of times have we, in this manner, been put on our guard against the selfish designs which others were harboring to our disadvantage, of which no tongue had informed us, and of which, afterwards, we had tangible proof. And, on careful inquiry among persons of thought and sensibility, we have become convinced that the principle holds good to a very considerable extent among others; and that attention to the subject is only wanting to make it a generally received opinion. It was this principle that now affected Mrs. Elwood: not that she had the most distant idea that her son harbored aught of wrong intention toward any of his family, but she felt that his mind was somehow becoming subservient to schemes which existed somewhere in the minds of others, which concerned her or her family. But she *felt* rather than thought this; and, knowing she could give no reason for her singular impression, prudently kept it to herself.

"Good-morning, good-morning, gentlefolks," rang out the cheery voice of the hunter, who now looked in at the door as the Elwoods were rising from their breakfast. "Things look a little altered round here, this morning. I should hardly have known the place without the king pine, which, in its prime, was a tree of a thousand."

"That tree was an old acquaintance of yours, I suppose," remarked Elwood.

"Yes, of twenty years' standing; and I shall miss and mourn it as an old friend. But it died like a monarch, yielding only under the direct blow of the Almighty."

"Then you consider the lightning more especially the instrument of Heaven than the wind, fire, and other elements, do you?"

"To be sure I do. Wind, we know what it is; fire we know; water we also know; because we can see them, touch them, measure them. But who can see a piece of lightning when not in motion? who can find the least fragment of it after it has struck? It rends a tree, makes a smooth hole through a board, and ploughs up the ground. But go to the tree, and there is nothing there; look under the board, it is the same; and dig along the furrow it has ploughed to where it stopped, and it is not there, as it would be if it was any material thing, like a bullet, an axe, knife, or other instrument that produces such effects, in all other instances. No, 'tis not matter; it is the power of God; and your philosophers, who pretend to explain it, don't know what they are talking about. But enough of that. I came here to rally you out to go up the river with the rest of us, for the moose. You will both go, won't you?"

"Claud will, doubtless," replied Mr. Elwood. "Indeed, I have half a mind to go myself."

"Perhaps Claud, having had a fatiguing excursion yesterday, will stay at home, and let his father go, to-day," suggested Mrs. Elwood.

"It was not at all fatiguing, mother," responded Claud.

"The wind blows up the river to-day, ma'am," said the hunter, with a knowing look.

Little more was said; but the result was that Claud and the hunter now soon went off together on the proposed excursion. On reaching the mouth of the Magalloway, they found four others waiting for them, with their canoes, when the whole party commenced their little voyage up the river. After leisurely rowing against the here slow and gentle current of the stream for an hour or two, they reached their destination, and hauled up at a point most convenient for gaining the spot where the slaughtered moose had been left the evening before. Led on by the hunter, all now started for the place just named, except Claud, who, under pretence of taking a short gunning bout in the woods, and of soon coming round to join his companions, proceeded, as soon as the latter were out of sight, with slow and hesitating steps, up the river, for the opening and supposed residence of the fair unknown who had so long been the object of his wondering fancies, and who had, notwithstanding the exciting scenes he had witnessed at home, been the especial subject of his dreams after he retired to rest the night before. But what a strange, wayward, timid, doubting, and inconsistent thing is the tender passion in its incipient stages, especially when that passion has principally been wrought up by the imagination! He soon came to the clearing of which he was in quest, and obtained a clear view of the, to him, charmed cottage. But, instead of entering the opening directly, he went nearly round it, frequently pausing and advancing nearly to the edge of the woods; but as often retreating, being unable quite to make up his mind to show himself at all to the inmates of the cottage. Once he gave it up entirely, and started off for his companions. But, after he had proceeded a dozen rods, he came again to a stand, hesitated a while, and, as if ashamed of his irresolution, wheeled rapidly about, proceeded, with a quick, firm step, to the border of the woods, struck directly for the house, and, with assumed unconcern, marched up to the door,—where he was met, not by the young lady he expected first to see, but by her father. But who was that father? To his utter surprise, it was *his* father's old tempter and ruiner, the dark and inscrutable Gaut Gurley!

With a manner, for him, unusually gracious, Gurley extended his hand to Claud; ushered him into the house; formally introduced him to his wife, an ordinary, abject-looking woman; and then to his daughter, the fair, dark-eyed, tall, shapely, and every way magnificent Avis Gurley, the girl who had so long, but unwittingly, been the object of the young man's dreamy fancies.

"I have but very lately discovered," remarked Gurley, who seemed to feel himself called on to lead off in the conversation, after the usual commonplace remarks had been exchanged, "I have but lately discovered that I had, by a singular coincidence, again cast my lot in the same settlement with your family. Having made up my mind, a few months ago, to try a new country, and coming across the owner of this place, who was on a journey in New Hampshire, and who offered to sell and move off at once, I came on with him, struck a bargain, returned for my family, and brought them here about a fortnight ago. But, having been absent most of the time since, I didn't mistrust who my neighbors were."

"And you probably perceived, sir," said Avis, turning to Claud, with a smile, "you probably perceived, in your yesterday's adventure up here in the woods, that I have been in as bad a predicament as my father."

"How is that, Avis?" asked Gurley.

"Why, father," responded the other, "Mr. Elwood will readily suppose that I should not have been straying into the wood for flowers and berries, had I known we had any such neighbors as the one from whose pursuit he so kindly rescued me last evening."

"I was as much surprised at the ferocity of the animal as you were, I presume," said Claud, in reply. "And I was far more indebted to the hunter, Phillips, for my *own* rescue, than *you* were to *me* for *yours*. I merely turned the furious brute aside. It was he who, coming up in the nick of time, brought him dead to the earth."

"I supposed there were two of you," remarked Gurley. "I was half a mile up the river, yet I heard the firing plain enough; and, returning soon after, and hearing my daughter's story, I went to the place; but, by that time, you had dressed the animal and were gone. By the voices I heard in the woods, a short time ago, I concluded you came up, with others, for the beef."

"We did. You here should certainly be entitled to a liberal share. Will you not go up there?"

"Yes; I was thinking about it before you came in. I will go; but, as I wish to go a short distance into the woods, partly in another direction, I will now walk on and come round to the spot; and, if I don't meet you there, you may just tell your father how surprised I have been to find myself again in the same neighborhood with himself."

"Umph!" half audibly exclaimed the hitherto mute wife, with a look that seemed to say, "What a bouncer he is telling now!" and she was evidently about to say something, comporting with the significant exclamation, but a glance from her husband, as he passed out of the door, quelled her into silence.

On the departure of Gurley, his wife rose and left the room; when Claud, unexpectedly finding himself alone with his fair companion, instead of entering into the easy conversation with her which the dictates of common gallantry would seem to require, soon began to manifest signs of constraint and embarrassment, which did not escape the eye of the young lady, and which caused her no little surprise and perplexity. She knew nothing of what had been passing in his mind, nor once dreamed of the circumstance which had first impressed her image there. She had, indeed, known nothing of the Elwoods, except what she had heard her father say of them as a family, with whose head he had in some way been formerly connected in business. Had she been asked, she would doubtless have recalled the fact that her father had, the year before, employed an artist to paint a miniature likeness of her, which he subsequently pretended to have sent to a relative of his residing in Quebec, and she never entertained the least suspicion that it was not thus properly disposed of. She had never seen Claud till yesterday, when he so opportunely appeared for her rescue; and, even then, she had no idea who it was to whom she had thus become indebted. She, however, had been much prepossessed with his appearance and manly bearing, and felt a lively sense of gratitude for the voluntary service; and when, by the introduction of her father, she became apprised of the character of her deliverer, she felt doubly gratified that he had turned out to be one who, she believed, would not take any mean advantage of the obligation. For these reasons, she could not understand why he should appear so reserved, unless it was that she had failed to interest him; and, finally concluding that this must be the case, she did that which, with her maidenly pride and high spirit, she would otherwise have scorned to do, she exerted herself to the utmost to interest and please him; and, when he rose to return to his companions, she followed him into the yard, and smilingly said:

"You are fond of gunning excursions, are you not, Mr. Elwood?"

"Yes, O yes, quite so," replied Claud, with awkward hesitation.

"And would not an occasional excursion in *this* direction be as pleasant as any other?" she asked, with playful significance.

But, instead of replying in the same spirit, the bewildered young man turned, and sent a gaze into the depths of her lustrous dark eyes, so serious and intense that it brought a blush to her cheek; when, stammering out his intention of often taking her house in his way in future, he hurriedly bade her good-by, and departed, leaving her more perplexed than ever.

As for Claud, it would be difficult to describe his sensations on leaving the house, or make any thing definite out of the operations of his mind. Both heart and brain were working tumultuously, but not in unison. The train which his imagination had been laying was on the point of being kindled into, a blaze by the reality. He knew it; he felt it; but he knew also that it was the part of wisdom to smother the flame while it yet might be controlled. The unexpected and startling discovery which he had just made, that the girl who had so wrought upon his fancy, both when seen in the picture and met in the original, was the daughter of Gaut Gurley, raised difficulties and dangers in the path he found himself entering, which his judgment told him could only be avoided by his immediate desistance. For he was well aware how deeply rooted was his mother's aversion to this man, and how fatal had been his influence over his father, who had but a few months before escaped from his toils, and then only, perhaps, because there was no more to be gained by keeping him in them any longer. A connection with the daughter, therefore, however opposite in character from her father, would not only greatly mar his mother's happiness, but in all probability lead to a renewal of the intimacy between his father and Gurley; an event which he himself felt was to be deprecated. But the Demon of Sophistry, who first taught self-deceiving man how to make "the wish father to the thought," here interposing, whispered to the incipient lover that his father had reformed, and why not then Gaut Gurley? This reasoning, however, could not be made to satisfy his judgment; and again commenced the struggle between head and heart, one pulling one way and the other in another way,—too often an unequal struggle, too often like one of those contests between man and wife, where reason succumbs and will comes off triumphant.

Such were the fluctuating thoughts and purposes which occupied the agitated bosom of Claud Elwood, in his solitary walk to the place where the boats had been left, and where the subject was now driven from his mind, for a while, by the appearance of his companions and the merry jokes of the hunter. They had cut up the moose meat, which they had found in good condition, and brought all they deemed worth saving down to the landing. And, being now ready to embark, they apportioned the meat among the different canoes, and rowed with the now favoring current rapidly down the river together till they reached its mouth, when they separated, and bore their allotted portions of the moose to their respective homes.

For the two succeeding days and nights the hapless Claud was the prey of conflicting emotions,—the more oppressive because he carefully kept them pent up in his own bosom. He dared not make the least allusion before his parents to the lady whom they knew he had rescued, or his visit to her home, for he could not do so without revealing the fact that the dreaded Gaut Gurley, with his family, had found his way into the vicinity; while, if he did disclose this fact, he felt that he could not hold up his head before them till he had conquered his feelings towards the daughter. And sometimes he thought he had conquered them, and resolved that he would never see her again. But, brooding over his feelings in the solitudes of the woods, he only cherished and fanned the flame he was thinking to extinguish; and he again relapsed,—again paused,—again "resolved, re-resolved, and *did* the same;" for, on the third day, under the excuse of taking another excursion on the lake, he was drawn, as surely as the vibrating needle to the pole, to the beautiful load-star of the Magalloway.

Suspecting the state of young Elwood's feelings towards her, and fearing that she might have been too forward in her advances at their last interview, Avis Gurley, this time, received him with a dignity and maidenly reserve, which, when contrasted with her former sociability and cordiality of manner, seemed to him like studied coolness. This soon led him, in turn, to sue for favor. And so earnestly did he pursue his object, that, before he was aware of what he was saying, he had revealed the secret of his heart. She received his remarks in respectful silence, but gave no indication by which he could judge whether the inadvertent disclosure was pleasing or otherwise, except what might be gathered from her increased cordiality on other subjects, to which she now adroitly turned the conversation. This was just enough to encourage him, and at the same time leave him in that degree of doubt and suspense which generally operate as the greatest incentive to persevere in the pursuit of an object. It proved so in his case; and, to this natural incentive to persevere, was now added another, that of respect for her character,—a respect which every hour's conversation with her enhanced, and which he might accord to her with entire justice. Gaut Gurley, like many other bad men, was proud of having a good daughter. He early perceived that she inherited all that was comely and good in him, physically and morally, without any of his defects or faults of character. And, desirous so to rear her as to make the most of her natural endowments, and so, at the same time, that her character should not be marred by his example, he had been at considerable expense with her education, and had even deported himself with much circumspection in her presence. This, as will be readily inferred of one of his designing character, he did from a mixed motive: partly from parental pride and affection, and partly to make her, through some advantageous marriage, subservient to his own personal interests.

In this state of affairs between Claud and Avis, closed this, their second interview. Another, and another, and yet another, succeeded at brief intervals. And so rapid is the course of love, when springing up in solitudes like these, where nothing occurs to divert the gathering current, but every thing conspires to increase it,—where to our young devotees all around them seemed to reflect their own feelings,—where the aeolian music of the whispering pines that embowered their solitary walks seemed but to give voice to the melody that filled their own hearts,—where to them the birds all sang of love,—where love smiled upon them in the pensive beams of the moon, glistened in the stars, and was stamped on all the expanse of blue sky above, and on all the forms of beauty on the green earth beneath,—so rapid, we repeat, is the course of love, thus born, and thus fostered, that a fortnight had scarcely elapsed before they had both yielded up heart and soul to the dominion of the well-named blind god, and uttered their mutual vows of love and constancy.

This was the sunshine of their love; but the storms were already gathering in the distance.

CHAPTER VIII.

"The sigh that lifts her breastie comes.
Like sad winds frae the sea,
Wi' sic a dreary sough, as wad
Bring tears into yer e'e."

When Claud Elwood reached home, on the eventful visit to the Magalloway which resulted in the exchange of vows between him and Avis Gurley, as intimated at the close of the last chapter, he at once suspected, from the sad and troubled looks of his mother and the disturbed manner of his father, that the secret of his late visits abroad, as well as of the unexpected advent of the family visited, had, in some way, become known to them in his absence. A feeling of mingled delicacy and self-condemnation, however, prevented him from making any inquiries; and, with a commonplace remark, which was received in silence, he took a seat, and, with much inward trembling, awaited the expected *denouement*. But it did not come so soon nor in so harsh terms as he expected. There are occasions when we feel so deeply that we are reluctant to begin the task of unburdening our minds; and, when we do speak out, it is oftener in sorrow than in anger. It was so in the present instance. Mr. Elwood had that day been abroad among the settlers, and, for the first time, learned not only that Gaut Gurley had moved with his family into the settlement, but that Claud was courting his daughter, and a match already settled on between them. On his return home, Elwood felt almost as much reluctance in making known his discoveries to his wife as Claud had before him; for he well knew how deeply they would disquiet her. But, soon concluding there would be no wisdom in attempting concealment, he told her what he had heard. As he had anticipated, the news fell like a sudden thunderclap on her heart. She had experienced, indeed, many strange misgivings respecting her son's late mysterious absences; but she was not prepared for such a double portion of ill-omened news as she deemed this to be, and it struck her mute with dismay, for it at once brought a cloud over the future, which to her eye was dark with portents. Elwood himself was also obviously considerably disquieted by the news, showing no little uneasiness and excitement,—an excitement, perhaps, resembling that which is said to be manifested by a bird in the presence of the devouring reptile. He doubtless would gladly have been relieved from any further connection with Gaut. He doubtless would gladly have avoided even the slightest renewal of their former acquaintance. But, for reasons which he had never disclosed, he felt confident he should not long be suffered to enjoy any such exemption. And feeling, for the same reasons, how weak he should be in the hands of that man, he was troubled, far more troubled than he would have been willing to own, at the discoveries of the day, even if that part of it relating to the intimacy of his son and Gaut's daughter should prove, as he believed, a mere conjecture.

It was at this juncture, and before a word of comment had been offered either by Mrs. Elwood or her husband on the news he had related, that Claud arrived and entered the room.

"Well, God's will be done!" sadly uttered Mrs. Elwood, at length breaking the embarrassing silence, but without raising her eyes from her work, which lay neglected in her lap.

"What does mother mean?" doubtfully asked Claud, turning to his father.

"I have been telling her some unexpected news, which greatly disturbs her mind,—more than is necessary, perhaps," replied the other, with poorly assumed indifference.

"What news?" rejoined the son, having made up his mind that, if his own secret was involved, as he supposed, the long dreaded *eclaircissement* might as well come now as ever.

"Why, that Gaut Gurley has moved with his family into the settlement. And that is not all; but the rest of it, which relates to a lately-formed intimacy between you and Gaut's daughter, I presume is mere guess-work."

Mrs. Elwood turned a searching glance to the face of her son, and waited to hear his reply to the last remarks, but he was silent; and the last gleam of hope, which had for the moment lighted up the mother's countenance, faded like a moon-beam on the edge of an eclipsing cloud; and, after a long pause and silence which no one interrupted, she slowly and sadly said:

"When I consented to leave the comforts and social blessings to which I had been accustomed, and come into this lone wilderness, with its well-known hardships and privations, my great and indeed only motive was, to see my family placed beyond the temptations of the city, and especially beyond the fatal, and to me always mysterious, influence of that wicked and dangerous man, Gaut Gurley. And with this object I came cheerfully, gladly. And when I reached this place, fondly hoping and believing we had escaped that man, and were forever secure from his wiles, I became happy,—happier than since I left my native hills in New-Hampshire. It soon became to *me*, lone and dreary as it might appear to others,—it soon became to *me*, in my fancied security from the evils we had fled, a second Paradise. But to me it is a Paradise no longer; the Serpent has found his way into our Eden; and, not content with having beguiled and ruined one, must now have the other so entangled in the toils that both will be kept in his power."

"You are going a great ways to borrow trouble, it appears to me, Alice," remarked Elwood, after a pause.

"It certainly seems so to me, also, mother," said Claud. "You cannot know but Gurley comes here with as honest purposes as father. But, were it otherwise, the daughter should not be held responsible for the faults of the father, nor, without good reason, be accused of favoring any sinister designs he may entertain."

"Claud takes a just view of the case, on both points, I presume," rejoined Mr. Elwood. "As to Gurley, I know not how, or why, he came here; nor do I wish or expect to have any thing to do with him. And as to Claud, I trust he knows enough to take care of himself."

"You have both evaded the spirit of my remarks," responded Mrs. Elwood. "When I speak of Gaut Gurley's motives and designs, you must know I judge from his past conduct. Have either of you as safe grounds of judging him? And when I allude to his daughter, I do so with no thought of holding her amenable for the faults of her father, or even of assuming the ground that she has inherited any of his objectionable traits of character. I intend nothing of the kind, for I know nothing of her. But I do say, that, whenever she marries, she becomes the connecting link between her husband and her father, the chain extending both ways, so as to bind their respective families together, and give one the power and means of evil which could in no other way be obtained. In view of all these circumstances, then, I feel that a calamity is in store for us. God grant that my fears and forebodings may prove groundless."

The husband and son were saved the difficult and embarrassing task of replying, by the arrival of Philips, who, in his free and easy manner, entered and took a seat with the family.

"I came, gentlefolks," said the hunter, after a few commonplace remarks had been exchanged,—"I came to see if you know what a 'bee' means?"

"A bee? what, honey-bees?" asked Mr. Elwood, in surprise at the oddness of the question.

"No, not a honey-bee, exactly, or a humble-bee, but a sort of work-meeting of men or women, to help a neighbor to husk his corn, for instance, build him a log house, or do off some other job for him in a day, which alone would take him perhaps weeks. These turn-outs we new settlers call 'bees.' Nothing is more common than for a man to get up a bee to knock off at once a pressing job he wants done. And, when a new-comer appears to be delicate about moving in the matter, the neighbors sometimes volunteer, and get up a bee for him, among themselves."

"I may have heard of the custom; but why do you say you came to ask me if I know any thing about it?"

"Well, I kinder thought I would. You have a pretty stiff-looking burnt piece here to be logged off soon, have you not?"

"Why, yes."

"And it would be a hard and heavy month's job for you and the young man to do it, would it not?"

"The best part of a month, perhaps; but I was intending to go at it in season, that we might get it all cleared and sown by the middle of September; which must be done, if I join you and the rest of the usual company in the fall trapping and hunting expedition."

"Of course you will join us. It is our main and almost only chance here of getting any money."

"So I have always understood, and therefore made up my mind to go into it, if I can get ready. I have been down the river to-day and engaged my seed wheat. To-morrow I thought of going abroad again, to try to engage some help for clearing the piece."

"Well, you need not go a rod for that purpose."

"Why not?"

"Because we have got up a bee for you in the settlement, large enough, we think, to log off your whole piece in a day."

"Indeed! Who has been so kind as to start such a project?"

"Several of us: Codman, that you may have seen, or at least heard of, as the best trapper in the settlement, took upon himself to enlist those round the southerly end of the lake, where he lives; and I have arranged matters a little in this section and on the river below. But, in justice, I should name, as the man who has taken the most interest in the movement, the new settler who has this summer come into the parts, and made his pitch over on the Magalloway. His name is Gurley."

A dead silence of several minutes ensued, during which Mrs. Elwood looked sadly and meaningly from the husband to the son, both of whose countenances seemed to fall and shrink before her significant glances.

"Well," at length resumed the hunter, perceiving no response was to be made to his last remark, "seeing we had got all arranged and ready, I came to notify you, so that you should not be taken by surprise. We propose to be on the ground, men and oxen, early day after to-morrow. There will be fifteen or twenty of us, perhaps, with five or six yoke of oxen, and like enough a stiff horse or two."

"But how can I provision such a company on so short notice?"

"No trouble about that. You have salt pork?"

"A good supply."

"Corn meal?"

"Yes; and wheat flour, with fine new potatoes."

"All right. I will take care of the rest. I will take the young man, here, into my largest canoe, to-morrow morning, if he be so disposed, and we will go up the lake, perhaps into the upper lake, and it will be a strange case if we don't return at night with fish, and I think flesh, enough to victual the company; and, in the mean time, my women will come up and be on hand to-morrow and next day, to help Mrs. Elwood do the baking and cooking."

The friendly movement of the neighbors, thus announced, was not, of course, to be opposed or questioned by those for whose benefit it was intended, any further than Mr. Elwood had done in relation to his ability to entertain the company so well as their kindness deserved. Mr. Elwood and his son, indeed, who had been dreading the hard job of clearing off their land, were greatly gratified at the unexpected kindness. And even Mrs. Elwood, pained and annoyed as she was by the part taken by Gaut Gurley, whose only motive she believed was to gain some advantage for meditated evil, entered cheerfully into the affair, and joined her husband in handsome expressions of acknowledgment to the hunter, and assurances of doing their best to provide properly for the company. The matter was therefore considered as settled; and the hunter departed, to call, as he had proposed, early the next morning for Claud, for an excursion up the lake, to procure fresh provisions for the coming occasion.

The family were early astir the next morning, intent on their respective duties in preparation for the appointed logging bee. They had scarcely dispatched their breakfast, before the hunter, as he had promised, called for Claud; when the two departed together, with their guns and fishing gear, for the lake, whither we propose to accompany them.

"Well, now, let us settle the order of the day," said Phillips, after they had reached the landing and deposited their luggage in the canoe selected for the purpose.

"I am a companion of the voyage, to-day, and, as you know, but a learner in these sports," responded Claud. "You have but to name your plan."

"Well, my plan is this: to steer across and get up the lake to the inlet and rapids which connect this to the next upper lake, called by the Indians the Molechunk-a-munk; up these rapids into that lake, where we will take a row of a few hours, and home again by nightfall. In these rapids, going or returning, we may safely count, at this season, on a plenty of trout; and, on the borders of the lake beyond, I know of several favorite haunts of the deer, one of which I propose to take into the canoe as ballast to steady it for running the rapids, on our way back."

"What is the whole distance?"

"Four or five miles of this lake, as many of the river or rapids, and as far into the upper lake as we please."

"You are laying out largely for one day, are you not?"

"No, 'tis nothing. You see, I have brought round for our use my best birch bark canoe. I have rowed her fifty miles a day round the lakes many a time. We shall bound over the lake in almost no time, and the rapids, which are the only drawback, can soon be surmounted, by oar or setting-pole, or, what may be cheapest, carrying the canoe round those most difficult of passage. The boat does not weigh an hundred. I could travel with it a mile on my head, as fast as you would wish to walk without a pound of luggage. So, in with you, and I'll show you how it is done."

Accordingly they launched forth in their primitive craft, which, as before intimated, was the once noted birch bark canoe built by the hunter agreeably to the exact rules of Indian art. Few, who have never seen and observed the process of constructing this canoe, which, for thousands of years before the advent of the white man, was the only craft used by the aborigines in navigating the interior waters, have any idea how, from such seemingly fragile materials, and with no other tools than a hatchet, knife, and perhaps a bone needle, the Indian can construct a canoe so extremely light and at the same time so tough and durable. In building his canoe, which is one of the greatest efforts of his mechanical skill, the Indian goes to work systematically. He first peels his bark from a middle-sized birch tree, and cuts it in strips five or six inches wide, and twelve, fifteen, or twenty feet long, according to the length and size of the designed canoe. He then dries them thoroughly in the sun, after which he nicely scrapes and smooths off the outside. He next proceeds to soak these strips, which are thus made to go through a sort of tanning process, to render them tough and pliable, as well as to obviate their liability to crack by exposure to the sun. After the materials are thus prepared, he smooths off a level piece of ground, and drives around the outside a line of strong stakes, so that the space within shall describe the exact form of the boat in contemplation. Inside of these stakes he places and braces up the wet and pliable pieces of bark, beginning at the bottom and building up and bending into form the sides and ends, till the structure has attained the required height. In this situation it is left till it is again thoroughly dried and all the pieces become fixed in shape. A light inside framework is then constructed, resembling the skeleton of a fish, and of dimensions to fit the canoe already put in form in the manner we have described. The pieces of cured material are then numbered and taken down; when the architect, beginning at the bottom, lapping and sewing together the different pieces, proceeds patiently in his work, till the sides are built, the ends closed nicely up, and each piece lashed firmly to the framework, which, though of surprising lightness, is made to serve as keel, knees, and ribs of the boat. Every seam and crevice is then filled with melted pitch. The Indian then has his canoe fit for use; and he may well boast of a boat, which, for combined strength and lightness, and especially for capacity of burden, no art of the shipbuilder has ever been able to surpass, and which, if it has not already, might serve for a model of the best lifeboat ever constructed, in these days of boasted perfection in marine arts and improvements.

Bounding over the smooth waters like a seabird half on wing, our voyagers soon found themselves on the northerly side of the lake; when, rounding a point, they began to skirt the easterly shore of the bay that makes up to the inlet, at a more leisurely pace, for the purpose of being on the lookout for deer, which might be standing in the edge of the water round the coves, to cool themselves and keep off the flies. Not seeing any signs of game, however, they steered out so as to clear the various little capes or woody points of land inclosing the numerous coves scattered along the indented shore, and struck a line for the great inlet at the head of the lake, which they now soon reached, and commenced rowing against the at first gentle and then rapid current, which here pours down from, the upper lakes, through the rocky and picturesque defiles, in the form of a magnificent river, rivalling in its size the midway portions of the Connecticut or Hudson.

"Now, young man," said the hunter, laying aside his paddle and taking up the strong, elastic setting-pole he had provided for the occasion, "now you must look out for your balance. The river, to be sure, is quite low, and the current, of course, at its feeblest point; but we shall find places enough within the next mile where the canoe, to go up at all, must go up like the jump of a catamount. So, down in the bottom of the boat, on your braced knees, with your haunches on your heels, and leave all to me."

"What! do you expect to force the canoe up rapids like these?" asked Claud, in surprise, as he cast his eye over the long reach of eddying, tumbling waters, that looked like a lessening sheet of foam as it lay stretched upward in the distant perspective.

"I expect to try," coolly replied the hunter; "and, if you lay asleep in the bottom of the canoe, I should expect to succeed. And, as it is, if you can keep cool and obey orders, we will see what can be done."

Claud implicitly obeyed the directions of the hunter, without much faith, however, in the success of his bold attempt. But he soon perceived he had underrated the skill and strength of arm which had been relied on to accomplish the seemingly impossible feat. Standing upright and slightly bracing in the bottom of his canoe, the hunter first marked out with his eye his course through a given reach of the rock-broken and foaming waters above; then, nicely calculating the resisting force of each rapid to be overcome, and the required impetus, and the direction to be given to his canoe to effect it, he sharply bid Claud be on his guard, and sent the light craft like an arrow into the boiling eddies before him. And now, by sudden and powerful shoves, he was seen shooting obliquely up one rapid; tacking with the quickness of light, and darting off zigzag among the rocks and eddies towards another, which was in turn surmounted; while the boat was forced, surging and bounding forward, with increasing impetus, now up and now athwart the rushing currents, till he had gained a resting-place in the still water of some sheltering boulder in the stream, when he would mark off, with a rapid glance, another reach of falls, and shoot in among them as before. Thus, with the quick tacks and turns and sudden leaps of the ascending salmon, and almost with the celerity, he made his way up the long succession of rapids, until the last of the series was overcome, and he found himself safely emerging into the smooth waters of the beautiful lakelet or pond which divides, in the upper portion of its course, this remarkable stream. Another row of a mile or so now brought the voyagers where the water again took the form of a swift river, tumbling and foaming over the rocks, in the last series of rapids to be overcome. These also were surmounted in the same manner and with the same success as the former.

But this part of the voyage was marked with an unexpected adventure, and one which seemed destined to lead to the operation of new and singular moral agencies, both in the near and more distant future, having an important bearing on the fate and fortunes of young Elwood. They had reached the last and most difficult of all the rapids yet encountered, and were resting, preparatory to the anticipated struggle, in a smooth piece of water under the lee of a huge rock, on either side of which the divided stream rushed in two foam-covered torrents, with the force and swiftness of a mill-race; when they were startled by the shrill exclamations of a female voice, in tones indicative of surprise and alarm. The sounds, which came from some unseen point not far above them in the stream, were evidently drawing near at a rapid rate. Presently a small Indian canoe, with a single female occupant, whose youth and beauty, even in the distance, were apparent, shot swiftly into view, and came tossing and whirling down the stream, unguided, and wholly at the mercy of the crooked and raging currents along which it was borne with the speed of the wind. The imperilled maiden uttered a cry of joy at the appearance of our voyagers, and held up the handle of a broken oar, to indicate to them at once the cause of her fearful dilemma and need of assistance.

"I will throw her one of our paddles, and she will best take care of herself," hurriedly exclaimed the hunter, seizing the implement, and awaiting her nearest approach to throw it within her reach.

The critical point was the next instant reached, but the hunter, in his nervous anxiety and haste, made his throw a little too soon and with too much force. The paddle struck directly under the prow of the canoe, and shot beyond, far out of reach of the expectant maiden's extended hands. Another oar was hurled after her, with no better effect; when, for the first time, a shade of despair passed over her agitated countenance; for she saw herself rapidly drifting directly into the jaws of a wild and fearful labyrinth of breakers not fifty yards below, where, in all probability, her fragile canoe would be dashed to pieces, and herself thrown against the slippery and jagged rock, drawn down, and lost. Claud, who had witnessed, with trembling anxiety, the hunter's vain attempts to place the means of self-preservation in the hands of the maiden, and who now perceived, in their full light, the perils of the path to which she was helplessly hastening, could restrain his generous impulses no longer; and, quickly throwing off his hat and coat, he leaped overboard, dashed headlong into the current, and struck boldly down it to overtake the receding canoe.

"Hold! madness! They will both perish together!" rapidly exclaimed the hunter, surprised and alarmed at the rash attempt of his young companion. "But I will share in their dangers,—perhaps save them, yet."

Accordingly he hastily headed round his canoe, and, hazardous as he knew must be the experiment, sent it surging down the current after his endangered young friends; for the one, as will soon appear, was no less his favorite than the other. In the mean time, Claud, in swimming over a sunken rock, luckily gained a foothold, which enabled him to rise and plunge forward again with redoubled speed; and, so well-timed and powerful were his exertions, that he came within reach of the stern of the fugitive canoe just as it was whirling round sideways in the reflux of the waves caused by the water dashing against a high rock standing partly in the current. It was a moment of life or death, both to the man and maiden; for the boat was on the point of going broadside over the first fall into the wild and seething waters, seen leaping and roaring in whirlpools and jets of foam among the intricate passes of the ragged rocks below. Making sure of his grasp on the end of the canoe that had been thus fortunately thrown within his reach, the struggling Claud made an effort to draw it from the edge of the abyss into which it was about to be precipitated; but, with his most desperate exertions, he was barely enabled to keep it in position, while his strength was rapidly giving way. The unequal contest was quickly noticed by the hapless girl; and, after watching a moment, with a troubled eye, the fruitless efforts and wasting strength of the young man, she calmly rose to her feet, exhibiting, as she stood upright in the boat, with the spray dashing over her marble forehead and long flowing hair, in the faultless symmetry of her person, the beautiful cast of her features, and the touching eloquence of her speaking countenance, a figure which might well serve as a subject for the pencil of the artist.

"Let go, brave stranger," she cried, in clear, silvery tones, after throwing a grateful and admiring glance down upon her gallant rescuer; "let me go, and save yourself. I can die as befits a daughter of my people."

"Hold on, there, Claud! Courage, girl! I see a way to save you both," at that critical instant rang above the roar of the waters the sharp voice of the hunter, who, with wonderful tact and celerity, had shot down obliquely across the main current, out of it through a narrow side pass, down that and round the intervening rocks, and was now driving with main strength up another pass, abreast of the objects of his anxiety. "There: now seize the head of my canoe, and hold on to both; and, on your life, be quick!" he continued, shouting to the exhausted young man, while he himself was struggling with all his might to get and keep his boat in the right position among the battling currents.

After one or two ineffectual attempts, Claud, with a last desperate effort, fortunately succeeded in securing his grasp on the hunter's boat, without losing his hold on the other; when, with one mighty effort of the latter, they were all drawn out of the vortex together, and soon brought safely to shore.

"Fluella, my fair young friend," said the hunter, taking a long breath, and respectfully turning to the rescued girl, as the party stepped on to the dry beach, "I have not often—no, never—felt more rejoiced than now, in seeing you stand here in safety."

"I know the danger I have been in," responded the maiden, feelingly. "O yes, know to remember, and know to remember, also, those who made my escape. Mr. Phillips, I am grateful much."

"Don't thank *me*," promptly replied the hunter. "I am ashamed not to have been the first in the rescue, when the chief's daughter was in danger."

"But, Mr. Phillips," rejoined the other, with an expressive smile, "you have not told me who this stranger is, who seemed to measure the value of his own life by such a worthless thing as mine."

"True, no," returned the hunter; "but this gentleman, Fluella, is young Mr. Claud Elwood, who, with his father and mother, has recently moved into the settlement; and they are now my nearest neighbors, at the foot of the lower lake. And to you, Claud, I have to say, that this young lady is the daughter of Wenongonet, the red chief, the original lord of these lakes, and still living on the one next above."

Both the maiden and her gallant young preserver seemed equally surprised, at the announcement of each others' name and character: the former, because it suggested questions in the solution of which she felt an interest, but which, with the characteristic prudence of her race, she forbore to ask; and the latter, because he found it hard to realize that the fair-complexioned and every way beautiful girl, who stood before him, readily speaking his own language, and neatly and even richly arrayed in the usual female habiliments of the day, with the single exception of the gay, beaded moccasins, that enveloped her small feet and ankles,—found it extremely difficult to realize that one of such an exterior, and of so much evident culture, could possibly have descended from the tawny and uncultivated sons of the forest.

"You two should hereafter be friends, should you not?" observed the hunter, perceiving their mutual restraint, of which he wished to relieve them.

Rousing himself, with a prompt affirmative reply to the question, Claud gallantly advanced, and extended his hand to his fair companion, who, with evident emotion, and a slight suffusion of the cheek, gave him her own in return, as she said:

"O yes. Mr. Phillips' friend is my friend, and, I—I—why, I can't thank him *now*; the words don't come; the thanks remain unshaped in my heart."

"Excuse me," replied Claud, "excuse me if I say, Miss Fluella, as Mr. Phillips calls you, that you have already expressed, and in the finest terms, far more than I am entitled to; so let that pass, and tell us how your mishap occurred?"

"O, naturally enough, though rather stupidly," responded the other, regaining her ease and usually animated manner. "You must know that I sometimes play the Indian girl, in doing my father's trouting. And, having rowed down to the rapids this morning for that purpose, I ran my canoe on to a rock, up here at the head of the falls, and threw into an eddy below, till I had taken a supply. But, like other folks, I must have the *one more*,—a large one I had seen playing round my hook; and, in my eagerness to take him, I did not notice that my canoe had slipped off the rock till I found it drifting down the current. I seized my oar, but, with the first blow in the water it snapt in my hands. You know the rest, unless, perhaps, the number of fish I caught," she added, pointing to a string of fine trout still lying safely in the bottom of her canoe.

"Brave girl!" exclaimed the hunter, going up to the boat with Claud, to inspect the fish, which they had not before noticed. "A good ten pounds, and fine ones, too. Claud shall remain here while I go a piece up the lake for a deer, and follow your example, except the race down the rapids; but that he can't do, for I shall take our canoe with me, and make him fish from the shore, which will be just as well. Are you agreed to that arrangement, young man?"

This proposition being accepted, and it being also settled by common consent that no further attempt should, at this time, be made to ascend the remaining rapids with either of the boats the hunter and Claud, accompanied by the light-footed Fluella, took up her canoe and set off with it, along shore, towards a convenient landing in the lake above, then not more than sixty or seventy rods distant. In a short time the proposed landing was reached, and the boat let down into the water. The maiden, with an easy and sprightly movement, then flung herself into her seat, and, with a paddle hastily whittled for her out of a piece of drift-wood, by the ever ready hunter, sent her little craft in a curving sweep into the lake; when, facing round to her preservers, while a sweet and grateful smile broke over her dimpling features, she bade and bowed them adieu, and went bounding over the undulating waves towards her home, on an island some miles distant, near the southeastern border of this romantic sheet of water.

"Can it be," half-soliloquized Claud, as he stood rivetting his wondering gaze on the beauteous figure, which, gracefully bowing with the lightly-dipping oar, was receding from his rapt view, and gradually melting away in the distance; "can it be that she is but a mere Indian girl, one of those wild, untutored children of the forest?"

"It is even so, young man," responded the hunter, rousing himself from the reverie into which he also seemed to have fallen at the departure of his fair favorite; "it is even so; but, for all that, the very flower of all the womankind, white or red, according to my ideas, that ever graced the borders of these lakes."

"But how came she by those neatly-turned English features, and that clear, white complexion?"

"Why, her mother, who is now dead, was an uncommon handsome woman for a squaw, and had, as I perhaps should have qualified when I answered so about this girl, some white blood in her veins; or rather had, as the old chief once told me, somewhere away back among the gone-by generations, a female ancestor, a pure white woman, who was made captive by the Indians, and married into their tribe, and who was as handsome as a picture. But the white blood seemed to have been pretty much lost among the descendants, till the appearance of this nonsuch of a girl, in whom every drop of it seemed to have again been collected."

"Some might, perhaps, draw different conclusions in the case."

"Yes, and draw them very wrongfully, too, as I have no doubt many people do in such cases; for I have often noticed it among families, and ascertained it as a fact, that where a person of particular looks and character once lived, his or her like, though not coming out visibly in any of the descendants for a long time, is sure sooner or later to appear, and so will frequently leap out in a child four or five generations off; a complete copy, in looks, blood, and character, of the original (as far as can be judged from family tradition), who may have been dead an hundred years. This is my notion; and I hold that every person is destined to be at least once reproduced among some of his descendants. I, or the exact like of me, will likely enough be seen in some of my blood descendants, fifty or an hundred years hence, building dams or mills on these very falls, or even riding in a carriage around these wild lakes, where I have spent nearly my whole life in hunting moose, and the other wild animals known only in the unbroken forest."

"Your theory may be true, but it does not quite account, I think, for the evident intelligence and culture of this remarkable girl. To appear and converse as she does, she must have seen considerable of good society out of the forest, and, I should think, schools."

"She has, both. Her father, one fall, when she was a girl of ten or eleven, took her along with him to a city on the coast, where he went to sell his furs and nice basket-work, and where she, some how, excited the lively interest of a good family, and particularly of a wealthy gentleman then living in the family. Well, the short of the matter is, that they persuaded the chief to leave her through the winter; and, she becoming a favorite with them all, they instructed her, sent her to school, and dressed her as they would an own daughter, and would only part with her in the spring on condition of her returning in the fall. And so it has gone on till now, she living with them winters, and here with her father summers; for, though they would like to take her entirely out of the woods, she would not desert her father, who loves her as his life, and calls her the light of his lodge,—no, not for all the gold in the cities."

"You must then be well acquainted with this Indian family, and can give me their history."

"As far as is proper for me to tell, as well as anybody, perhaps. When I was a young man, I at times used to live with the chief, who always made me welcome to his lodge, and gave me his confidence. He was then but little past his prime, and one of the smartest men, every way, I ever knew. He was then worth property, and lived with his first wife, this girl's mother, who, as I told you, was very good-looking and intelligent. But his second wife was as homely as his first was handsome. As to Wenongonet himself, who has now got to be, though still active, an old man, he claims to have been a direct descendant of Paugus,—a grandson, I believe, of that noted chief,—who was slain in Lovewell's bloody fight, and whose tribe, once known as the Sokokis or Saco Indians, who were great fighters, it is said, were then forever broken up, the most of them fleeing over the British highlands and joining the St. Francis Indians in Canada. The family of Paugus, however, with a few of the head men, who survived the battle, concluded to remain this side of the mountain, and try to keep up a show of the tribe on these lakes, where they lived till Paugus' son, who on the death of his father became their sagamore or chief, died, when they gradually drew off into Canada, leaving Wenongonet, the last chief's son, the only permanent Indian resident, after a while, on these lakes. But come, young man, enough of Indian matters for to-day: we must now be stirring, or our day's work may come short. Help me to take my canoe up here into the lake; and, within four hours, the time to which I will limit my absence, we will see what can be done by each, in our different undertakings."

The employment of another half-hour fully sufficed to place the canoe of the hunter in the smooth water above the rapids; when the latter, with a cheery "heigh ho," at each light dip of his springy oar, struck off towards the foot of the pine-covered hills that lift their green summits from the western shores of the lake, leaving his young companion to proceed to his allotted portion of the sports or labors of the day. Preparing his long fishing-rod and tackle, according to the instructions which the hunter had given him for adapting his mode of fishing to the locality and season, Claud made his way along down the edge of the stream to a designated point, a short distance above the place where, on the occurrence of the incident before described, they had ceased to ascend the rapids in their canoes. He here found, as he had been told, below a traversing reach of bare breakers, a large, deep eddy of gently revolving water, in the centre of which lay tossing on the swell a broad spiral wreath of spotless foam. The hunter, in selecting these rapids, and especially this resting-spot of the ascending fish, as the place where he could safely warrant the taking of the needed supply of trout, had not spoken without knowledge; for it may well be doubted whether there could be found, in all the regions of the north, a reach of running water of equal length with this wild and singularly picturesque portion of the Androscoggin river, containing such quantities of this beautiful fish as are found about midsummer, swarming up the rapids on their way from the Umbagog to the upper lakes.

So, at least, Claud then found it; for, having passed to the most outward point of rocks inclosing the eddy, he no sooner threw in and drew his *skip bait* round the borders of the foam-island just named, than a dozen large trout shot up from beneath, and leaped splashing along the surface, in keen rivalry for the prize of the bait. With a second throw, he securely hooked one of a size which required all his strength to draw it, as he at length did, flapping and floundering to a safe landing. And for the next three hours he pursued the sport with a success which, notwithstanding the great number that broke away from his hook, well made good the augury of his beginning. By that time he had caught some dozens, of sizes varying from one to seven pounds, and enough, and more than he needed. But still he could not forego his exciting employment, and, insensible of the lapse of time, continued his drafts on the seemingly inexhaustible eddy, till roused by the long, shrill *halloo* of the returned hunter, summoning him to the landing above. Throwing down his pole by the side of his proud display of fish, he hastened up to the lake, where he found the hunter complacently employed in removing, for lightness of carriage, the head and offal of a noble fat buck; when the two, with mutual congratulations on their success, took up canoe, and, with a stop only long enough to take in the trout, carried and launched their richly-freighted craft at a convenient place in the stream below. Seeing Claud securely seated in the bottom of the canoe, and the freight nicely balanced, the hunter took his paddle, instead of setting-pole, the better to restrain the speed of the boat at the most rapid and dangerous passes, and struck out into the current, adown which, under the quick and skilful strokes of its experienced oarsman, it was borne with almost the swiftness of a bird on the wing, till it reached the quiet waters of the pond; and, this being soon passed over, they entered and descended the next reach of rapids with equal speed and safety. All the dangers and difficulties were now over; and, leisurely rowing homeward, they were, by sunset, at the cottage of the Elwoods, displaying the fruits of their enterprise, and recounting their singular adventures to the surprised and gratified inmates.

CHAPTER IX

"Then came the woodman with his sturdy-team
Of broad-horned oxen, to complete the toil
Which axe and fire had left him, to redeem,
For culture's hand, the cold and root-bound soil."

The next morning, it being the day appointed for the "logging bee," the Elwoods were again up betimes, to be prepared for the reception of the expected visitants. On going out into the yard, while yet the coming sun was only beginning to flush the eastern horizon, Mr. Elwood perceived, early as it was, a man, whom he presumed, from the handspike and axe on his shoulder, to be one of the company, entering the opening and leisurely approaching, with an occasional glance backward along the road from the settlements below. Not recognizing the man as an acquaintance, Elwood noted his appearance closely as he was coming up. He was a rather young-looking man, of a short, compactly built figure, with quick motions, and that peculiar springy step which distinguishes men of active temperament and hopeful, buoyant spirits; while the fox like cut of his features, the lively gray eyes that beamed from them, and the evidently quick coming and going thoughts that seemed to flash from his thin-moving nostrils and play on his curling lips, served to indicate rapid perceptions, shrewdness, and a kind and perhaps fun-loving disposition.

"Hillo, captain,—or captain of the house, as I suppose you must be," he sang out cheerily, as with slackening step he approached Elwood; "did you ever hear spoken of, a certain rough-and-ready talking sort of a chap they call Jonas Codman?"

"I have heard of a Mr. Codman, and was told that he would probably be here to-day," doubtfully replied Elwood.

"Well, I am he, such as he is, pushed forward as a sort of advanced guard,—no, herald must be the book-word,—to tell you that you are taken. Did you mistrust it?"

"No, not exactly."

"You *are*, nevertheless. But I'll tell you a story, which, if you can see the moral, may give you some hints to show you how to turn the affair to your advantage without suffering the least inconvenience yourself; and here it is:

"There was once a curious sort of a fellow, whose land was so covered with stones, which had rolled down from a mountain, that little or nothing could grow among them; and the question was, how he should ever remove them. Well, one day, when he was thinking on the matter, he found in the field an old Black-Art book, on the cover of which he read, '*One chapter will bring one, two chapters two, and so on; but set and keep them at work, lest a worst thing befall.*' So, to see what would come of it, he read one chapter; when a great, stout, dubious-looking devil made his appearance, and asked what he should go about? 'Go to throwing these stones over the mountain,' said the man. The devil went at it. But the man, seeing the poor devil was having a hard job of it, read on till he had raised about a dozen of the same kind of chaps, and set them all at work. And so smashingly did they make the stones fly that, by sunset, the last were disappearing; and the man was about to set them to pulling up the stumps on his newly-cleared land. But they shook their heads at this, and, being pretty well tuckered out, agreed to quit even, if he would, and go off without the usual pay in such cases made and provided in devildom; when, he making no objections, they, with another squint at the green gnarly stumps, cut and run; and all the chapters he could read after that—for he began to like the fun of having his land cleared at so cheap a rate—would never bring them back again."

So saying, the speaker turned; and, without the explanation or addition of a single word, retraced his steps and disappeared in the woods, leaving the puzzled Elwood to construe the meaning of his story as he best could. Very soon, however, sounds reached his ears which enabled him to form some conjecture what the man intended by his odd announcement. The mingling voices of ox-team drivers, with their loud and peculiarly modulated "*Haw Buck! gee! and up there, ye lazy loons!*" were now heard resounding through the woods, and evidently approaching along the road from the settlement. And soon an array of eight sturdy pair of oxen, each bearing a bundle of hay bound on the top of their yoke with a log chain, and each attended by a driver, with a handspike on his shoulder, marching by their side, emerged one after another from the woods, and came filing up the road towards the spot where he stood. As the long column approached, Elwood, with a flutter of the heart, recognized in the driver most in advance, the erect, stalwart figure and the proud and haughty bearing of Gaut Gurley.

"Good-morning, good-morning, neighbor Elwood, as I have lately been pleased to find you," exclaimed Gurley, with an air of careless assurance, as he came within speaking distance. "We have come, as you see, to give you a lift at your logging. So show us right into your slash, and let us go at it, at once. We shall find time to talk afterwards."

Elwood, with some general remark expressive of his obligation to the whole of the company at hand for their voluntary and unexpected kindness, led the way to the burned slash, and went back to meet and salute the rest of the company, as they severally came up. Having performed this ceremony with those having the immediate charge of the oxen, till the whole had passed on to their work, he turned to the rest of the company, whom, though before unnoticed by him, he now found following immediately behind the teams.

These consisted of some half-dozen sturdy logmen, with their implements, appointed to pair off with the drivers of the teams, so as to provide two men to each yoke of oxen; the hunter, Phillips, with his brisk wife and buxom daughter, bearing a basket of plates, knives, forks, spoons, and extra frying-pans, to supply any deficiency Mrs. Elwood might find in furnishing her tables or in cooking for so large a company; and lastly, Comical Codman, as he was often called by the settlers, who, though the first to come forward to meet Elwood, was now bringing up the rear.

"A merry morning to you," exclaimed the hunter, as the logmen turned off to the slash; "a merry morning to you, neighbor Elwood. This looks some like business to-day. You were not expecting us a very *great* sight earlier than this, I conclude," he added, with a jocular smile.

"Earlier? Why, it is hardly sunrise yet, and I am wholly at a loss to know how men living at such distances could get here at this hour."

"Well, that is easily explained. They haven't had to travel so far this morning as you imagine. They came on as far as my place last night, mostly, and such as could be accommodated nestled with me in my house. The rest camped out near by in the bush, which is just as well generally with us woodsmen. But you, having no mistrust of this, as it seems, were taken, I suppose, by surprise at our appearance so early."

"I should have been, wholly so, but for the coming ahead of this gentleman," replied Elwood, pointing to Codman; "and then, I was rather at loss to know what he intended by his queer way of announcing you."

"Very likely. He never does or says any thing like other folks. Jonas," continued the hunter, turning to the odd genius of whom he was speaking, "you are a good trapper, but I fear you make a bad fore-runner."

"Well, I am all right now here in the rear, I suppose," replied the other, with an oddly assumed air of abashment. "A man is generally good for one thing or t'other. If I ain't a good forerunner, it then follows that I am a good hind-runner."

"You see he must have his fol-de-rol, Mr. Elwood," said the hunter. "But, for all that, he is a good fellow enough at the bottom, if you can ever find it: ain't all that so, Jonas?"

"Sort of so and sort of not so; but a little more not than sorter, they may say, perhaps. And I don't think, myself, there is much either at the top or bottom to brag on," rejoined Codman, suddenly darting off to join his companions in the slash; and now whistling a tune, as he went, and now crowing like a cock, in notes and tones each of its kind so wondrous loud and shrill that the whole valley of the lake seemed wakened by the strange music.

The operations of the day having been thus auspicuously commenced in the slash, Elwood, retaining the hunter with him at the house to advise and assist in such arrangements and preparations for breakfast as might render the meal most acceptable to the company, entered at once upon his duties as host; and, it being found that neither the room nor tables in the house were sufficient to seat all the company, it was decided, for the purpose of avoiding every appearance of invidious distinction, to prepare temporary tables and seat the whole of them, except the females, in the open air near the house. Accordingly the hunter, who, from his experience as a woodman, was ever ready at such contrivances, went to work; and, clearing and levelling off a smooth place, driving into the ground three sets of short stout crotches, laying cross-pieces in each, and then two new pine planks longitudinally over the whole, he soon erected a neat and substantial table, long enough to seat a score of guests. Seats on each side were then supplied by a similar process; when Mrs. Elwood, who had watched the operation with a housewife's interest, made her appearance with a roll of fine white tablecloths, the relics of her better days, and covered the whole with the snowy drapery, making a table which might vie in appearance with those of the most fashionable restaurants of the cities. Upon this table, plates, knives and forks, with all other of the usual accompaniments, were speedily arranged by the quick-footed females; while the sounds of boiling pots, and the hissing frying-pans spreading through the house and around the yard the savory fumes of the cooking trout, betokened the advanced progress of the culinary operations within, which were now soon completed; when the fact was announced by Mr. Elwood by several long and loud blasts on his "tin horn" to the expectant laborers in the field, who, while the meal was being borne smoking on to the table, chained their oxen to stumps and saplings about the field, parcelled out to them the hay, and repaired to their morning banquet.

Banquet! A banquet among backwoodsmen? Yes; and why not? It is strange that a thousand generations of epicures should have lived, gluttonized, and passed away from the earth, without appearing to understand the chief requisite for that class of animal enjoyments which they seem to make the great end and aim of their lives,—without appearing to realize that it is the appetite, not the quality of the food, that makes the feast; that there can be no such thing as a feast, indeed, without a *real* not factitious appetite; and that there can be no real appetite without toil or some prolonged and vigorous exercise. Nero ransacked his whole kingdom, and expended millions for delicacies; and yet he never experienced, probably, one-half the enjoyments of the palate that were experienced from the coarsest fare by his poorest laboring subject. No, the men of ease and idleness may have surfeits, the men of toil can only have banquets. And it is doubtless a part of that nicely balanced system of compensations which Providence applies to men, that the appetites of the industrious poor should make good the deficiencies in the quality of their food, so that it should always afford equal enjoyment in the consumption with that experienced by the idle rich over their sumptuous tables.

The meal passed off pleasantly; and when finished, the gratified and chatty workmen, with their numbers now increased by the addition of the two Elwoods and the hunter, returned, with the eager alacrity of boys hurrying to an appointed game of football, to their voluntary labors in the field, in which they had already made surprising progress.

The business of the day was now resumed in earnest. The teamsters having quickly scattered to their respective teams and brought them with a lively step on to the ground, and having there each received their allotted quota of log-rollers, to pile up the logs as fast as drawn, at once penetrated at different points into the thickest parts of the blackened masses of timber before them, awaiting their sturdy labors. Here the largest log in a given space, and the one the most difficult to be removed, was usually selected as the nucleus of the proposed pile. Then two logs of the next largest size were drawn up on each side, and placed at a little distance in a line parallel with the first, when the intermediate spaces were filled with limbs, knots, and the smallest timber at hand; so that a fire, when the process of burning the piles should be commenced, communicated at the centre thus prepared, would spread through the whole, and not be likely to go out till all the logs were consumed. When this foundation was laid, the next nearest surrounding logs were drawn alongside and rolled up on skids, by the logmen stationed there with their handspikes for the purpose. Then generally commenced a keen strife between the teamster and the log-rollers, to see which should first do their part and keep the others the most closely employed. And the result was that in a very short time a large pile of logs was completed, and a space of ten or fifteen square rods was completely cleared around it. This done, an adjoining thicket of timber was sought out, another pile started, and another space cleared off in the same manner. And thus proceeded the work, with each team and its attendants, in every part of the slash; while the same spirit of rivalry which had thus began to be exhibited between the members of each gang soon took the form of a competition between one gang and another, who were now everywhere seen vieing with each other in the strife to do the most or to build up the largest and greatest number of log-heaps in the shortest space of time. The whole field, indeed, was thus soon made to exhibit the animated but singular spectacle of men, engaged in a wholly voluntary labor, putting forth all the unstinted applications of strength and displaying all the alertness and zeal of men at work for a wager. But, among all the participants in the labors of the day, no one manifested so much interest in advancing the work, no one was so active and laborious, as Gaut Gurley. Not only was he continually inciting and pressing up all others to the labor, but was ever foremost in the heaviest work himself, generally selecting the most difficult parts for himself, and often performing feats of strength that scarcely any two men on the ground were able to perform. Nor was the Herculean strength which he so often displayed before the eyes of the astonished workmen, ever made useless, as is sometimes the case with men of great physical powers, by any misapplication of his efforts. He seemed perfectly to understand the business in which they were engaged; and, while all wondered, though no one knew, where he had received his training for such work, it was soon, by common consent, decided that he was much the most efficient hand on the ground, many even going so far as to declare that his equal was never before seen in that part of the country.

"You see that, don't you, captain?" said Codman, coming up close to Elwood, and speaking in a half whisper, as he pointed to Gaut Gurley, who, having noticed two of the stoutest of the hands vainly trying to roll up a large log, rushed forward, and, bidding them stand aside, threw it up single-handed without appearing to exert half his strength. "You see that, don't you, captain?" he repeated, with an air of mingled wonder and waggishness. "Now, what do you think of my story, and the great, stout, black-looking devil that came, on reading the first chapter, and made the big stones fly so?"

"I haven't thought much about it," carelessly replied Elwood, evidently wishing not to appear to understand the allusion of the other. "But why do you ask such a question?"

"Don't know myself, it's a fact; but I happened to be thinking of things. But say, captain, you haven't been reading any chapters in any strange book yourself, lately, have you?" said Codman, with a queer look.

"No, I guess not," replied Elwood, laughingly, though visibly annoyed by the subject.

"No? Nor none of the family?" persisted the other, glancing towards Claud Elwood, who was standing near by. "Well, I wish I knew what put that story into my head, when I let it off this morning. It is de-ive-lish queer, at any rate, considering." So saying, he walked off to his work, croaking like a rooster at some questionable object.

Although none of the settlers present seemed disposed to attribute the extraordinary physical powers, which Gaut Gurley had so unmistakably shown, to any supernatural agency, as the trapper, Codman, whose other singularities were not without a smart sprinkling of superstition, was obviously inclining to do, yet those powers were especially calculated, as may well be supposed of men of their class, to make a strong impression on the minds of them all, and invest the possessor with an importance which, in their eyes, he could in no other way obtain. Accordingly he soon came to be looked upon as the lion of the day, and suddenly thus acquired, for the time being, as he doubtless shrewdly calculated he could do in this way, a consequence and influence of which no other man could boast, perhaps, in the whole settlement.

Meanwhile the work of clearing off the logs was prosecuted with increasing spirit and resolution. And so eagerly intent had all the hands become, in pressing forward to its completion their self-imposed task, which all could see was now fast drawing to a close, that they took no note of the flight of time, and were consequently taken by surprise when the sound of the horn summoned them to their midday meal.

"Why! it can't yet be noon," exclaimed one, glancing up at the sun.

"No" responded another. "Some of us here have been counting on seeing the whole job nearly done by noon, but it will take three hours yet to do that. No, the women must have made a mistake."

"Well, I don't know about that: let us see," said the hunter, turning his back to the sun, and throwing out one foot as far as he could while keeping his body perpendicular. "Now my clock, which, for noon on the 21st of June, or longest day of summer, is the shadow of my head falling on half my foot, and then passing off beyond it about half an inch each day for the rest of the season, makes it, as *I* should calculate the distance between my foot and the shadow of my head, now evidently receding,—makes it, for this last day of August, about a quarter past twelve."

"I am but little over half past eleven," said Codman, pulling out and inspecting an old watch. "Phillips, may be, is thinking of that deer that he has been promising himself and us for dinner; and, before I take his calculation on shadows and distances, I should like to know how many inches he allowed for the hurrying influence of his appetite."

"What nonsense, Comical! But what you mean by it is, I suppose, that I can't tell the time?"

"Not within half an hour by the sun."

"Why, man, it is the sun that makes the time; and, as that body never gets out of order or runs down, why not learn to read it, and depend directly upon it for the hour of the day? If half the time men spend in bothering over timepieces were devoted to studying the great clock of the heavens, they need not depend on such uncertain contrivances as common clocks and watches to know the time of day."

"But how in cloudy weather?"

"Tell the time of day by your feelings. Take note of the state of your appetite and general feelings at the various hours of the day, when it is fair and you know the time, and then apply the rule when you have no other means of judging; and you may thus train yourself, so that you need not be half an hour out of the way in your reckoning through the whole day."

"Well, supposing it is night?"

"Night is for sleep, and it is no consequence to know the time, except the time waking. And, as to that, none need be in fault, if they had you anywhere within two miles to crow for them."

"A regular hit! I own it a hit, Mr. Hunter. But here comes Mr. Elwood: we will leave the question of the time of day to him."

"We have a correct noon-mark at the house, and the women are probably right," replied Elwood. "At all events, men who have worked like lions, as you all have this forenoon, must by this time need refreshment. So, let us all drop work, and at once be off to dinner."

With such familiar jokes and converse, the light-hearted backwoodsmen threw off their crocky frocks, and, after washing up at a runlet at hand, marched off in chatty groups to the house, where they found awaiting their arrival the well-spread board of their appreciating hostess, this time made more tempting to their vigorous and healthy appetites by the addition, to the fine trout of the morning, of the variously-cooked haunches of the hunter's venison. And, having here done ample justice to their excellent meal, they again hastened back to their labor in the field, unanimously declaring for the good husbandman's rule, "Work first and play afterwards," and saying they would have no rest nor recreation till they had seen the last log of the slash disposed of. And with such animation did they resume their labors, and with such vigor continue to apply themselves in carrying out their resolution, and in hastening the hour of its fulfilment, that by the middle of the afternoon their task was ended; and the gratified Mr. Elwood had the satisfaction of seeing the formidable-looking slash of the morning converted into a comparatively smooth field, requiring only the action of the fire on the log heaps, with a few days' tending, to make it fit for the seed and harrow.

"Come, boys," said the hunter to the company, now all within speaking distance, except two or three who had somehow disappeared; "come, boys," he repeated, after pausing to see the last log thrown up in its place, "let us gather up here near the middle of the lot. Comical Codman and some others, I have noticed, have been putting their heads together, and I kinder surmise we may now soon expect some sort of christening ceremony of the field we have walked through in such fine style to-day; and, if they make out any thing worth the while, it may be well to give them a good cheer or two, to wind off with."

While the men were taking their stand at the spot designated by the hunter, Codman was seen mounting a conspicuous logheap at the southerly end of the field; and two more men, at the same time, made their appearance on the tops of different piles on opposite sides of the lot, and nearly abreast of the place where the expectant company were collected and standing, silently awaiting the commencement of the promised ceremony. Presently one of the two last-named, with a preliminary flourish of his hand, slowly and loudly began:

"Since we see the last logs fairly roll'd,
And log-heaps full fifty, all told,
   We should deem it a shame
If so handsome and well-cleared a field,
Bidding fair for a hundred-fold yield,
   Be afforded no name."

To this, the man standing on the opposite pile, in the same loud and measured tone promptly responded:

"Then a name we will certainly give it,
If you'll listen, and all well receive it,
   As justly you may:

We will call it the thing it will make,
We will name it the Pride of the Lake,
   Or the Job of a Day."

Before the last words of this unique duet had died on the ear, Comical Codman on his distant perch straightened up, and, triumphantly clapping his sides like the boastful bird whose crowing he could so wonderfully imitate, raised his shrill, loud, and long-drawn *kuk-kuk-ke-o-ho* in a volume of sound that thrilled through the forest and sent its repeating echoes from hill to hill along the distant borders of the lake.

"There, the dog has got the start of us!" exclaimed the hunter, joining the rest of the company in their surprise and laughter at the prompt action of the trapper as well as at the striking character of his performance,—"fairly the start of us; but let's follow him up close, boys. So here goes for the new name!"

And the prolonged "hurra! hurra! hurra!" burst from the lips of the strong-voiced woodmen in three tremendous cheers for the "*Pride of the Lake and the Job of a Day.*"

All the labors and performances of the field being now over, the company gathered up their tools, and by common consent moved towards the house, where, it was understood, an hour or so, before starting for their respective homes, should be spent in rest, chatting with the women, or other recreation, and a consultation also be held, among those interested, for forming a company, fixing on the time, and making other arrangements for the contemplated trapping and hunting expedition of the now fast-approaching season.

As the company were proceeding along promiscuously towards the house, Gaut Gurley, who had thus far through the day manifested no desire for any particular conversation with Mr. Elwood, nor in any way deported himself so as to lead others to infer a former acquaintance between them, now suddenly fell in by his side; when, contriving to detain him till the rest had passed on out of sight, he paused in his steps and said:

"Well, Elwood, I told you in the morning, you know, that we would do the work first and the talking afterwards. The work has now been done, and I hope to your satisfaction."

"Yes—O yes—entirely," replied Elwood, hesitating in his doubt about what was to follow from the other, whose unexpected conduct and stand for his benefit he hardly knew how to construe. "Yes, the neighbors have done me a substantial favor, and you all deserve my hearty thanks."

"I was not fishing for thanks," returned Gaut, half-contemptuously, "but wished a few words with you on private matters which concern only you and myself. And, to come to the point at once, I would ascertain, in the first place, if you know whether you and I are understood, in this settlement, to be old acquaintances or new ones?"

"New ones, I suppose, of course, unless it be known to the contrary through your means. *I* have not said a word about it, nor have my family, I feel confident," replied Elwood, demurely.

"Very well; our former acquaintance is then wholly unsuspected here. Let it remain so. But have you ever hinted to any of the settlers what you may have known or heard about me, or any former passages of my life, which occurred when I used to operate in this section or elsewhere?"

"No, not one word."

"All is well, then. As you have kept and continue to keep my secrets, so shall yours be kept. It is a dozen or fifteen years since I have been in this section at all. It is filling up with new men. There are but two persons now in the settlement that can ever have seen or known me. And they will not disturb me."

"Then there *are* two that *have* known you? Who can they be?"

"One is Wenongonet, an old Indian chief, as he calls himself, still living on one of the upper lakes, they say, but too old to ramble or attend to anybody's business but his own. The other is Phillips, the hunter."

"Phillips! Phillips, did you say? Why, as much as he has been at our house, he has never dropt a word from which one could infer that you were not a perfect stranger to him."

"I did not suppose he had. Phillips is a peaceable, close-mouthed fellow; pretends not to know any thing about anybody, when he thinks the parties concerned would rather have him ignorant; keeps a secret by never letting anybody know he has one; and never means to cross another man's path. I can get along with *him*, too. And the only question now is whether *you* and I can live together in the same settlement."

"It will probably be your fault if we can't. I shall make war on no one."

"My fault! Why I *wish* to be on good terms with you; and yet, Elwood, you feel out of sorts with me, and, in spite of all I can do, seem disposed to keep yourself aloof."

"If I do seem so, it may be because the past teaches me that the best way to avoid quarrels is to avoid intimacies. You know how we last parted in that gambling-room. I had no business to be there, I admit; but that was no excuse for your treatment."

"Treatment! Why, Elwood, is it possible you have been under a misapprehension about that, all this time?" responded Gaut, with that peculiar wheedling manner which he so well knew how to assume when he wished to carry his point with another. "My object then was to save the money for you and me, so that we could divide it satisfactorily between ourselves. I was angry enough at those other fellows, whom I saw getting all your money in that way, I confess; and, in what I said, I was whipping them over your shoulders. I thought you understood it."

"I didn't understand it in that way," replied Elwood, surprised and evidently staggered at the bold and unexpected statement. "I didn't take you so: could that be all you intended?"

"Certainly it was," resumed Gaut, in the same insinuating tone. "Had I supposed it necessary, I should have seen you and explained it at the time. But it is explained now; so let it go, and every thing go that has been unpleasant between us; let us forget all, and henceforth be on good terms. Our children, as you may have suspected, seem intent on being friends; and why should not we be friends also? It will be a gratification to them, and we can easily make it the means of benefiting each other. You know how much

I once did in helping you to property,—I can do so again, if we will but understand each other. What say you, Elwood? Will you establish the treaty, and give me your hand upon it?"

Elwood trembled as the other bent his fascinating gaze upon him, hesitated, began to demur feebly; but, being artfully answered, soon yielded and extended his hand, which Gaut seized and shook heartily; when at the suggestion of the latter they separated and proceeded by different courses, so that they might not be seen together, to join the company at the house, whom they found, as they expected, in consultation about the proposed trapping and hunting expedition to the upper lakes, the time of starting, and the names and number of those volunteering to join the association, only remaining to be fixed and ascertained. That time was finally fixed on the 15th of September, and the company was formed to consist of the two Elwoods, Phillips, Gurley, Codman, and such others as might thereafter wish to join them. This being settled, they broke up and departed for their respective homes.

CHAPTER X.

"All good to me is lost;
Evil, be thou my good"—

The next scene in the slowly unfolding panorama of our story opens at the house of Gaut Gurley, on the banks of the Magalloway. Gaut reached home, on the evening of the logging bee, about sunset; and, having put out his team, entered his house, where he found his wife alone, his daughter being absent on a visit to a neighbor. Contrary to what might have been expected, after the favorable impression he had so evidently made on the settlers that day, and the attainment of the still more important object with him, the regaining of his old fatal influence over Elwood, he appeared morose and dissatisfied. Something had not worked to his liking in the complicated machinery of his plans, and he showed his vexation so palpably as soon to attract the attention of his submissive but by no means unobservant wife, who, after a while, plucked up the courage to remark:

"What is the case, Gaut? Have you been working yourself to death for those Elwoods, to-day, or has something gone wrong with you, that makes you look so sour this evening?"

"I have worked hard enough, God knows; but that I intended, for I had objects in view, most of which I think I have accomplished, but—"

"But not all, I suppose you would say?"

"Well, yes, there is one thing that has not gone exactly to suit me, over there."

"What is that, Gaut?"

"It is of no consequence that you should know it. If I should name it, you would not see its bearing on my plans, I presume."

"Perhaps not, for I don't know what your plans are, these days. I used to be able to guess out the objects you had in view, before you came here, whether you told me or not. But, since you have been in this settlement, I have been at loss to know what you are driving at; I can't understand your movements at all."

"What movements do you mean, woman?"

"All of them; but particularly those that have to do with the Elwoods."

"What is there in my course toward them, since they came here, that you can't understand?"

"Well, I'll tell you, Gaut. When you believed Elwood to be rich, I could easily see that you thought it would be an object to bring about an acquaintance between his son and only heir, and our Avis; and I knew you was, those days, studying how it could be done, and I always suspected that you in some way disposed of that picture of her for the purpose, instead of sending it to your relations, and———"

"And what?" exclaimed Gaut, turning fiercely on his wife. "Suspected! What business had you to suspect? And you told Avis what you thought, I suppose?"

"Not a word, never one word; for I knew she was so proud and particular, that, if she mistrusted any thing of that kind to have been done, she would flounce in a minute. No, I never hinted it to her, or anybody else, and it was guesswork, after all," replied the abashed wife, in a deprecating tone,—she having been tempted, by the unusual mood which her stern husband had manifested for discussing his private affairs with her, to venture to speak much more freely than was her wont.

"Well, see that you don't hint any thing about that, nor any thing else you may take it into your silly head to guess about my objects," rejoined the other, in a somewhat mollified tone. "But now go on with what you were going to say."

"Well, I could understand your course before Elwood failed; but, when he did, I could see no object, either in following him here, or having any thing particular to do with him, or any of his family. But you seized on the first chance, after we came here, to court them, and have followed it up; first, in the affair of the young man and Avis, and then, in drumming up the whole settlement in getting up this logging bee for the old man. Now, Gaut, you don't generally drive matters at this rate without something in view that will pay; and, as I can see nothing to be gained worth so much pains, I don't understand it."

"I didn't suppose you did, and it is generally of little consequence whether you see through my plans or not; but, in this case—"

Here Gaut suddenly paused, rose, and took several turns across the room, evidently debating with himself how far it was policy to disclose his plans to his wife; when, appearing to make up his mind, he again seated himself and resumed:

"Yes, as this is a peculiar case, and coming, perhaps, in part within the range of a woman's help, if she knows what is wanted, and one which she may unintentionally hurt, if she don't, I suppose I must give you some insight into my movements, so that you can manage accordingly, help when you can, and do no mischief when you can't; as you probably will do, for you well know the consequences of doing otherwise."

"I will do all I can, if I can understand what you want, and can see any object in it," meekly responded the woman.

"Well, then, in the first place," resumed the other, "you know how many years I slaved myself, and what risks I run, to help Elwood make that fortune; how he threw me off with simple wages, instead of the share I always intended to have for such hard and dangerous services; and how he failed, like a fool, before I got it."

"I knew it all."

"Then you can easily imagine how much it went against my grain to be balked in that manner. At all events, it did; and I soon determined not to give up the game so, even if that was all. And ascertaining that Elwood, by allowances made by the creditors to his wife, and sales of furniture which they allowed the family to retain, brought quite a little sum of money into the settlement,—enough, at any rate, to pay for his place, put him well afloat, and make him a man of consequence in such a new place,—I soon made up my mind on buying and settling, for present purposes, here, too, as we did."

"Yes, but what do you expect to make here more than in any other new country? And what can you make out of the Elwoods, more than any other new settlers?"

"A good deal, if all things work to my mind. There is money to be made here. I could do well in the fur business alone, and at the worst. And, by the aid of one who could be made to favor my interests, there is no telling what could be done. Now, what claim had I on any other settler to be that one to aid me? On Elwood I had a claim to help *me* to property in turn; and I determined he should do it. But he must first be brought into the traces. He has got out with me, and must be reconciled before I can do much with him."

"Well, I should think he ought to be by this time, after what you have been doing for him, without his asking."

"Without asking? Why, that was just the way to do it. As I calculated, he was taken by surprise, disarmed, and yielded; so that object is accomplished, as well as making the right impression on the other settlers by beating them at their own work."

"I begin to understand, now."

"You will understand more, soon; that was only part of my object."

"What was the other part?"

"To insure the consummation of the match between Avis and young Elwood, which now seems in fair progress, but which would be liable to be broken off, if his family should continue to be unfriendly to me."

"Why, that was the thing I could understand least of all. The young man is well enough, I suppose, but I thought you had looked to have Avis make more of herself, and do better for us. She is still young, and we don't know what chances she may have. If she and the young man should keep on intimate, and set their hearts on it, I don't know that I should oppose it much; but what object we can have in helping it on, I can't, for the life of me, see. I have not said a word against it, because I saw that you were for it. But, if I had been governed by my own notions, I should have sooner discouraged than helped it on."

"I suspected so; and, for that reason, as well as others, I see I must tell you a secret, which the Elwoods themselves don't know, and which I meant should never pass my lips; and, when I tell it to you, see that it never passes yours. That young man, Claud Elwood, whom you think so ordinary a match, is heir to a large property. A will is already executed making him so."

"Is that so, Gaut?"

"Yes, I have known it for months. I made the discovery before I decided to move here."

"It is a wonder how you could keep it from me."

"Humph! It is a greater wonder how I came to tell you at all, and I fear I shall yet repent it; but things had come to a pass that seemed to make it necessary."

"But who is the man, and where, who is going to give the young man such a property?"

"It is not for you to know. I have told you enough for all my purposes. And this brings me back to your first question, when I admitted that there was one thing which had not gone to my liking. There *was*, indeed, one thing that disturbed and vexed me; and that was the discovery I made, over there, today, that Elwood's wife is an enemy to me. I contrived all ways to get speech with her, but she studiously avoided giving me a chance, nor was I able once even to catch her eye, that I might give her a friendly nod of recognition. I know she never wished me about, in former times, but I then attributed her coldness to the pride of the rich over the poor. But I now think it was because she hated me. I am satisfied she is an enemy, at heart; and will, for that reason, prove a secret and I fear dangerous opposer to a match which will connect me with her family, unless something is done to reconcile her."

"How can that be done?"

"Perhaps *you* can do something. We start, in about a fortnight, on the fall hunt,—both the Elwoods, myself, and others. When we are gone, you can go down into that neighborhood, get acquainted with some of the women, and get them to call with you on Mrs. Elwood; and, if Avis could be made to go and see her, so much the better. She would make an impression without trying. You would have to manage, but how, I am not now prepared to decide. I will think of it, and you may, and we will talk it over again. I have told you this, now, that you might understand the situation of affairs; and the object, which you will now see, is worth playing for. And, if we can carry this last point, the last danger will be removed,—unless Claud himself proves fickle."

"I guess there will not be much danger of that in *this* settlement. What girl is there that he could think of in comparison with Avis?"

"I think there is none; and still, there is one whom I would rather he would not see."

"Who can that be, I should like to know?"

"She is the daughter, or is claimed to be, of an old Indian chief, called Wenongonet, who lives up the lakes, and was once a man of some consequence, both with Indians and whites."

"An Indian girl! Fudge!"

"You might alter that tune, if you should see her. She is white as you are, and has, most of the time, of late years, lived in some of the old settlements, been schooled, and so on. I saw her, soon after we came here, with another woman, at the south end of the lake, where she was visiting in the family of one of the settlers, and I inquired her out, as she appeared so much above the common run of girls. But she is courted, they say, by a young educated Indian, called Tomah, from Connecticut-river way, where I used to see him. He *ought* to be able to take care of her. But hark! what was that? It sounded like the trotting of some heavy horse. I'll see."

So saying, Gaut rose and went to the window, when, after casting a searching look out into the road, and pausing a moment, in evident doubt and surprise at what met his gaze, he muttered: "The devil is always at hand when you are talking about him; for that must be the very fellow,—Tomah himself! But what a rig-out! Wife, look here."

The woman promptly came to the window, when her eyes were greeted with the appearance of a smart-looking and jauntily-equipped young Indian, mounted on the back of a stately, antlered moose, that, by some contrivance answering to a bridle, he was about bringing to a stand in the road, opposite to the house. Without heeding the exclamations of surprise and questions of his wife, who had never seen an animal of the kind, Gaut stepped out of the door, and, after pausing long enough to satisfy himself that he was not known to the other, said, after the distant greeting customary among strangers had been exchanged:

"That is a strange horse you are travelling on, friend."

"No matter that, when he carry you well," replied the Indian, whose language was a little idiomatic, notwithstanding his education.

"Perhaps not; but I should think he would be a hard trotter for most riders."

"Moose don't care for that: he say, he carry you ten miles an hour, you not the one to complain: if you no like, you no ride."

"How did you tame him to be so manageable?"

"Caught him a little calf, four years ago; trained him young to mind halter; then ox-work, horse-work. This year ride him. No trouble, you let him enough to eat."

"Where did you catch him?"

"Over the mountain. Live there. My name John Tomah. Been here to hunt some, but not see you before. Another man live in this house last spring."

"Yes, I am a new-comer. But I have heard some of the settlers speak of you,
I think. You are the Indian that has been to college?"

"Yes, been there some, but in the woods more. Love to hunt, catch beaver, sable, and such things. Come here to hunt now, soon as time. But must have moose kept when off hunting: thought the man lived here do that. May be you keep him, while I come back. Pay you, all right."

"Yes, if I could; but where could I keep him? He would jump any pasture or yard fence there is here, and then run away, would he not?"

"No. Stay, after week or two, and get wonted, same as horse or cow. I go to work, make yard, keep him in a while, and feed him with grass or browse. I tend him first. You keep him,—you keep me, till go hunting; then get boy. Pay well, much as you suit."

Gaut Gurley never acted without a strong secret motive. He had been intently studying the young Indian during the conversation just detailed, with a view of forming an opinion how far his subservience could be secured; and, appearing to become satisfied on this point, and believing the first great step for making him what was desired would be accomplished by yielding to his request gracefully, however much family inconvenience it might occasion, Gaut now turned cordially to him, and said:

"Yes, Tomah, I will do it. I like your looks, and I will do it for *you*, but wouldn't for anybody else. We can get along with your animal, somehow; and you shall stay, too, till our company start on our hunt, and then you shall go with us. I will see that you have fair play. I will be your friend; and perhaps I may want a good turn of you some time."

"Like that; go with you; show you how catch beaver. Do all I can."

"Very well; and perhaps I can help you in some way. You have an affair that you feel a peculiar interest in, with somebody on the upper lake, and—"

"You know that?" interrupted the startled but evidently not displeased Indian.

"Yes, I have heard something about it."

"But how you help there?"

"O, I can contrive a way for you to make the matter work as you wish, if you will only persevere."

"Persevere? Ah, means keep trying. Yes, do that; but she don't talk right, now; perhaps, will, you help, then we be great friends, sure."

The treaty being thus concluded, the gratified young Indian dismounted, with his rifle and pack, containing his blanket, hunting-suit, etc., which he carried before him, laid across the shoulder of his novel steed; and, under the guidance of Gaut, he led the animal into the cow-yard, where he was tied and fed, and the fence, already made high to exclude the wolves, as usual among first settlers, was topped out by laying on a few additional poles, so as to prevent the possibility of his escape. This being done, Gaut conducted his new-found friend into the house, and introduced him, to his wife and also to his daughter, who had by this time returned, as the young Indian that had been to college, but still had a liking for the woods.

"I have often thought I should feel interested in seeing an educated native of the forest," remarked Avis, after the civilities of the introduction had been exchanged. "Books, when you became able to read and understand them," she continued, turning to the Indian, "books must have opened a new world to you, and the many new and curious things you found in them must have been exceedingly gratifying to you, Mr. Tomah."

"Yes, many curious things in books," replied Tomah, indifferently.

"And also much valuable knowledge?" rejoined Avis, interrogatively.

"Valuable enough to some folks, suppose," replied the other, with the air of one speaking on a subject in which he felt no particular interest. "Lawyers make money; preachers get good pay for talking what they learn in books; so doctors."

"But surely," persisted the former, who, though disappointed in his replies, yet still expected to see, if she could draw him out, the naturally shrewd mind of the native made brilliant by the light of science, "surely you consider an education a good thing for all, giving those who receive it a great advantage over those who do not?"

"Yes, education good thing," responded Tomah, his stolid countenance beginning to lighten up at the idea which now struck him as involving the chief if not the sole benefit of his scientific acquirements; "yes, education good, very good, sometime. Instance: I go to Boston with my moose next winter; show him for pay, one, two days; then reckon up money—add; then reckon up expenses—subtract; tell how much I make. Make much, stay; make little, go to other place. Yes, education good thing."

"But I should think you might do better with your education than you could by following the usual employments of your kind of people," resumed the other, still unwilling to see the subject of her scrutiny fall so much below her preconception of an educated Indian. "You say, lawyers, preachers, and doctors make money from the superiority which their education has given them; now, why don't you profit by *your* education, and go into a profession like one of theirs, and obtain by it the same wealth and position which you see them enjoying?"

"Did try," replied Tomah, with an evident effort to elevate his language, and meet the question candidly. "When I came home from the school, people all say, Now you go and live like white folks, in village, and study to be doctor, make money, be great man. So went; study one year; try hard to like; but no use. Uneasy all the time; could not keep down the Indian in me; he always rising up, more every day, all the time drawing me away to the woods,—pull, pull, pull. I fight against him; put him down little some time; but he soon up again, stronger than ever. Found could not make myself over again; must be as first made; so gave up; left study for the woods; and said, Now let Indian be Indian as long as he like."

Satisfied, or rather silenced, by Tomah's reasons, Avis turned the conversation by asking him to relate to her how he caught and tamed his moose. She found him completely at home in this and other of his adventures in the forest, which he was thus encouraged to relate, and in which he often became a graphic and interesting narrator, and displayed the keen observation of the objects of nature, together with the other peculiar qualities of his race, to so much advantage that she soon relinquished her favorite idea of ever finding a philosopher in an educated Indian.

In presenting the above picture, drawn from one of the many living prototypes that have fallen within our personal observation, or come within our knowledge derived from reliable sources, we had no wish to disparage the praiseworthy acts and motives of those spirited and patriotic men who, like Moore, in establishing his well-known charity school, in connection with Dartmouth college, may have, in times past, founded and endowed schools for the education of the natives of the forest; nor would we dampen the faith and hopes of those philanthropists who still believe in the redemption of that dwindling race by the aids of science and civilization; but we confess our inability to perceive any general results, flowing from the attempts of that character, at all adequate to the pains and outlay bestowed on the experiment. And we think we cannot be alone in this opinion. We believe that those results, when gathered up so that all their meagreness could be seen, have sadly disappointed public expectations; that this once favorite object and theory, of elevating and benefiting the red man by taking him from his native woods and immuring him in the schoolroom, has been, in the great majority of the cases, a futile one; and that whole system, indeed, can now be regarded as but little less than a magnificent failure.

There have been, it is true, some brilliant exceptions to the application of our remarks, such as may be found in the pious and comparatively learned Samson Occom, the noted Indian preacher of the times of the Pilgrims; in the eloquent Ojibway chief of our own times, and a few others; as well as in the person we have already introduced into this work, the intelligent and beautiful Fluella. But *only* as exceptions to the general rule, we fear, can we fairly regard them,—for, where there is one Occom, there are probably ten Tomahs.

Education, or so much of it as he has the patience and ability to acquire, seems often to unsettle and confuse the mind of the red man; for, while his old notions and traditions are disturbed or swept away by it, he fails of grasping and digesting the new ones which science and civilization present to his mind; and he falters and gropes, like an owl in the too strong light of the unaccustomed sun. In his natural condition, he can *at least* realize the happy picture which the poet has drawn of him:

"Lo the poor Indian! whose untutored mind
Sees God in clouds, or hears him in the wind:
His soul proud science never taught to stray
Far as the solar walk or milky way;
Yet simple nature to his hope has given,
Behind the cloud-topt hill, an humbler heaven,

Some safer world in depth of wood embraced;
Some happier island in the wat'ry waste,

    Where slaves once more their native land behold,
No fiends torment, no Christian thirsts for gold.
To be content's his natural desire;
He asks no angel's wings, no seraph's fire;
But thinks, admitted to that equal sky,
His faithful dog shall bear him company."

    But now, in his new and anomalous position, even this happiness and this content is taken away, while he is unable to embrace an adequate substitute. His old faith is shaken, but no new one is established. Before, he could see God in clouds or hear him in the wind; but now he can scarcely see God in any thing. His physical system, in the mean while, deprived as it is of the forest atmosphere, in which it was alone fitted to exist and reach its greatest perfection, suffers even more than his mental one. And his whole man, both mental and physical, begins to degenerate, and soon dwindles into insignificance. Yes, it is only in his native forests that the Indian appears in his wild and peculiar dignity of character. There only can he become a being of romance, and there only a hero. And there, in conclusion, we would say, in view of the unsatisfactory results of the experiments made to elevate him by any of the methods yet adopted,—there we would let him remain.

    But we must now on with our tale, the main incidents of which we have only foreshadowed, not touched.

CHAPTER XI.

"Hearts will be prophets still."

The week succeeding the logging bee was an extremely busy one with the Elwoods, who still had a heavy task to perform on their new field, before it could be considered properly cleared or fitted for seeding and harrowing. Sixty days before, that field was covered with a heavy growth of primitive forest, standing in its native majesty, a mountain mass of green vigor and sturdy life, and as seemingly invincible against the assaults of man as it had been against those of the elements whose fury it had so long withstood. But the busy and fatal axe had done its work. That towering forest had been laid prostrate with the earth, and the first process of the Herculean task of converting the forest into the field had been completed. The second and third process, also, in the burning of the slash and the gathering the trunks of the trees into log-heaps, as we have seen, had been in turn successfully accomplished. But the fourth and last process still remained to be performed. Those unseemly log-heaps, cumbering no inconsiderable portion of the field, must be disposed of, to complete the work. This was now the first task of the Elwoods, and time pressed for its speedy execution. Accordingly, the next morning after the bee, they sallied out, each with a blazing brand in his hand, and commenced the work of firing the piles,—a work which, unlike that of firing a combustible and readily catching slash, required not only considerable time, but often the exercise of much skill and patience. But they steadily persevered, and, before sunset, had the gratification of beholding every one of those many scores of huge log-piles, that thickly dotted the ground, clearly within the grasp of the devouring element; and afterwards of seeing that grasp grow stronger and stronger on the solid material on which it had securely fastened, till, to the eye of fancy, the dark old forest seemed by day to be reproduced in the numerous, thickly-set columns of smoke that shot upward and spread out into over-arching canopies above, while, with the gathering darkness of the night, that forest seemed gradually to take the form of a distant burning city in the manifold tapering pillars of fire which everywhere rose from the field, fiercely illuminating the dark and sombre wood-wall of the surrounding forest, and dimly glimmering over the sleeping waters of river and lake beyond.

They had now made the fire their servant, and got it safely at work for them; but that servant, to insure its continued and profitable action, must be constantly fed and fostered. The logs, becoming by the action of the fire partially consumed, and, by thus losing their contact with each other, ceasing to burn, required, every few hours, to be rolled together, adjusted, and repacked; when, being already thoroughly heated and still partly on fire, they would soon burst out again into a brisk blaze. This tending and re-packing of the piles demanded, for many of the succeeding days, the constant attention of the Elwoods; who, going out early each morning, and keeping up their rounds at short intervals through the day and to a late hour at night, assiduously pursued their object, till they had seen every log-heap disappear from the field, and the last step of their severe task fully accomplished.

Few of those who live in cities, villages, or other places than those where agricultural pursuits prevail; few of those, indeed, who have been tillers only of the subdued and time-mellowed soils of the old States and countries, have any adequate conception of the immense amount of hard labor required to clear off the primitive forest, and prepare the land for the first crop; nor have they, consequently, any just appreciation of the degree of resolution, energy, and endurance necessary to insure continued perseverance in subduing one piece of forest-land after another, till a considerable opening is effected. It is the labor of one man's life to clear up a new farm; and few there be, among the multitudes found making the attempt, who have the sustaining will and resolution—even if the pecuniary ability is not wanting—to accomplish that formidable achievement. Probably not one in five of all the first pioneer settlers of a new country ever remain to become its permanent settlers. The first set of emigrants, or pioneers, are seen beginning with great resolution and energy, and persevering unfalteringly till the usual ten-acre lot is cleared, the log-house thrown up, and the settlement of the family effected. Another piece of forest is the next year attacked, but with a far less determined will, and the clearing prosecuted with a proportionate lack of energy and resolution; and the job, after being suffered to linger along for months beyond the usual period for completion, is finally finished. But, in view of the hard labors and prolonged struggles they have experienced in their two former trials for conquering the wilderness, they too often now falter and hesitate at a third attempt. Perhaps the lack of means to hire that help, which would make the toil more endurable, comes also into the case; and the result is that no new clearing is begun. They live along a while as they are; but, for want of the first crops of the newly-cleared land and the usual accessions to their older fields, they soon find themselves on the retrograde, and finally sell out to a new set of incoming settlers, who in their turn begin with fresh vigor, and with more means generally for prosecuting advantageously the work which had discouraged or worn out their predecessors. But even of this second set a large proportion fail to succeed, and, like the former, eventually yield their places to more enterprising and able men, who, with those of the two former sets of settlers that had succeeded in overcoming the difficulties and retaining their places, now join in making up the permanent settlers of the country.

Such is generally the history of the early settlement of every new country. Those who have endured the most hardship, encountered the greatest difficulties, and performed the hardest labor, do not generally reap the reward which might eventually crown their toils, but leave that reward to be enjoyed by those to whom such hardships and toils are comparatively unknown. This seems hard and unjust; but, from the unequal conditions and characters of men, it is doubtless a necessary state of things, and one which, though it may occasionally be somewhat modified, will never, probably, as a general thing, be very essentially altered.

The Elwoods, having now thus brought the labors of clearing to a successful close, next proceeded to the lighter and more cleanly task of taking the incipient step towards securing the ever-important first crop which was to reward them, in a good part, for their arduous toils. Accordingly, the previously engaged supply of winter wheat intended for seed was brought home, the requisite help and ox-work enlisted, the seed sown, and the harrows and hoes put in motion to insure its lodgment beneath the surface of the broken soil. And, by the end of the second day from its commencement, this task was also completed, leaving our two persevering settlers only the work of gathering in the small crops of grain and potatoes they had succeeded in raising on their older grounds, to be performed before leaving home on the contemplated trapping and hunting expedition; the appointed day for which was still sufficiently distant to allow them abundant time to do this, and also to make all other of the necessary arrangements and preparations for that, to them, novel and interesting event.

But how, in the meanwhile, stood that domestic drama of love and its entanglements, which was destined to be deeply interwoven with the other principal incidents of this singular story? All on the surface seemed as bright and unruffled as the halcyon waters of the sleeping ocean before the days of storm have come to move and vex it. But how was it within the vail of the heart and teeming mind, where the currents and counter-currents of that subtle but powerful passion flow and clash unseen, often gaining their full height and unmasterable strength before any event shall occur to betray their existence to the public. How was it there? We shall see.

While the events we have described in the last foregoing chapters were transpiring, Mrs. Elwood held her peace, studiously avoiding all allusion to what still constituted the burden of her mind,—the thickening intimacy between her family and the Gurleys; but, though she was silent on the subject, yet her heart was not any the less sad, nor her thoughts any the less busy. She had been made aware that a reconciliation had taken place between her husband and Gaut Gurley; and she had seen how artfully the latter had brought it about, and regained his old fatal influence over the former. She believed she fully understood the motives which actuated Gaut in all these movements. And she now looked on in helpless anguish of heart to see the toils thus drawn tighter and tighter around the unconscious victims, and those victims, too, her husband and son, with whose happiness and welfare her own was indissolubly connected. She saw it with anguish, because her feelings never for once were permitted even the alleviation of a doubt that it could result in aught else than evil to her family. She could not reason herself into any belief of Gaut's reformation. She felt his black heart constantly throwing its shadow on to her own; she *felt* this, but could not give to others, nor perhaps even to herself, what might be deemed a satisfactory reason for her impressions and forebodings; for in her was exemplified the words of the poet:

"The mind is capable to show
Thoughts of so dim a feature,
That consciousness can only know
Their presence and their nature."

Such thoughts were hers,—dim and flitting, indeed; but she felt conscious of their continued presence, of their general character, and deeply conscious what they portended. They took one shape, moved in one course, and all pointed one way, and that was to evil,—some great impending evil to the two objects of her love and solicitude.

"But is there no hope?" she murmured aloud, in the fullness of her heart, while deeply pondering the matter, one day, as she sat alone at her open window, looking out on her husband and son engaged in their harvest, which she knew they were hurrying on to a close, before leaving her on the contemplated long, and perhaps perilous, expedition into the wilderness,—a circumstance that doubtless caused the subject, in the thus awakened state of her anxieties, to weigh at this time peculiarly heavy on her mind. "Is there no hope," she repeated, with a sigh, "that this impending calamity may in some part be averted? Must they both be sacrificed? Must the faults of the erring father be visited on the innocent son, who had become the last hope of the mother's heart? Kind Heaven! may not that son, *at least*, be delivered from the web of toils into which he has so strangely fallen, and yet be saved? Grant, O grant that hope—that one ray of hope—in this my hour of darkness!"

But what sound was that which now fell upon her ear, as if responsive to her ejaculation? It was a light tap or two on the door, which, after the customary bidding of *walk in* had been pronounced, was gently opened, when a young female of extreme beauty and loveliness entered. Mrs. Elwood involuntarily rose, and stood a moment, mute with surprise, in the unexpected presence. Soon recovering, however, she invited the fair stranger to a seat, still deeply wondering who she could be and what had occasioned her visit.

"You are the good woman of the house?—the wife of the new settler?—the mother of Mr. Claud Elwood?" asked the stranger girl, pausing between each interrogatory, till she had received an affirmative nod from Mrs. Elwood.

"Yes," replied the latter kindly, but with an air of increasing curiosity, "yes, I am Mrs. Elwood. Would you like to see my son, Claud?"

"No," rejoined the girl, in the same subdued and musical accents. "No, it was not him, but you, I came to see and speak with," she added, carefully, withdrawing a screening handkerchief from a light parcel she bore in her hand, and displaying a small work-basket of exquisite make, which, advancing with hesitating steps, she presented to the other, as she resumed:

"I came with this, good lady, to see if you would be suited to have such an article?"

"It is very pretty," said Mrs. Elwood, examining the workmanship with admiration, "beautiful, indeed. Did you make it?"

"I did, lady," said the other modestly.

"Well, it certainly does great credit to your skill and taste," rejoined the other. "I should, of course, be pleased to own it, but I have little money to pay for such things. You ought to sell it for quite a sum."

"But I do not wish to sell it," responded the girl, looking up to Mrs. Elwood with an expostulating and wounded expression. "I do not wish to take money for it; but hoped you would like it well enough to accept it for a gift,—a small token."

"O, I should," said Mrs. Elwood, "if I was entitled to any such present; but what have I ever done to deserve it of you? I do not even know who you are, kind stranger."

"They, call me Fluella," responded the other, the blood slightly suffusing her fair, rounded cheek. "*You* have not seen me, I know. You have not done me the great favor that brings my gratitude. It is your brave son that has done both."

"O, I understand now," exclaimed Mrs. Elwood. "You are the chief's daughter, whom Claud and Mr. Phillips helped out of a difficulty and danger on the rapids, some time since. But your token should be given to Claud, should it not?"

"It would be unsuitable, too much," quickly replied the maiden, in a low, hurried tone. "I could not do a thing like that. But if you would accept such a small thing?"

"I cannot but appreciate and honor your delicacy," returned Mrs. Elwood, with a look of mingled admiration and respect. "I think you must be an excellent girl; and I will accept your present,—yes, thankfully,—and never forget the manner in which it was bestowed."

"Your words are in my heart, lady. I came, feeling much doubtful; I return, much happy," said the maiden, rising to depart.

"Do not go yet," interposed the matron, who was beginning to feel a lively interest in the other; "do not go yet. Claud should know you are here. I will call him," she added, starting for the door.

"O no, no,—do not, do not. He would not wish to be troubled by one like me," hurriedly entreated the maiden, with a look of alarmed delicacy.

"O, you are mistaken. He would be pleased to see you, and expect to be called," said Mrs. Elwood, in a tone of gentle remonstrance, while pausing at the unexpected objection. "But it is unnecessary; for I see that he is already coming, and in a moment will be here," she added, glancing out of the window.

Having made the announcement, she turned encouragingly to the maiden, to reassure her, believing her request that Claud should not be called in proceeded entirely from over-diffidence. But one glance of her quick and searching eye was sufficient to apprise the former that there was a deeper cause for those tender alarms. The cheeks of the beautiful girl were deeply suffused with crimson, her bosom was heaving wildly, and her whole frame was trembling like an aspen. As her eyes met the surprised gaze of the matron, she became conscious that her looks had betrayed the secret she was the most anxious to conceal; and she cast an imploring look on the face of the other, as if to entreat the mercy of shielding the weakness.

Mrs. Elwood understood the silent appeal; and, approaching and laying her hand gently on the shoulder of the other, said, in a low, kindly tone:

"Have no fears. You have made a friend of me."

The girl silently removed the hand, brought it to her lips, and, as a bright tear-drop fell upon it, kissed it eagerly. The two then separated, and resumed their respective seats, to compose themselves before the expected entrance should be made.

In a few moments Claud carelessly entered the house; but stopped short in surprise, at the threshold, on so unexpectedly seeing the well-remembered face and form of the heroine of his late romantic adventure on the rapids, in the room with his mother. But, almost instantly recovering his usual manner, he gallantly advanced to the trembling maiden, took her by the hand, and respectfully inquired about her welfare, and pleasantly adverted to the singular circumstances under which they had become acquainted. Soon becoming in a good measure assured, by a reception so much more condescending and cordial than she had dared hope for, from one whose image she had been cherishing as that of some superior being, the grateful and happy girl, now forgetful of her wish to depart, gradually regained her natural ease and vivacity, and sustained her part in the general conversation that now ensued, with an intelligence and instinctive refinement of thought and expression that equally charmed and surprised her listeners. She at length, however, rose to depart, observing that her father, who was in waiting for her at the landing, would chide her for her long delay; when Claud offered to attend her to the lake. To this she at first objected; but, on Claud's assurance that he should be pleased with the walk, and that it would afford him the opportunity of meeting her father, whom he had a curiosity to see, she blushingly assented, and the couple sociably took their way to the lake together, leaving Mrs. Elwood deeply revolving in her mind the new train of thoughts that had been awakened by the remarkable personal beauty and evident rare qualities of her fair visitor, and the discovery of the state of her feelings,—thoughts which the matron laid up in her heart, but forbade her tongue to utter.

On reaching the landing, Fluella drew a bone whistle from her pocket, and blew a blast so loud and shrill that the sound seemed to penetrate the inmost depths of the surrounding forest. The next moment a similar sound rose in response from the woods, apparently about half a mile distant, on the right.

"He has heard me; that was my father's whistle. He has been taking a short bout in the woods with his rifle, but will now soon be here. And Mr. Elwood will wait, I know, for the chief wishes to thank the brave that rescued his daughter," said the maiden, looking inquiringly at Claud.

"Yes," replied Claud, "yes, certainly; for, even without company, I am never tired of standing on this commanding point, and looking out on this beautiful lake and its surrounding scenery."

"Ah! then you think, Mr. Elwood," exclaimed Fluella, with a countenance sparkling with animation, "you think of our woods life, like one of your great writers, whom I have read to remember, and who so prettily says:

'And this our life, exempt from public haunt,
Finds tongues in trees, books in running brooks,
Sermons in stones, and good in every thing.'

One would almost think this wise writer must be one of my people, he describes our ways of becoming instructed so truly; for we Indians, Mr. Elwood, read few other books than those we see opened to us on the face of nature, or hear or read few other sermons than those in the outspread pages of the bright lake, the green woods, and the grand mountain."

"You Indians!" said Elwood, looking at the other with a playful yet half-chiding expression. "Why, Fluella, should a stranger look at your fair skin, hear you conversing so well in our language, and quoting so appropriately from our books, he would hardly believe you an Indian, I think, unless you told him."

"Then I would tell him, Mr. Elwood," responded the maiden, with dignity, and a scarcely perceptible spice of offended pride in her manner. "I *am* one,— on my father's side, at least, wholly so; and, for the first ten or twelve years of my life, was but a child of the woods and the wigwam; and I will never shame at my origin, so far as that matters."

"But you did not learn to read in the wigwam, Fluella?" said Claud, inquiringly.

"No," replied the girl; the proud air she had assumed, while speaking of her origin, quickly subsiding into one of meekness. "No; but I supposed that Mr. Phillips, who knows, might have told you that, for many years past, I have lived much with your people, learned their ways, been to their schools, and read their books. And, in owning my natural red father, may be I should have also said, I have a good white father, who has done every thing for the poor, ignorant, Indian girl."

"But where does this good and generous white father live, and what is his name?" asked Claud.

"He lives near the seaside city," answered she, demurely; "I may say so far. But I do not name him, ever. We think it not best. But, if he comes here sometime, as he may, you shall see him, Mr. Elwood."

At this point of the dialogue, the attention of its participants was arrested by the sound of breaking twigs and other indications of the near approach of some one from the forest; and, the next moment, emerging through the thick underbrush, which he parted by the muzzle of his rifle as he made his way, the expected visitant came into view. Seemingly unmindful of the presence of others near by, or of the curious and scrutinizing gaze of Claud, he advanced with a firm, elastic tread, and stately bearing, exhibiting a strong, erect frame, a large, intellectual head, and handsomely moulded features, with a countenance of a grave and thoughtful cast, but now and then enlivened by the keenly-glancing black eyes by which it was particularly distinguished. With the exception of moccasins and wampum belt, he was garbed in a good English dress; and, so far as his exterior was in question, might have easily been mistaken, at a little distance, for some amateur hunter from the cities; while, from the vigor of his movements, and other general appearance, he might have equally well passed for a man of the middle age, had not the frosts of time, which were profusely sprinkled over his temples, and other visible parts of his head, betrayed the secret of his advanced age.

"My daughter is not alone," he said, in very fair English utterance, coming to a stand ten or twelve yards distant from the young couple.

"No" promptly replied the daughter, assuming the dignified tone and attitude usual among those engaged in the ceremonies of some formal presentation, or public introduction. "No, but my father will be pleased to learn that this is the Mr. Claud Elwood, who did your daughter such good service in her dangers on the rapids, and whom she has now conducted here, that he might have the opportunity to see the chief, and receive the thanks which it is more fitting for the father than the daughter to bestow."

"My daughter's words are good," said the chief. "The young brave has our thanks to last; but the Red Man's thanks are acted, the White Man's spoken. Does the young man understand the creed of our people?"

Fluella looked at Claud as if he was the one to answer the question, and he accordingly remarked:

"I have ever heard, chief, that your people always notice a benefit done to them, and that he who does them one secures their lasting gratitude."

"The young man," rejoined the chief, considerately, "has heard words that make, sometime, too much; they make true, the good-doer doing no wrong to us after. But when he takes advantage of our gratitude he wipes out the debt; he does more,—he stands to be punished like one an enemy always."

The maiden here cast an uneasy glance at Claud, and a deprecating one at her father, at the unnecessary caution, as she believed it, which she perceived the latter intended to convey by his words to the former. But, to her relief, Claud did not appear as if he thought the remarks had any application to himself, for he frankly responded:

"Your distinction is a just one, chief. Your views about these matters are my own views. Your creed is a good creed, so far as the remembrance of benefits is concerned; and I wish I could see it observed as generally among my people as I believe it to be among yours. But, chief, your daughter makes too much out of my assistance, the other day. I did only a common duty,— what I should have been a coward not to have done. I have no claim for any particular gratitude from her or you."

"Our gratitude was strong before; the young man now makes stronger," remarked the other, exchanging appreciating glances with his daughter.

"No, chief," resumed Claud, "I did not come here to boast of that small service, nor claim any thanks for it, but to see a sagamore, who could give me the knowledge of the Red Man which I would like to possess; to see one who, in times gone by, was as a king in this lake country. His own history, and that of his people especially, I would like to hear. They must be full of interest and instruction to an inquirer like me. Will not the chief relate it briefly? I have leisure,—my ears are open to his words."

"Would the young man know the history of Wenongonet, alone?" said the other, with a musing and melancholy air. "It may be told easier than by words. Does the young man see on yonder hill that tall, green pine, which stands braced on the rocks, and laughs at the storms, because it is strong and not afraid?"

"I do."

"That is Wenongonet fifty winters ago. Now, does the young man see that tall, dry pine, in the quiet valley below, with a slender young tree shooting up, and tenderly spreading its green branches around that aged trunk, so it would shield its bare sides in the colds of winter, and fan its leafless head in the heats of summer?"

"Yes, I see that, also."

"That dry tree, already tottering to its fall, is Wenongonet now."

"But what is the young tree with which you have coupled it?"

"The young man has eyes," said the speaker, glancing affectionately at his blushing daughter.

"But the young man," he resumed after a thoughtful pause, "would know more of the history of the Red Men who once held the country as their own? Let him read it in the history of his own people, turned about to the opposite. Let him call the white man's increase from a little beginning, the red man's decrease from a great,—the white man's victories, the red man's defeats,—the white man's flourishing, the red man's fading; and he will have the history of the red men, and the reasons of their sad history, in this country.

"Two hundred year-seasons ago, the Abenaques were the great nation of the east. From the sea to the mountains they were the lords of Mavoshen. [Footnote: The name by which the Province of Maine was designated by the early voyagers, and the Indian word probably from which the present name of the State of Maine was derived.] They were a nation of warriors and a wise and active people. But, of all the four tribes—the Sokokis, the Anasquanticooks, the Kenabas, the Wawenocks—who made up this great nation, the Sokokis were the wisest and bravest. Wenongonet is proud when he thinks of them. They were his tribe. All the land that sent its waters through the Sawocotuc [Footnote: The Indian appellation of the river Saco, which is doubtless an abbreviation of the Indian name here introduced.] to the sea was theirs. They stood with their warriors at the outposts against the crowding white settlers from the west and south. They were pleased to stand there, because it was the post of danger and of honor in the nation. And there they bravely kept their stand against that wide front of war, and took the battle on themselves, till the snows of more than a hundred winters were made red by their rifles and tomahawks. But those who court death must often fall into his embrace. So with the Sokokis. They were at first a great and many people; but they wasted and fell, as time, the bringer of new and strange things, wore away, before the thick and more thick coming of their greedy and pushing foes,—by their fire-water in peace and their bullets in war, till the many became few, the great small. What the bloody Church, with his swarm of picked warriors, had left after his four terrible comings with fire and slaughter, the bold Lovewell finished, on that black day when the great Paugus and all the flower of the tribe found red graves round their ancient stronghold and home,—their beloved Pegwacket. [Footnote: The name of a once populous Indian village, which occupied the present beautiful site of the village of Fryeburg, Me., near Lovewell's Pond, where the sanguinary conflict here alluded to occurred in 1725.] This was the last time the tribe was ever assembled as a separate people. The name of the Sokokis, at which so many pale faces had been made paler, was buried in the graves of the brave warriors who had here died to defend its glory. The feeble remnant, panic-struck and heart-broken, fled northward, and, like the withered leaves of the forest flying before the strong east wind, were scattered and swept over the mountains into Canada; all but the family of Paugus, who took their stand on these lakes, where his son, Waurumba, took the empty title of chief and, dying, left it still more empty to Wenongonet, the last of the long line of sagamores,—the last ever to stand here to tell the young white man the story of their greatness, and the fate of their tribe."

On concluding his story, the chief turned to his daughter and significantly pointed to the lengthening shadows of the trees on the water, with a motion of his head towards their home up the lakes.

"The chief thinks," said Fluella, arousing herself from the thoughtful attitude in which she had been silently listening to the conversation,—"the chief thinks it time we were on the water, on our way home. We shall have now to bid Mr. Elwood a good-evening."

So saying, she stepped lightly into the canoe and took her seat. She was immediately followed by the chief, who, quickly handling his oar, sent the light craft, with a single stroke, some rods into the lake, when, partially turning its bow towards the spot where Claud was standing on the shore, he said:

"Should the young man ever stray from his companions in the hunt, or find himself weary, or wet, or cold, or in want of food, when out on the borders of the Molechunk-a-munk, let him feel, and doubt not, that he will be welcome to the lodge of Wenongonet."

"And, if Mr. Elwood should be in the vicinity of our lake this fall, and *not* happen to be in a so very sad condition, he might, perhaps, find a good welcome on calling,—so, especially, if he come before the time of the first snows," added Fluella, playfully at first, but with a slight suffusion of the cheek as she proceeded to the close.

"I thank the chief," responded Claud with a respectful bow. "And I thank you, my fair friend," he continued, turning more familiarly to Fluella. "I hope to come, some time. But why do you speak of the first snows?"

"O, the birds take wing for a warmer country about that time, and perhaps some who have not wings may be off with them," replied Fluella, in the same tone of playfulness and emotion.

A stately bow from the father, and another with a sweetly eloquent smile from the daughter, completed, on their part, the ceremonies of the adieu; when the canoe was headed round, and, by the easy and powerful paddle-strokes of the still vigorous old man, sent bounding over the waters of the glassy lake.

Slowly and thoughtfully Claud turned and took his way homeward. "Who could have expected," he soliloquized, "to witness such an exhibition of intellect and exalted tone of feeling in one of that despised race, as that proud old man displayed, in his eloquently-told story? And that daughter! Well, what is she to me? My faith is given to another. But why feel this strange interest? Yet, after all, it is probably nothing but what any one would naturally feel in the surprise occasioned on beholding such qualities in such a place and person. No, no, it can be nothing more; and I will whistle it to the winds."

And he accordingly quickened his steps, and literally began to whistle a lively tune, by way of silencing the unbidden sensation which he felt conscious had often, since he first met this fair daughter of the wilds, been lurking within. But, though he thus resolved and reasoned the intruding feeling into nothing, yet he felt he would not like to have Avis Gurley know how often the sparkling countenance and witching smile of this new and beautiful face had been found mingling themselves with the previously exclusive images of his dreams. But, if they did so before this second interview, would they do it less now? His head resolutely answered, "Yes, less, till they are banished." His heart softly whispered, "No." And we will not anticipate by disclosing whether head or heart was to prove the better prophet.

CHAPTER XII.

"Away! nor let me loiter in my song,
For we have many a mountain path to tread,
And many a varied shore to sail along,—
By truth and sadness, not by fiction, led."

The day agreed on, by the trappers, for starting on their expedition into the unbroken wilds around and beyond the upper lakes to the extreme reservoirs of the lordly Androscoggin, had at length arrived. All the married men belonging to the company, not having sons of their own old enough, had engaged those of their neighbors to come and remain with their families during their absence from home, which, it was thought probable, would be prolonged to nearly December. Steel-traps and rifles had been put in order, ammunition plentifully provided, and supplies of such provisions as could not be generally procured by the rifle and fish-hook in the woods and its waters, carefully laid in; and all were packed up the night previous, and in readiness for a start the next morning.

It had been agreed that the company should rendezvous on the lake-shore, at the spot which we have already often mentioned, and which, by common consent, was now beginning to be called Elwood's Landing. And, accordingly, early on the appointed morning, Mark Elwood and his son Claud, having dispatched their breakfast, which Mrs. Elwood had been careful to make an unusually good and plentiful one, shouldered their large hunting packs, with their blankets neatly folded and strapped outside; and, having bid that anxious and thoughtful wife and mother a tender farewell, left the house and proceeded with a lively step to the border of the lake. On reaching their canoe at the landing, they glanced inquiringly around them for some indications of the presence or coming of their expected companions. But not a living object met their strained gaze, and not the semblance of a sound greeted their listening ears. A light sheeted fog, of varying thickness and density in the different portions of the wide expanse,—here thin and spray-like, as if formed of the breath of some marine monster, and there thickening to the appearance of the stratiform cloud,—lay low stretched, in long, slow-creeping undulations, over the bosom of the waveless lake.

"The first on the ground, after all," exclaimed Mr. Elwood, on peering out sharply through the partially-obstructing fog in the direction of the outlet of the lake, up through which most of the company, who lived on the rivers below, were expected to come. "That is smart, after so much cautioning to us to be here in season. But they cannot be very far off, can they, Claud?"

"One would suppose not," replied the latter; "but sounds, in this dense and quiet state of the atmosphere, could be distinguished at a great distance, and, with all that my best faculties can do, I cannot hear a single sound from any quarter.—But stay, what was that?"

"What did you think you heard, Claud?" asked Mr. Elwood, after waiting a moment for the other to proceed or explain.

"Why, I can hardly tell, myself," was the musing reply; "but it was some shrill, long-drawn sound, that seemed to come from a great distance in the woods off here to the south-east, or on the lake beyond."

"Perhaps it was a loon somewhere up the lake," suggested Mr. Elwood.

"It may be so, possibly," rejoined Claud, doubtfully; "but, if there were any inhabitants near enough in that direction, I should think it must be—hark, there it is again! and, as I thought, the crowing of a rooster."

"A rooster! then it must be the echo of one, that has somehow struck across from Phillips' barn; but how could that be? Ah, I have just thought: your rooster must be Codman coming down the lake. You know how curiously he imitated that creature at the logging bee, don't you?"

"No; I happened to be in a noisy bustle in the house, just at the time of those queer performances of his, and heard them imperfectly. But, if the sound I heard was not that of a veritable rooster, I never was so deceived in my life respecting the character of a sound."

"Well, I think you will find I am right, but we will wait, listen, and see."

The event soon proved the truth of Mr. Elwood's conjecture. Suddenly a canoe, rounding a woody point a half-mile to the right, shot into view, and the old loud and shrill *Kuk-kuk-ke-o-ho* of Comical Codman rang far and wide over the waters to the echoing hills beyond. But, before Claud had sufficiently recovered from his surprise to respond to the triumphant "*I told you so*" of his father, the strange salute was answered by a merry, responsive shout of voices in the opposite direction; and presently two canoes, each containing two men, emerged into view from the fog hanging over the outlet, and, joining in a contest of speed, to which they seemed to perceive the single boatman was, by his movements, challenging them, rapidly made their way towards the understood goal of the landing.

"The race is run. The vict'ry won!"

exclaimed the trapper, in his usual cheery tone and inimitable air of mock gravity, as he drew up his oar, to let the impulse of his last stroke send his canoe in to the shore of the landing, as it did, while the foremost of his competitors in the friendly race was yet fifty yards distant. "Mighty smart fellows, you!" he resumed, waggishly cocking his eye towards the hunter, who had charge of the boat most in advance. "*What bright and early* chaps, living only from two to five miles off, to let one who has ten miles to come be in first at the rendezvous!"

"Well, Codman, I suppose we must give in," responded the hunter. "But, to do all this, you must have risen long before day; how did you contrive to wake up?"

"Why, crowed like the house a-fire, and waked myself up, to be sure!" replied Codman, promptly. "How did you suppose I did it? But let that all go; I want to look you over a little. You have brought some new faces with you, this time, haven't you, Mr. Hunter?"

"Yes, here is one," answered Phillips, pointing to a tall, sandy-complexioned, but good-looking man of about thirty, who, having occupied the forward seat of the canoe, now quietly stepped ashore; "yes, gentlemen," added the hunter, addressing himself to the Elwoods, standing on the bank, as well as to the trapper, "I make you acquainted with Mr. Carvil,—a man, if I ain't a good deal out in my reckoning, who might be relied on in most any circumstances."

The customary salutations were then exchanged with the stranger; when the hunter, instinctively understanding that often violated rule of true politeness which requires of the introducer some accompanying remark, giving a clue to the position and character of the introduced, so as to gratify the natural curiosity felt on such occasions, and to impart more freedom to the conversation, quickly resumed:

"Mr. Carvil is a Green Mountain boy, who loves hunting, partly for the health it gives, and partly for the fun of it. His old range has usually been round the Great Megantic, the other side of the highlands, in Canada, where I have heard of him through the St. Francis Indians. But, having a mind to see and try this side, he came on a few days ago, inquired me out, and turned in with me. We from below have invited him to join our company; are you all here agreed to that?"

"Certainly," said Mark Elwood, in his usual off-hand manner.

"Certainly," added Claud, more specifically, "I think we ought to be gratified in such an acquisition to our company."

"And you, Codman?" said the hunter, turning inquiringly to the trapper. "It is your turn to speak. But don't show the gentleman so many of your bad streaks, to begin with, as to put him out of conceit of you before he has time to find out your good ones."

"Well, I don't see but I must run the risk, then," said the trapper; "my streaks always come out as they come up, I never pick any of them out as samples for strangers. But to the question,—well, let's run him over once, if he won't be mad: high cheek bones, showing him enough of the Indian make to be a good hunter; a crank, steady eye, indicating honest motives, and a good resolution, that won't allow a man to rest easy till his object is carried out; and lastly, a well-put-together, wiry frame, to bear fatigues, and do the work which so large a head must often lay out for it. Yes, he passes muster with me bravely: let him in, with a welcome."

Carvil rewarded these good-natured running commentaries on his person and supposed qualities, with a complacent bow; when the trapper turned to the other canoe, which, with Gaut Gurley and the young Indian described in a preceding chapter on board, now came within speaking distance, and sang out:

"Hil-lo! there, you, captain, who made the big logs fly so like the de-i-vel, the other day, whether the old chap had any hand in it or not, what red genius is that you have brought along with you?"

"It's Tomah, the young red man from the Connecticut-river region, who hunted some in this section last fall, I understand. I supposed you had met him before," replied Gaut.

"O, ah, well, yes," responded Codman; "I bethink me, now, it is the young Indian that went to college, but couldn't be kept there long enough to make any thing else, though long enough, may be, to spoil him for a hunter."

"May be not, too," retorted Tomah, with a miffed air, which showed he did not so readily appreciate the half-serious, half-sportive manner of the trapper as the other stranger had done. "May be, when you out with me catching beaver, one, two month, you no crow so loud."

"That's right," interposed the hunter; "the Indian gives you what you deserve for your nonsense, Codman. But a truce to jokes. Let us all aboard, strike out, and be on our way over the lake."

In compliance with this suggestion, those not already in the boats took to their seats, handled their oars, pushed off, and, headed by the hunter and his boat companion, and falling, one after another, into a line, rowed steadily on across, the broadest part of the lake, taking a lofty pine, whose attenuated top looked like a reed rising over the fog in the distance, as a guide and landmark to the great inlet, where the most arduous task of their expedition was to be encountered,—the surmounting of the long line of rapids leading to the great lakes above. But that task, after a pleasant rowing of a couple of hours had brought them to it, was, by dint of hard struggles against the current, with oars as long as oars could be made to prevail; with setting-poles when oars ceased to serve the purpose; and with ropes attached to the boats and drawn from point to point or rock to rock, when neither oars nor poles were of any avail; together with the carrying both boats and baggage by land round the last and most difficult ascent,—that task was at length accomplished, and, before one o'clock in the afternoon, all the boats, with their loading, were safely launched on the broad bosom of the wild and picturesque Molechunk-a-munk.

Here, however, the company decided on taking their mid-day's lunch, and an hour's rest, before proceeding on their voyage. But, not deeming it expedient to incur the trouble and delay which the building of fires and the new cooking of provisions would require, they drew out only their bread and cold meats, for the occasion; and these, as the company were seated in an irregular circle on the rocks, were discussed and dispatched with that keen relish which abstinence and a toil-earned appetite alone could have brought them.

After they had finished their repast, they, at the suggestion of Phillips and Codman, the only persons of the company who were familiar with the lakes and country above, took up a question which they had before discussed, without settling, but which, they were told by the persons just named, must now, before proceeding any farther, be definitely settled and understood. This question was that of the expediency of establishing a general head-quarters for the season, by building a large, storm-proof camp, and locating it at some central point on the shore of one of the two great lakes opening still above the one on which they were now about to embark. The object of this was to insure the company comfortable quarters, to which they could resort in case of falling sick, or encountering long storms, at which their furs could be collected and more safely kept, their more cumbrous stores left, and from which their provisions could be distributed, with the least trouble and travel, to the smaller and more temporary camps that each of the company, or any two of them, might make at the nearest terminations, on the neighboring waters, of the different ranges of woods they should select for their respective fields of operations. The main part of the question, that of the necessity of establishing general head-quarters, was at once, and unanimously, decided in the affirmative. The remaining part, that of the most eligible location for these quarters, was then fully discussed, and finally settled by fixing the point of location about midway of the eastern side of the Mooseeluk-maguntic, the next great lake above, and, counting from the south, the third in this unique chain of secluded lakes and widely clustering lakelets, through which the far-spanning Androscoggin pours its vast volume of wild waters to the distant bosom of the welcoming ocean.

"Wisely arranged," remarked the hunter, at the close of the discussion. "The next object in view, then, is to reach there this evening, in season to work up something in the shape of a camp, that will serve for the night, and until the good one we propose to build can be completed."

"That can be done easily enough," said Codman, "that is, if we will tax our marrow-bones a little extra in pulling at the oars. The distance over this lake, up the narrows, or river, and across the end of the Maguntic to the mouth of that second stream we have talked of, can't be much more than a dozen miles, and all smooth sailing. Lord, yes! if we put in like decent oarsmen, I warrant we make fetch come, so as to be there by the sun an hour high, which will give time to build a comfortable camp, and for cooking up the jolly good supper I'm thinking to have, to pay us for all these sweats and hard pulls up these confounded rapids and over these never-ending lakes."

"Well, let us put in, then, boys," responded Gaut Gurley. "I am as much for the go-ahead principle as the best of you. Let us try the motion, and *earn* the good supper, whether we get it or not. But, to make the supper quite the thing for the occasion, it strikes me we ought to have something a little fresher than our salt junk."

"True, O King, and Great Mogul of the lubber-lifts," rejoined the trapper; "thou talkest like one not altogether without knowledge of the good living of the woods. That something fresher we will have, if it be only a mess of fish, which I think I can take out of that stream in a short time after we get there."

"That could be done as we go along, if these lakes are as well stocked with large trout as they are reputed," observed Carvil, in the calm, deliberate manner which characterized him on all occasions.

"But we mustn't stop for that," said the trapper.

"There is no need of stopping," quietly replied the former.

"That's a queer idea," said the trapper, evidently at fault. "How are we to put in and wait for bites, without stopping, I would like to know?"

"Perhaps I may be able to demonstrate the matter, as we proceed on our way. At all events, since the question is raised, I will try," replied Carvil, drawing from his pocket a roll of small silk cord, to which a fish-hook, without any sinker, was attached. "Can any of you handily get at your pork, so as to cut off and throw me a small bit? There, that will do," he continued, taking the proffered bit of meat, and baiting his hook with it. "Now, the experiment I propose to try is what in my region we call 'troulling,' which consists of throwing out a baited hook and paying out, as the boat moves on, a hundred feet, or so, of line, that is left to trail, floating on the surface of the water behind; when most large fish, like bass, or trout, especially if you make a sharp tack, occasionally, so as to draw the line across an undisturbed portion of the water, will see, and, darting up, sieze it, and hook themselves. And, if you have many large trout *here*, and they are any related to those I have found in the Great Maguntic, and other large bodies of fresh water, they will some of them stand a pretty good chance to be found adding to our supper to-night."

"Sorry to hear it," said the trapper, "for I have always considered the trout a sensible fish, and I should be sorry to lose my respect for them. But, if they will do that, they are bigger fools than I took them to be. But you'll find they just won't."

"Well, I don't know about that, now. I am not so sure but there may be something in it," remarked the hunter, who had been listening to Carvil with evident interest. "Though we have never tried that method in this region, to my knowledge, yet my experience rather goes to confirm the notion. I remember to have caught several fine trout, when I had laid down my pole, and was moving off with my boat, but had left my line trailing behind. Those great fellows are not very bashful about seizing any thing they think they can eat, which they can see on the surface. I have known them do a stranger thing than to come up and seize a piece of pork."

"What was that?" asked the trapper.

"Well, I don't know as you will believe the story," answered the other, "but it will be equally true, if you don't. Some years ago I was out on the Umbagog, for a mess of trout, but couldn't get a bite; and, seeing a flock of black ducks in a neighboring cove, I hauled in my line, and rowed off towards them, thinking I might get a shot, and so have something to carry home, by way of mending my luck at fishing. But, before I got near enough to count with much certainty on the effect of a shot, if I fired, they all flew up, but one, which, though it seemed to be trying hard enough, could not raise its body out of the water. As my canoe drifted in nearer, I once or twice raised my rifle to fire at it; but it acted so strangely, flapping the water with its wings, and tugging away at swimming, without appearing to gain scarce a single foot, that I soon laid down my piece and concluded I would try to take it alive, supposing it must have got fast tangled with something, but with what, I was wholly unable to conceive. So, taking up my oar, and gunning my canoe, so as to send it by within reach of the bird, I gave two or three strong pulls, threw down the oar, put out my hand, and sat ready for the grab, which the next moment I made, seizing the panting and now sinking duck by one of its outspread wings, and pulling it in, with a big trout fastened to its foot and leg so tight by the teeth that the hold did not give way till the greedy fish was brought slapping over the side, and landed safely in the bottom of the canoe. That trout, when I got home, weighed just seven pounds and nine ounces."

"Wheugh! whiz! kak! ke-o-ho!" exclaimed, whistled, and crowed Comical Codman.

"I do not doubt it in the least," said Carvil.

"Nor can I, of course, on Mr. Phillips' statement," added Mark Elwood; "but, if I had not known his scrupulousness in matters of fact, I should not have believed that so strange a circumstance had ever happened in the world."

"So the story is voted gospel, is it?" rejoined the trapper. "Well, then, I propose we commission its author to cruise along the coves this afternoon, so that he may bring into camp to-night trout enough caught in that way to make up what Mr. Carvil may miss taking by *his* method, together with a brace or two of nice ducks, which would be a still further fine addition to our supper."

"Yes, ducks or some other kind of flesh, to go with the fish, we may now safely count on being secured, by some of the various proposed methods," here interposed Claud Elwood, seriously. "And I second the motion of such a cruise along the shores, by Mr. Phillips, who so seldom fails of killing something. And if he, Mr. Carvil, and father, will agree to an exchange of boat companions for the afternoon, I should like to go with him. I have chosen him my schoolmaster in hunting, and I should have a chance for another lesson before we go into the separate fields of our approaching operations."

Gaut Gurley started at the suggestion, and cast a few quick, searching glances at Claud and the hunter, as if suspecting a concert of action between them, for some purpose affecting his secret plans; but, appearing to read nothing in either of their countenances to confirm such suspicions, and seeing all the rest of the company readily falling in with the proposal, he held his peace, and joined the others in handling the oars for their immediate departure; which was now in a few minutes taken, the main part of the company striking in a direct line across the middle of the lake for their destination, leaving the hunter and Claud moving off obliquely to the right, for a different and farther route among the intervening islands, and along the indented shores beyond,—where it will best comport with the objects of our story, we think, to accompany them in their solitary excursion.

"Where away, as the sailors have it?" said Claud, after the two, each with a single oar, had rowed on a while in silence; "where away, Mr. Phillips, or in the line of what object in sight would you lay your course?"

"Why, I had proposed, in my own mind," replied the hunter, "to steer direct across, so as to graze the east side of the great island you see yonder in the distance; but, as we shall pass so near the cove which lies snuggled away between two sharp, woody points here, a little ahead to the right, we might as well, perhaps, haul in and take a squint round it."

"What shall we find there?"

"Perhaps nothing. It is the place, however, where I found that deer which I killed when we were here before."

"Well, if you can count on another, we should turn in there now."

"We will; but a hunter, young man, must never talk of certainties when going to any particular spot in search of such roving things as the animals of the forest. He must learn to bear disappointment, and be prepared to find nothing where he or others had before found every thing. He must have patience. Loss of patience is very apt to be fatal to success in almost any business, but especially so in hunting. You spoke of taking lessons of me in the craft: this is the very first grand lesson I would impress on your mind. But we are now close upon the point of land, which we are only to round to be in the cove. If you are disposed to row the boat alone, now, keep in or out, stop or move on, as I from to time give the word, I will down on my knees in the bow of the boat, with cocked rifle in hand, ready for what may be seen."

Readily complying, Claud carefully rowed round the point and entered the dark and deep indenture constituting the cove, whose few acres of surface were thrown almost wholly into the shade, even at sunny noonday, by the thickly-clustered groups of tall, princely pines, which, like giant warriors in council, stood nodding their green plumes around the closely-encircling shores. Closely hugging the banks, now stopping behind some projecting clump of bushes, now in some rock-formed nook, and now in the covert of some low-bending treetop, to give the keen-eyed hunter a chance to peer round or through these screening objects into the open spaces along the shore beyond, he slowly pushed along the canoe till the whole line of the cove was explored, and they reached the point corresponding to the one at which they commenced their look-out for game, and all without seeing a living creature.

"Pshaw! this is dull business," exclaimed Claud, as they came out into the open lake, where he was left free to speak aloud. "This was so fine a looking place for game that I felt sure we should see something worth taking; and I am quite disappointed in the result."

"So that, then, is the best fruit you can show of my first lesson in hunting, is it, young man?" responded the hunter, with a significant smile.

Claud felt the implied rebuke, and promised better behavior for the future; when both seated themselves at the oars, and, as men naturally do, after an interval of suppressed action, plied themselves with a vigor that sent their craft swiftly surging over the waters in the line of their original destination.

They now soon reached, and shot along the shore of, a beautifully-wooded island, nearly a half-mile in extent, about midway of which the hunter-rested on his oars, and, after Claud, on his motion, had done the same, observed, pointing through a partial opening among the trees, along a visible path that led up a gentle slope into the interior of the island:

"There! do you catch a glimpse of a house-like looking structure, in an open and light spot in the woods, a little beyond where you cease to trace the path?"

"Yes, quite distinctly. What is it?"

"That belongs to the chief, and might properly enough be called his summer-house, as he generally comes here with his family to spend the hot months. He raises fine crops of corn in his clearing on there beyond the house, and saves it all, because the bears, coons, and squirrels, that trouble him else-where, are so completely fenced out by the surrounding water."

"Are the family there, now?"

"No; they have moved back to his principal residence, a mile or two distant, on a point of land over against the opposite side of this island, and not far out of our course."

"Indeed! what say you, then, to giving them a call as we pass by?"

"We shall not have time, which is a good reason for not calling now, if there were not still stronger ones."

"What stronger reasons, or what other reasons at all?"

"Well, perhaps there are none. But, supposing two of the company we left behind, who might happen to conceive they have some secret interest at stake, should ever suspect that your leading object in leaving them was to make the very visit you are now proposing, would you not prefer that we should have it in our power to set their minds at rest, when we join them to-night, by telling them all the places we *did* touch at?"

"It is possible I should, in such a case," replied Claud, looking surprised and puzzled; "but, 'suspected,' did you say? *Why* should they suspect? and what if they do?"

"Three questions in a heap, when one is more than I could wisely attempt to answer," evasively answered the cautious hunter.

"But you must have some reasons for what you said," persisted the other.

"Reasons founded upon guesses are poor things to build a statement on," rejoined the hunter. "Half the mischief and ill-feeling in the world comes from statements so made. And, guessing aloud is often no better. I rather think, all things considered, we had better not stop at the chief's, this time. I can show you where he lives, as we pass; and, if that will do, we will now handle oars, and be on our way."

Much wondering at the enigmatical words of the other, Claud, without further remark, put in his oar and thoughtfully rowed on, till they had passed round the head of the island; when, on the indication of the hunter, they stretched away towards a distant promontory, on the northeastern shore of the lake. A steady and vigorous rowing of half an hour brought them within a few hundred yards of the headland, for which they had been steering; when the hunter lifted his oar, and said:

"There! let the canoe run on alone, a while, and give me your attention. Now, you see," he continued, pointing in shore to the right, "you see that opening in the woods, yonder, on the southern slope extending down near the lake, eighty rods or such a matter off, don't you? Well, that, and divers other openings, where the timber has been cut down and burnt over, for planting corn, scattered about in the woods in different places, as well as a large tract of the surrounding forest-land, are the possessions of the chief."

"But where is their house?"

"Down near the lake, among the trees. You can't see much of it, but it is a smart, comfortable house, like one of our houses, and built by a carpenter; for the chief used formerly to handle considerable money, got by the furs caught by himself, and by the profits on the furs he bought of the St. Francis Indians, who came over this way to hunt. But stay: there are some of the family at his boat-landing. I think it must be Fluella and her Indian half-brother. She is waving a handkerchief towards us. Let us wait and see what she wants."

The female, whose trim figure, English-fashioned dress, and graceful motions went to confirm the hunter's conjectures, now appeared to turn and give some directions to the boy, who immediately disappeared, but in a few minutes came back, entered a canoe, and put off towards the spot where our two voyagers were resting on their oars. In a short time the canoe came up, rowed by an ordinary Indian boy of about fourteen, who, pulling alongside, held up a neatly-made, new, wampum-trimmed hunting pouch, and said:

"The chief send this Mr. Claud Elwood,—gift. Fluella say, wish Mr. Phillips and Mr. Claud Elwood good time."

And so saying, and tossing the article to Claud, he wheeled his canoe around, and, without turning his head or appearing to hear the compliments and thanks that both the hunter and Claud told him to take to the chief and his daughter, sped his way back to the landing.

"There, young man!" exclaimed the obviously gratified hunter, "that is a present, with a meaning. I would rather have it, coming as it does from an Indian, and that Indian such a man as the chief,—I would rather have it, as a pledge of watchfulness over your interests in the settlement, whether you are present there or absent,—than a white man's bond for a hundred dollars; and I would also rather have it, as a token of faith, given when you are roaming this northern wilderness, than a passport from the king of England. The chief's *Totem*, the bald eagle, is woven in, I see, among the ornaments. Every Indian found anywhere from the great river of Canada to the sea eastward will know and respect it, and know, likewise, how to treat the man to whom it was given."

"But how," asked Claud, "could stranger Indians, whom I encountered, know to whom it was given, or that I did not find, buy, or steal the article?"

"Let an Indian alone for that. You have but three fingers on your left hand, I have noticed."

"True, the little finger was accidentally cut clean off by an axe, when I was a child; but what has that to do with the question?"

"Enough to settle it. Do you notice something protruding as if from under the protecting wing of the eagle of the *Totem*, there?"

"Yes; and surely enough it resembles a human hand, with only three fingers."

"That is it; and you may yet, in your experiences in these rough and sometimes dangerous wilds, know the value of that gift."

"At any rate, I feel gratified at this mark of the chief's good will; the more because I was so little expecting it, especially at this time. How could they have possibly made out who I, or indeed either of us, was, at such a distance?"

"A very natural inquiry, but answered when I tell you that Fluella has a good spy-glass, that a year or two ago she brought, among other curious trinkets, from her other home in the old settlement. And she makes it often serve a good purpose, too. She has spied out, for her father's killing, many a moose or deer that had come down to the edge or into the water of the lake round the shores to drink, eat wild-grass, or cool themselves, as well as many a flock of wild geese, lighting here on their fall or spring passages. She knew, I think, about the day we were to start, and, being on the lookout, saw the rest of our company passing off here to the west, an hour or two ago, and, not seeing us among them, expected us to be along somewhere in this direction. Now, is all explained?"

"Yes, curiously but satisfactorily."

"Then, only one word more on the subject: let me advise you not to show that hunting-pouch when we join the company, nor wear it till we are off on our separate ranges. I have my reasons, but mustn't be asked to give them."

"All this is odd, Mr. Phillips; but, taking it for granted that your reasons are good ones, I will comply with your advice."

"Very well. The whole matter being now disposed of, let us move on round the point, and into the large cove we shall find round there. We mustn't give up about game so. No knowing what may yet be done in that line."

Having risen to his feet, raised his hunting-cap, and bowed his adieu to the still lingering maiden on shore, Claud now joined his companion at the oars; when they rapidly passed round the headland, and soon entered the bay-like recess of water, which, sweeping round in a large wood-fringed circle, opened upon the view immediately beyond. After skirting along the sometimes bold and rocky, and sometimes low and swampy, thickly-wooded shore, with a sharp lookout for whatever might come within range of the eye, but without stopping for any special examination till they had reached the most secluded part of the cove, the hunter suspended his oar, and signified his intention of landing. Accordingly, running in their canoe by the side of an old treetop extending into the water, and, throwing their mooring-line around one of its bare limbs, they stepped noiselessly ashore, and ascended the bank, when the hunter, pausing and pointing inward, said, in a low, suppressed tone:

"There, within a short distance from us, commences one of the thickest windfall jungles in these parts, and extends up nearly to the chiefs outermost cornfield, about half a mile off. I have been threatening to come here some time; and if, as I will propose, we go into the tangle, and get through, or half through, without encounter of some kind, I confess I shall be uncommonly disappointed. But, before entering, let us sit down on this old log a few minutes, and, while looking to our flints and priming, keep our ears open for such sounds as may reach them."

And, bending low his head, with closed eyes, and an ear turned towards the thicket, the hunter listened long and intently in motionless silence, after which he quickly rose, and, while glancing at his gun-flint and priming, said:

"There are no distinct sounds, but the air is disturbed in the kind of way that I have frequently noticed when animals of some size were in the vicinity. Let us forward into the thicket, spreading out some ten rods apart, and worming ourselves among the windfalls, with a stop and a thorough look every few rods of our progress. Should you start up a panther, which ain't very likely, you had better whistle for me, before firing; but, if any thing else, blaze away at it."

Nodding his assent, and starting off in a course diverging to the right of the one he perceived his companion to be taking, Claud slowly, and as he best could, made his way forward, sometimes crawling underhand sometimes clambering over the tangled masses of fallen trees, which, with a thick upshooting second growth, lay piled and crossed in all conceivable shapes and directions before him. After proceeding in this manner thirty or forty rods, he paused, for the third or fourth time, to look and listen; but lastly quite as much for his companion as for game, for, with all his powers, he could detect no sound indicating that the latter could be anywhere in the vicinity. While thus engaged, he heard a small, shrill, plaintive sort of cry, as of a little child, coming from somewhere above him; when, casting up his eyes, he beheld a large raccoon sidling round a limb, and seemingly winking and nodding down towards him. With the suppressed exclamation of "Far better than nothing," he brought his piece to his face and fired; when the glimpse of a straight-falling body, and the heavy thump on the ground that followed, told him that the object of his aim was a "*dead coon.*" But his half-uttered shout of exultation was cut short by the startling report of a rifle, a little distance to the rear, on his left. And the next moment a huge old bear, followed by a smaller one, came smashing and tearing through the brush and tree-tops directly towards him. And with such headlong speed did the frightened brutes advance upon him, that he had scarce time to draw his clubbed rifle before the old one had broke into the little open space where he stood, and thrown herself on her haunches, in an attitude of angry defiance. Recoiling a step in the only way he could move, and expecting the next moment to find himself within the fatal grasp of the bear, if he did not disable her, Claud aimed and struck with all his might a blow at her head. But, before the swiftly-descending implement reached its mark, it was struck by the fending paw of the enraged brute, with a force that sent its tightly-grasping owner spinning and floundering into the entangled brushwood, till he landed prostrate on the ground. And, ere he had time to turn himself, the desperate animal had rushed and trampled over him, and disappeared through a breach effected in one of the treetops that had hemmed him in and prevented his retreat from such a doubtful, hand-to-hand encounter. As the discomfited young huntsman was rising to his feet, his eyes fell upon Phillips, hurrying forward, with looks of lively concern; which, however, as he leaped into the small open space comprising the battle-ground, and saw how matters stood, at first gave place to a ludicrous smile, and then to a merry peal of laughter.

"I can't say I blame you much for your merriment," said Claud, joining, though rather feebly, in the laugh, as he brushed himself and picked up his rifle; "for, to be upset and run over by a bear would have been about the last thing I should have dreamed of myself."

"O well," said the other, checking his risibles, "it had better turn out a laughing than a crying matter, as it might have done if you had kept your footing; for, if you had not been overthrown and run over, you would have probably, in this cramped-up place, stood up to be hugged and scratched in a way not so very agreeable; and I rather guess, under the circumstances, you may as well call yourself satisfied to quit so; for the bears have left you with a whole skin and unbroken ribs, though they have escaped themselves where, with our time, it will be useless to follow them. But, if you had not fired just as you did, we would have had all three of them."

"What! have you killed one?" asked Claud, in surprise.

"To be sure I have," answered the hunter. "Then you supposed it was one of your rough visitors I fired at, and missed? No, no. I had got one of the black youngsters in range, and was waiting for a chance at the old one, knowing if I killed her first the young ones would take to the trees, where they could easily be brought down. Seeing them, however, on the point of running at the report of your rifle, I let drive at the only one I was sure of; when the two others, they being nearly between us, tacked about and ran towards you. But go get your 'coon, and come along this way, to look at my black beauty."

"How did you know I had killed a 'coon?" inquired the other.

"Heard him squall before you fired, then strike the ground afterwards with a force that I thought must have killed him, whether your bullet had or not," replied the hunter, moving off for his bear, with which, tugging it along by a hind leg, he soon joined Claud, who was threading his way out with his mottled trophy swung over his shoulder.

"Why, a much larger one than I supposed," exclaimed the latter, turning and looking at the cub; "really, a fine one!"

"Ain't he, now?" complacently said the hunter. "There, heft him; must weigh over half a hundred, and as fat as butter,—for which he is doubtless indebted to the chiefs cornfield. And I presume we may say the same of that streaked squaller of yours, which I see is an uncommonly large, plump fellow. Well," continued the speaker, shouldering the cub, "we may now as well call our hunt over, for to-day,—out of this plaguey hole as soon as we can, and over the lakes to camp, as fast as strong arms and good oars can send us."

On, after reaching and pushing off their now well-freighted canoe, on,— along the extended coast-line of this wild lake, westward to the great inlet, up the gently inflowing waters of that broad, cypress-lined stream, to the Maguntic, and then, tacking eastward, around the borders of that still wilder and more secluded lake,—on, on, they sped for hours, until the ringing of the axe-fall, and the lively echo of human voices in the woods, apprised them of their near approach to the spot which their companions had selected, both for their night's rest and permanent head-quarters for the season.

CHAPTER XIII.

"And now their hatchets, with resounding stroke,
Hew'd down the boscage that around them rose,
And the dry pine of brittle branches broke,
To yield them fuel for the night's repose;
The gathered heap an ample store bespoke.
They smite the steel: the tinder brightly glows,
And the fired match the kindled flames awoke,
And light upon night's seated darkness broke.
High branch'd the pines, and far the colonnade
Of tapering trunks stood glimmering through the glen;
So joyed the hunters in their lonely glade."

"Hurra! the stragglers have arrived!" exclaimed Codman, the first to notice the hunter and Claud as they shot into the mouth of the small, quiet river, on whose bank was busily progressing the work of the incipient encampment. "Hurra for the arrival of the good ship Brag, Phillips, master; but where is his black duck, with a big trout to its foot? Ah, ha! not forthcoming, hey? Kuk-kuk-ke-oh-o!"

"Don't crow till you see what I have got, Mr. Trapper," replied the hunter, running in his canoe by the sides of those of his companions on shore. "Don't crow yet,—especially over the failure of what I didn't undertake: you or Mr. Carvil was to furnish the big trout, you will recollect."

"That has been attended to by me, to the satisfaction of the company, I rather think," remarked Carvil, now advancing towards the bank with the rest. "Not only one big trout, but two more with it, was drawn in by my method, on the way."

"O, accident, accident!" waggishly rejoined the trapper; "they were hooked by mere accident. The fact is, the trouts are so thick in these lakes that a hook and line can't be drawn such a distance through them without getting into some of their mouths. But, allowing it otherwise, it don't cure but half of your case, Mr. Hunter. Where is the black duck?"

"*Here* is the black duck," responded the hunter, stepping ashore and drawing his cub out from under some screening boughs in the bow of the boat.

A lively shout of laughter burst from the lips of the company at the disclosure, showing alike their amusement at the practical way in which the hunter had turned the jokes of the teasing trapper, and their agreeable surprise at his luck in the uncertain hunting cruise along the shores, on which they, without any expectation of his success, had banteringly dispatched him.

"Ah, I think you may as well give up beat, all round, Mr. Codman," observed Mark Elwood, after the surprise and laughter had subsided. "But come up here, neighbor Phillips, and see what a nice place we are going to have for our camp."

Leaving the game in charge of Claud and Carvil, who volunteered to dress it, the rest of the company walked up with the hunter to the spot where the new shanty was in progress, wishing to hear his opinion of the location selected, and the plan on which it had been commenced.

The location to which the company had been guided by the trapper was a level space, about ten rods back from the stream here falling into the lake from the east, and at the foot of a rocky acclivity forming a portion of the southern side of a high ridge that ran down to the lake. The first ten feet of the rise was formed by the smooth, even face of a perpendicular rock, which from the narrow shelf at the top fell off into a less precipitous ascent, extending up as far as the eye could reach among the stunted evergreens and other low bushes that partially covered it. About a dozen feet in front of this abutting rock, equidistant from it, and some fifteen feet apart, stood two spruce trees, six or eight inches in diameter at the bottom, but tall, and tapering towards the top. These, the company, who had reached the place about two hours before, had contrived, by rolling up some old logs to stand on, to cut off, and fell, six or seven feet from the ground; so that the tall stumps might serve for the two front posts of the proposed structure. And, having trimmed out the tops of the two fallen trees, and cut them into the required lengths, they had laid them from the top of the rock to the tops of the stumps, which had been first grooved out, so as to receive and securely fasten the ends of the timbers. These, with the stout poles which they had then cut and laid on transversely, at short intervals, made a substantial framework for the roof of the shantee. And, in addition to this, rows of side and front posts had been cut, sharpened, driven into the ground at the bottom, and securely fastened at the top to the two rafters at the sides and the principal beam, which had been notched into them at the lower ends to serve for the front plate.

"Just the spot," said the hunter, after running his eye over and around the locality a moment, and then going up and inspecting the structure in progress. "I thought Codman could not miss so remarkable a place. I have been thinking of building a camp here for several years; but it never seemed to come just right till this fall. Why, you all must have worked like beavers to get along with the job so well, and to do it so thoroughly. The bones of the thing are all now up, as far as I can see, and made strong enough to withstand all the snows and blows of half a dozen winters. So, now, nothing remains but to put on the bark covering."

"But how are we to get the bark covering?" asked Gaut Gurley. "Bark will not peel well at this season, will it?"

"No, not very well, I suppose," replied the former. "But I will see what I can do towards hunting up the material, to-morrow. A coat of these spruce boughs, spread over this framework above, and set up here against the sides, will answer for to-night. And this rigging up, gathering hemlock boughs for our beds, building a good fire here in front, and cooking the supper, are all we had better think of attempting this evening; and, as it is now about sunset, let us divide off the labor, and go at it."

The encampment of these adventurous woodsmen presented, for the next hour, a stirring and animated scene. The different duties to be performed having been apportioned by mutual agreement among the company, they proceeded with cheerful alacrity to the performance of their respective tasks. Phillips and Carvil set busily to work in covering, inclosing, and rigging up the camp,—to adopt the woodsman's use of that word, as we notify the critic we shall do, as often as we please, albeit that use, contrary to Noah Webster, indicates the structure in which men lodge in the woods, rather than the place or company encamping. Mark Elwood, Gaut Gurley, and the young Indian Tomah, proceeding to a neighboring windfall of different kinds of wood, went to work in cutting and drawing up a supply of fuel, among which, the accustomed backlog, forestick, and intermediate kindling-wood, being adjusted before the entrance of the camp, the fire from the smitten steel and preserving punkwood was soon crackling and throwing around its ruddy glow, as it more and more successfully competed with the waning light of the departing day. Claud and Codman, in fulfilment of their part of the business on hand, then unpacked the light frying-pans, laid in them the customary slices of fat salted pork, and shortly had them sharply hissing over the fire, preparatory to receiving respectively their allotted quotas of the tender and nutritious bearsteaks, or the broad layers of the rich, red-meated trout.

In a short time the plentiful contents of the pans were thoroughly cooked, the pans taken from the fires, the potatoes raked from the glowing embers, in which they had been roasting under the forestick, the brown bread and condiments brought forward, and all placed upon the even face of a broad, thin sheet of cleft rock, which they had luckily found in the adjacent ledge, and brought forward and elevated on blocks within the camp, to serve, as it well did, for their sylvan table. Gathering round this, they proceeded to help themselves, with their camp knives and rude trenchers, split from blocks of the freely-cleaving basswood, to such kinds and portions of the savory viands, smoking so invitingly in the pans before them, as their inclinations severally prompted. Having done this, they drew back to seats on broad chips, blocks of wood, piles of boughs, or other objects nearest at hand, and began upon their long anticipated meal with a gusto which made them for a while too busy for conversation, other than an occasional brief remark on the quality of the food, or some jocose allusion to the adventures of the day. After they had finished their repast, however, and cleared away the relics of the supper, together with the few utensils they had used in cooking and eating it, they replenished their fire; and, while the cheerful light of its fagot-fed blaze was flashing up against the dark forest around, and shooting away through the openings of the foliage in long glimmering lines over the waters below, they all placed themselves at their ease,—some sitting on blocks, some leaning against the posts, and some reclining on piles of boughs,—and commenced the social confab, or that general conversation, in which woodsmen, if they ever do, are prone to indulge after the fatigues of the day are over, and the consequent demands of appetite have been appeased by a satisfactory meal.

"Now, gentlemen, I will make a proposition," said Mark Elwood, in a pause of the conversation, which, though it had been engaged in with considerable spirit, yet now began to flag. "I will propose, as we have an hour or two on hand, to be spent somehow, before we shall think of rolling ourselves up in our blankets for the night,—I propose that you professional hunters, like Phillips, Codman, and Carvil, here, each give us a story of one of your most remarkable adventures in the woods. It would not only while away the hour pleasantly for us all, but might furnish useful information and timely hints for us beginners in this new life, upon which we are about to enter. For my part, I should like to listen to a story, by these old witnesses, of the strange things they must have encountered in the woods. What say you, Gurley, Claud, and Tomah? Shall we put them on the stand?"

"Yes, a good idea," replied Gaut, his habitual cold reserve relaxing into something like cordiality; "I feel just in the humor to listen,—more so than to talk, on this hearty supper. Yes, by all means let us have the stories."

"O, I should be exceedingly gratified," joined in Claud, in his usual frank and animated manner.

"I like that, too; like to hear hunting story, always, much," added Tomah, with a glistening eye.

"Well, no particular objection as far as I am concerned," responded the trapper, seriously; but adding, with his old waggish gleam of the eye: "that is, if you will take what I give, and swallow it as easily as you did Phillips' fish story. But let Carvil, who must be the youngest, go on with *his* story first; I will follow; and Phillips shall bring up the rear."

Carvil, after making a few excuses that were not suffered to avail him, commenced his narration, which we will head

THE AMATEUR WOODSMAN'S STORY.

"I call myself a woodsman, and a pretty good one, now; but, four years ago, I was almost any thing else but one of *any* kind. I should have then thought it would have certainly been the death of me to have lain out one night in the woods. And I had no more idea of ever becoming a hunter or trapper, to remain out, as I have since done, for weeks and months in the depths of the wilderness, with no other protection than my rifle, and no other shelter than what I could fix up with my hatchet for the night, where I happened to be, on the approach of darkness, than I now have of undertaking to swim the Atlantic. And, as the circumstances which led to this revolution in my opinions and habits, when *out* of the woods, may as much interest you, in the account, as any thing that happened to me after I got into them, I will first briefly tell you how I came to be a woodsman, and then answer your call by relating a hunting incident which occurred to me after I became one; which, if not very marvellous, shall, at least, have the merit of truth and reality.

"I was brought up rather tenderly, as to work; and my parents, absurdly believing that, with my then slight frame, any employment requiring any labor or physical exertion would injure me, put me to study, and assisted me to the means of entering college at eighteen, and of graduating at twenty-two. Well, I did not misimprove my opportunities for knowledge, I believe; but, instead of gaining strength and manhood by my exemption from labor, I grew feebler and feebler. Still, I did not know what was wanting to give me health and constitution, nor once think that a mind without a body is a thing not worth having; and so I went on, keeping within doors and studying a profession, until I found myself a poor, nervous, miserable dyspeptic, and threatened with consumption. It was now plain enough that, if I would avoid a speedy death, something must be done; and, by the advice of the doctors, who were about as ignorant of the philosophy of health as myself, I concluded to seek a residence and livelihood in one of the Southern States. Accordingly, I packed up and took stage for Boston, timing my journey so as to get there the day before the ship, on which I had previously ascertained I could find a passage, was to sail for Savannah. But, the morning after I arrived, a severe storm came on, and the sailing of the ship was deferred till the next day; so, having nothing to do, knowing nobody to talk with, and the weather being too stormy to go out to see the city, I took to my solitary room in the hotel, where, fortunately, there were neither books nor papers to prevent me from thinking. And I *did* think, that day, almost for the first time in my life, without the trammels of fashionable book-theories, and more effectually than I had ever done before. I had a favorite classmate in college, whose name was Silas Wright, who had a mind that penetrated, like light, every thing it was turned upon, and who never failed to see the truth of a matter, though his towering ambition sometimes prevented him from following the path where it led. In recalling, as I was pacing the floor that gloomy day, my old college friends and their conversation, I happened to think of what Wright once said to me on the subject of health and long life.

"'Carvil,' said he, 'did you know that we students were committing treason against the great laws of life which God has laid down for us?'

"'No.'

"'Well, we are. Man was made for active life, and in the open air.'

"'But *you*, it seems, are not observing the theory about which you are so positive?'

"'No, and don't intend to. To observe that, I must relinquish all thought of mounting the professional and political ladder, even half way to the mark I *must* and *will* reach. I have naturally a strong constitution, and I calculate it will last, with the rapid mounting I intend, till I reach the top round, and that is all that I care for. But I shall know, all the while, that I am going up like a rocket, whose height and brilliancy are only attained by the certain and rapid wasting of the substance that composes it. But the case is different with you, Carvil. You have a constitution yet to make, or your rocket will go out, before you can get high enough, in these days of jostling and severe competition, to warrant the attempt of mounting at all.'

"Such was one of Wright's intuitive grasps at the truth, hid under the false notions of the times, or the artificial theories of books, which he was wasting his life to master, and often only mastering to despise. And I, being now earnestly in search of the best means of health, eagerly caught at his notion, which placed the matter in a light in which I had never before seriously viewed it, and, indeed, struck me with a force that soon brought me to a dead stand in all my calculations for the future. 'What is it,' thought I, running into a sort of mental dialogue with myself, and calling in what little true science I had learned, to aid me in fully testing the soundness of the notion, before I finally gave in to it; 'what is it that hardens the muscles, and compacts the human system?'—'Thorough exercise, and constant use.'—'Can these be had in the study-room?' 'No.'—'And what is the invigorating and fattening principle of the air we breathe?'—'Oxygen.'—'Can this be had in the close or artificially-heated room?'—'No, except in stinted and uncertain proportions. It can be breathed in the open fields, but much more abundantly in the woods.'—'Well, what do I need?'—'Only hardening and invigorating.'—'But shall I go to the relaxing clime of the South for this?'—'No; the northern wilderness were a hundred times better.'—'It is settled, then.'—'Landlord,' I cried aloud, as I saw that personage at that moment passing by my partly open door, 'when does the first stage, going north, start?'

"'In twenty minutes, and from my door.'

"'Order on my luggage, here; make out your bill; and I will be on hand.'

"And I was on hand at the time, and the next hour on my way home, which I duly reached, but only to start off immediately to the residence of a hunter acquaintance, a dozen miles off, who, I knew, was about to start for the head-waters of the Connecticut, on his annual fall hunting expedition. I found him, joined him, and within ten days was entering, with pack and rifle, the unbroken wilderness, by his side, though with many misgivings. But my first night out tested and settled the matter forever. We had had a fatiguing march, at least to me, and the last part of it in the rain. We had to lay down in a leaking camp, and I counted myself a dead man. But, to my astonishment, I awoke the next morning, unhurt, and even feeling better than I had for a month. And I constantly grew better and hardier, through that and my next year's campaign in that region, and through the two succeeding ones I made on the Great Megantic; where the incident which I propose to relate to you, it being my best strike in moose-hunting, occurred, and which happened in this wise:

"It was a raw, gloomy day in November, and I had been lazily lying in my solitary camp, on the borders of this magnificent lake, all the forenoon. But, after dinner, I began to feel a little more like action, and soon concluded I would explore a sort of creek-looking stream, four or five rods wide, which I had noticed entering the lake about a mile off, but which I had never entered. Accordingly, I loaded my rifle, took my powder-horn, put two spare bullets in my vest-pocket, not supposing I could have use for more, entered my canoe, and pulled leisurely away for the place. After reaching and entering this sluggish stream, I went on paddling and pushing my way along through and under the overhanging bushes and treetops, something like half a mile, when I came to higher banks and a series of knolls jutting down to the stream, which, with frequent sharp curves and crooks, wound its way among them. On turning one of these sharp points, my eyes suddenly encountered a sight that made my heart jump. On a high, open, and almost bare bluff, directly before me, and not fifteen rods distant, stood two tremendous moose, as unconcernedly as a pair of oxen chewing their cuds, or dozing in a pasture. The last was unusually large, the biggest a monster, appearing, to my wide-opened eyes, with his eight or nine foot height, and ten or eleven foot spread of antlers, as he stood up there against the sky, like some reproduced mastodon of the old legends. Quietly falling back and running in under a screening treetop, I pulled down a branch and put in under my foot to hold and steady my canoe. When I raised my rifle, I aimed it for the heart of the big moose, and fired. But, to my great surprise, the animal never stirred nor moved a muscle. Supposing I had somehow unaccountably missed hitting him, even at all, I fell, with nervous haste, to reloading my piece; and, having got all right, as I supposed, I raised it this time towards the smaller moose, standing a little nearer and presenting a fairer mark; took a long and careful aim, and again let drive; but again without the least effect. Utterly confounded to have missed a second time, with so fair a shot, I stood half confused a moment, first querying whether something was not the matter with my eyes, and then thinking of stories I had heard of witches turning away bullets from their object. But I soon mechanically began to load up again; and, having got in my powder, I put my hand in my pocket for a bullet, when I found there both the balls I had brought with me from camp, and consequently knew that in my eager haste in loading for my last shot, I had neglected to put in any bullet at all! But I now put in the bullet, looked at it after it was entered, to make sure it was there, and then felt it all the way down, till I had rammed it home. I then raised the luckless piece once more, uncertain at first which of the two moose I should take, this time. But, seeing the smaller one beginning to move his head and lay back his horns, which I well enough knew was his signal for running, I instantly decided to take *him*, took a quick, good aim, and fired. With three dashing bounds forward, the animal plunged headlong to the ground. Knowing that one to be secure, at least, I then turned my attention to the big one. To my astonishment, he was still there, and, notwithstanding all the firing, had not moved an inch. But, before I got loaded for another trial upon him, I looked up again, when a motion in his body had become plainly visible. Presently he began to sway to and fro, like a rocking tower, and, the next moment, went over broadside, with a thundering crash, into the bushes. My first shot, it appeared, had, after all, done the business, having pierced his lungs and caused an inward flow of blood, that stopped his breath at the time he fell. All was now explained, except the wonder that such shy animals should stand so much firing without running. But the probability is, that, not seeing me, they took the reports of my rifle for some natural sound, such as that of thunder, or the falling of a tree; while, perhaps, the great one, when he was hit, was too much paralyzed to move, by the rupture of some important nerve. But, however that may be, you have the facts by which to judge for yourselves. And I have now only to add, that, having gone to the spot, bled, partially dressed the animals, and got them into a condition to be left, I went off to the nearest camps and rallied out help; when, after much toil and tugging, we got the carcases home to my shanty, for present eating, curing, and distributing among the neighboring hunters, who soon flocked in to congratulate me on my singular good luck, and receive their ever freely-bestowed portions, and who unanimously pronounced my big prize the largest moose ever slain in all the regions of the Great Megantic."

THE TRAPPER'S STORY.

"My story," commenced the trapper, who was next called on for his promised contribution to the entertainment of the evening, "my story is of a different character from the one you have just heard. It don't run so much to the great and terrible as the small and curious. It may appear to you perhaps a little queer, in some parts; but which, after the modest drafts that have been made on my credulity, you will, of course, have the good manners to believe. It relates to an adventure in beaver-hunting, which I met with, many years ago, on Moosehead Lake, where I served my apprenticeship at trapping. I had established myself in camp, the last of August, about the time the beavers, after having collected in communities, and established their never-failing democratic government, generally get fairly at work on their dams and dwelling-houses, for the ensuing cold months, in places along the small streams, which they have looked out and decided on for the purpose. I was thus early on the ground, in order to have time, before I went to other hunting, to look up the localities of the different societies, so that I need not blunder on them and disturb them, in the chase for other animals, and so that I should know where to find them, when their fur got thick enough to warrant the onslaught upon them which I designed to make.

"In hunting for these localities in the vicinity around me, I soon unexpectedly discovered marks of what I thought must be a very promising one, situated on a small stream, not over half a mile in a bee-line over the hills from my camp. When I discovered the place,—as I did from encountering, at short intervals in the woods, two wolverines, always the great enemy and generally the prowling attendant of assembled beavers,— these curious creatures had just begun to lay the foundation of their dam. And the place being so near, and the nights moon-light, I concluded I would go over occasionally, evenings,—the night being the only time when they can ever be seen engaged on their work,—and see if I could gain some covert near the bank, where, unperceived, I might watch their operations, and obtain some new knowledge of their habits, of which I might thereafter avail myself, when the season for hunting them arrived. Accordingly, I went over that very evening, in the twilight, secured a favorable lookout, and laid in wait for the appearance of the beavers. Presently I was startled by a loud rap, as of a small paddle struck flatwise on the water, then another, and another, in quick succession. It was the signal of the master workman, for all the workers to leave their hiding-places in the banks, and repair to their labors in making the dam. The next moment the whole stream seemed to be alive with the numbers in motion. I could hear them, sousing and plunging in the water, in every direction,—then swimming and puffing across or up and down the stream,—then scrambling up the banks,—then the auger-like sound of their sharp teeth, at work on the small trees,—then soon the falling of the trees,— then the rustling and tugging of the creatures, in getting the fallen trees out of the water,—and, finally, the surging and splashing with which they came swimming towards the ground-work of the dam, with the butt end of those trees in their mouths. The line of the dam they had begun, passed with a curve up stream in the middle, so as to give it more strength to resist the current; across the low-water bed of the river some five rods; and extended up over the first low bank, about as much farther, to a second and higher bank, which must have bounded the water at the greatest floods. They had already cut, drawn on, and put down, a double layer of trees, with their butts brought up evenly to the central line, and their tops pointing in opposite directions,—those of one layer, or row, pointing up, and those of the other, down stream. Among and under this line of butts had been worked in an extra quantity of limbs, old wood, and short bushes, so as to give the centre an elevation of a foot or two, over the lowest part of the sides, which, of course, fell off considerably each way in the lessening of the tops of the trees, thus put down. Over all these they had plastered mud, mixed in with stones, grass, and moss, so thick as not only to hold down securely the bodies of the trees, but nearly conceal them from sight.

"Scarcely had I time to glance over these works, which I had not approached near enough to inspect much, before the beavers from below, and above came tugging along, by dozens on a side to the lower edges of their embankment, with the loads or rafts of trees which they had respectively drawn to the spot. Lodging these on the solid ground, with the ends just out of water, they relinquished their holds, mounted the slopes, paused a minute to take breath, and then, seizing these ends again, drew them, with the seeming strength of horses, out of the water and up to the central line on top; laid the stems or bodies of the trees parallel, and as near together as they could be got; and adjusted the butt ends, as I have stated they did with the foundation layers, so as to bring them to a sort of joint on the top. They then all went off for new loads, with the exception of a small squad, a part of which were still holding their trees in a small space in the dam, where the current had not been checked, and the other part bringing stones, till they had confined the trees down to the bottom, so that they would not be swept away. This task of filling the gap, however, after some severe struggling with the current, was before long accomplished; when those engaged upon it joined in the common work, in which they steadily persevered till this second double layer of trees, with the large quantities of short bushes which they brought and wove into the chinks, near the top, was completed, through the whole length of their dam. They then collected along on the top of the dam, and seemed to hold a sort of consultation, after which they scattered for the banks of the stream, but soon returned, walking on their hind legs, and each bringing a load of mud or stones, held between his fore paws and throat. These loads were successively deposited, as they came up, among the stems and interlacing branches of the trees and bushes they had just laid down, giving each deposited pile, as they turned to go back, a smart blow with the flat of their broad thick tails, producing the same sound as the one I have mentioned as the signal-raps for calling them out to work, only far less loud and sharp, since the former raps were struck on water, and the latter on mud or rubbish. Thus they continued to work,—and work, too, with a will, if any creatures ever did,—till I had seen nearly the whole of the last layers plastered over.

"Thinking now I had seen all that would be new and useful to me, I noiselessly crept away and returned to camp, to lay awake half the night, in my excitement, and to dream, the other half, about this magnificent society of beavers, whose numbers I could not make less than three dozen. I did not go to steal another view of the place for nearly a week, and then went in the daytime, there now being no moon, till late,—when, to my surprise, I found the dam finished, and the river flowed into a pond of several acres, while on each side, ranged along, one after another, stood three family dwellings in different states of progress; some of them only rising to the surface of the water, showing the nature of the structure, which, you know, is built up with short, small logs, and mud, in a squarish form, of about the size of a large chimney; while others, having been built up a foot or two above the water, and the windows fashioned, had been arched over with mud and sticks, and were already nearly finished.

"Knowing that the establishment was now so nearly completed that the beavers would not relinquish it without being disturbed by the presence of a human foe,—which they will sometimes detect, I think, at nearly a quarter of a mile distance,—I concluded to keep entirely away from them till the time of my contemplated onslaught, which I finally decided to begin on one of the first days of the coming November.

"Well, what with hunting deer, bear, and so on, for food, and lynx, otter, and sable, for furs, the next two months passed away, and the long anticipated November at length arrived; when, one dark, cloudy day, having cut a lot of bits of green wood for bait, got out my vial of castor to scent them with, and got my steel traps in order, with these equipments and my rifle I set off, for the purpose of commencing operations, of some kind, on my community of beavers. On reaching the spot, I crept to my old covert with the same precautions I had used on my former visits, thinking it likely enough that, on so dark a day, some of the beavers might be out; and, wishing to know how this was, before proceeding openly along, the banks to look out the right places to set my traps, I listened a while, but could hear no splashing about the pond, or detect any *other* sounds indicating that the creatures were astir; but, on peering out, I saw a large, old beaver perched in a window of one of the beaver-houses on the opposite shore. I instinctively drew up my rifle,—for it was a fair shot, and I knew I could draw him,—but I forbore, and contented myself with watching his motions. I might have lain there ten minutes, perhaps, when this leader, or judge in the beaver Israel, as he soon showed himself to be, quietly slid out into the water, swam into a central part of the pond, and, after swimming twice or three times round in a small circle, lifted his tail on high, and slowly and deliberately gave three of those same old loud and startling raps on the water. He then swam back to his cabin, and ascended an open flat on the bank, where all the underbrush had been cut and cleared off in building the dam. In a few minutes more, a large number of beavers might be seen hastening to the spot, where they ranged themselves in a sort of circle, so as just to inclose the old beaver which came first, and which had now taken his stand on a little moss hillock, on the farther side of the little opening, to which he had thus called them, and, evidently, for some important public purpose. Soon another small band of the creatures made their appearance on the bank above, seeming to have in custody two great, lubberly, cowed-down looking beavers, that they were hunching and driving along, as legal officers sometimes have to do with *their* prisoners, when taking them to some dreaded punishment. When this last band reached the place, with these two culprit-looking fellows, they pushed them forward in front of the judge, as we will call him, and then fell into the ranks, so as to close up the circle. There was then a long, solemn pause, in which they all kept still in their places round the prisoners, which had crouched sneaking down, without stirring an inch from the places where they had been put. Soon, however, a great, fierce, gruff-appearing beaver left the ranks, and, advancing a few steps within them, reared himself on his haunches, and began to sputter and gibber away at a great rate, making his fore-paws go like the hands of some over-heated orator; now motioning respectfully towards the judge, and now spitefully towards the prisoners, as if he was making bitter accusations, and demanding judgment against them. After this old fellow had got through, two or three others, in turn, came forward, and appeared also to be holding forth about the matter, but in a far milder manner than the other, which I now began much to dislike for his spitefulness, and in the same proportion to pity the two poor objects of his evident malice. There was then another long and silent pause, after which, the judge proceeded to utter what appeared to be his sentence; and, having brought it to a conclusion, he gave a rap with his tail on the ground. At this signal, the beavers in the ranks advanced, one after another, in rapid succession toward the prisoners, and, circling round them once, turned and gave each one of them a tremendous blow with their tails over the head and shoulders; and so the heavy blows rapidly fell, whack, whack, whack, till every beaver had taken his part in the punishment, and till the poor prisoners keeled over, and lay nearly or quite dead on the ground. The judge beaver then quietly left his stand and went off; and, following his example, all the rest scattered and disappeared, except the spiteful old fellow that had so raised my dislike, by the rancor he displayed in pressing his accusations, and, afterwards, by giving the culprits an extra blow, when it came his turn to strike them. He now remained on the ground till all the rest were out of sight, when,—as if to make sure of finishing what little remains of life the others, in their compunction, might have left in the victims, so as to give them, if they were not quite killed by the terrible bastinadoing they had received, a chance to revive and crawl off,—he ran up, and began to belabor them with the greatest fury over the head. This mean and malicious addition to the old fellow's previously unfair conduct was too much for me to witness, and I instantly drew my rifle and laid him dead beside the bodies he was so rancorously beating. Wading the stream below the dam, I hastened to my prizes, finished their last struggles with a stick, seized them by their tails, and dragged them to the spot I had just left; and then, after concealing my traps, with the view of waiting a few days before I set them, so as to give the society a chance to get settled, I tugged the game I had so strangely come by, home to camp, where a more particular examination showed them to be the three largest and best-furred beavers I had ever taken.

"This brings me to the end of the unaccountable affair, and all I can say in explanation of it; for how these creatures, ingenious and knowing as they are, should have the intelligence to make laws,—as this case seems to presuppose,—get up a regular court, try, sentence, and execute offenders; what these offenders had done,—whether they were thievish interlopers from some other society, or whether they had committed some crime, such as burglary, bigamy, or adultery, or high treason, or whether they had been dishonest office-holders in the society and plundered the common treasury, is a mystery which you can solve as well as I. Certainly you cannot be more puzzled than I have always been, in giving the matter a satisfactory explanation.

"And now, in conclusion, if you wish to know how I afterwards succeeded in taking more of this notable society of beavers, I have only to say, that, having soon commenced operations anew, I took, before I quit the ground that fall, by rifle, by traps, by digging or hooking them out of their hiding places in the banks, and, finally, by breaking up their dwelling-houses, twenty-one beavers in all; making the best lot which I ever had the pleasure of carrying out of the woods, and for which, a month or two after, I was paid, in market, one hundred and sixty-eight hard dollars."

THE OLD HUNTER'S STORY.

"I never but once," commenced the hunter, who had announced himself ready with the last story, when called on for that purpose by his comrades, after they had commented to their liking on the trapper's strange adventure,—"I never but once, in my whole life, became afraid of encountering a wild beast, or was too much unnerved in the presence of one to fire my rifle with certainty and effect. But that, in one event, I *was* in such a sorry condition for a hunter, I freely confess. And, as you called for our most remarkable adventures, and as the occurrence I allude to was certainly the most remarkable one *I* ever met with in *my* hunting experience, I will relate it for the story you assign me.

"It was about a dozen years ago, and on the borders of lake Parmagena, a squarish-shaped body of water, four or five miles in extent, lying twenty-five miles or so over these mountains to the northwest of us, and making up the chief head-water of the river Magalloway. My camp was at the mouth of the principal inlet, and my most frequented hunting route up along its bank. On my excursions up that river, I had often noticed a deeply-wooded, rough, and singularly-shaped mountain, which, at the distance of four or five miles from the nearest point of the stream, westward, reared its shaggy sides over the surrounding wilderness, and which I thought must make one of the best haunts for bear and moose that I had seen in that region. So, once having a leisure day, and my fresh provisions being low, I concluded I would take a jaunt up to this mountain, thinking that I should stand a good chance to find something there, or on the way, to replenish my larder. And accordingly I rigged up, after breakfast, and, setting my course in what I judged would prove a bee-line for the place, in order to save distance over the river route, I took up my march through the woods, without path, trail, or marked trees to guide me.

"After a rough and toilsome walk of about three hours, I reached the foot of the mountain of which I was in search, and seated myself on a fallen tree, to rest and look about me. The side of the eminence next to me was made up of a succession of rocky, heavily-timbered steeps and shelves, that rose like battlements before me, while, about midway, it was pierced or notched down by a dark, wild, thicket-tangled gorge, which extended along back up the mountain, as far as the eye could penetrate beneath, or overlook above the tops of the overhanging trees.

"To think of trying to ascend such steeps was out of the question; and I was debating in mind whether I would attempt to go up through that forbidding and *pokerish*-looking gorge, or, giving up the job altogether, strike off in the direction of the river, and so go home that way, when a hideous yell, which brought me instantly to my feet, rose from an upper portion of the ravine, apparently about a hundred rods distant. I at once knew it came from a painter, or 'evil devil,' as the Indians justly call that scourge and terror of the woods; and, from the strength and volume of his voice, I also knew he must be a large one, while, from its savage sharpness, I further conjectured it must be a famine cry, which, if so, would show the animal to be a doubly ticklish one to encounter.

"Feeling conscious that it was but the part of wisdom to avoid such an encounter as I should be likely to be favored with if I remained where I was,

I soon moved off in an opposite direction, steering at once for the nearest point of the river, which was at the termination of a long, sharp sweep of the stream to the west, and nearer by a mile than in most other parts of its course. I had not proceeded more than a quarter of a mile before the same savage screech,—which was more frightful than I can describe, being seemingly made up of the mingling tones of a man's and a woman's voice, raised to the highest pitch in an agony of rage or pain,—the same awful screech, I say, rose and thrilled through the shuddering forest, coming this time, I perceived, from the mouth of the gorge, where the animal had so quickly arrived, found my trail, doubtless, and started on in pursuit. I now, though still not really afraid, quickened my steps into a rapid walk, hoping that, now he had got out of the thickets of the ravine, he would not follow me far in the more open woods; yet thinking it best, at all events, to put what distance I could between him and me, without too much disturbing myself. Another of those terrific yells, however, coming from a nearer point than before, as fast as I had made my way from him, told me that the creature was on my tracks, and rapidly gaining on me in the race. I then started off at a full run; but even this did not insure my escape, for I was soon startled by another yell, so near and fierce, that I involuntarily turned round, cocked my rifle, and stood on the defence. The next moment the animal met my sight, as he leaped up on to the trunk of a lodged tree, where he stood in open view, eagerly snuffing and glaring around him, about forty rods from the place where I had been brought to a stand,—revealing a monster whose size, big as I had conjectured it, perfectly amazed me. He could not have been much less than six feet from, snout to tail, nor much short of nine, tail included. But for his bowed-up back, gaunter form, and mottled color, he might have passed for an ordinary lioness. The instant he saw me, he began nervously fixing his paws, rapidly swaying his tail, like a cat at the first sight of her intended prey, and giving other plain indications that he was intent on having me for his dinner.

"I had my rifle to my shoulder: it was a fair shot, but still I hesitated about firing. My experience with catamounts, which, though of the same nature, are yet no more to be compared with a real panther, like this, than a common cur to a stout bulldog, had taught me the danger of wounding without killing them outright. If *those* were so dangerous under ordinary circumstances, what would this be, already bent on destroying me? And should I stand, at that distance, an even chance to finish him, which could only be done by putting a ball through his brain, or spine, or directly through his heart? I thought not. The distance was too great to be sure of any thing like that; and besides, my nerves, I felt, were getting a little unsteady, and I also found I was losing my faith, which is just the worst thing in the world for a hunter to lose. While I was thinking of all this, the creature leaped down, and, the next instant, I saw his head rise above the bushes, in his prodigious bounds towards me. With that glance, I turned and ran; ran as I never did before; leaping over logs, and smashing headlong through brush and bushes, but still distinctly hearing, above all the noise I made, the louder crash of the creature's footfalls, striking closer and closer behind me. All at once, however, those crashing sounds ceased to fall on my ear, and the thought that my pursuer had sprung one side into an ambush, from whence he would pounce on me before I could see him, flashing over my mind, I suddenly came to a stand, and peered eagerly but vainly among the bushes around me for the crouching form, of my foe. While thus engaged, a seeming shadow passing over the open space above caused me to glance upward, when, to my horror, I saw the monster coming down from a tree-top, with glaring eyes, open mouth, and outspread claws, directly upon me! With a bound, which at any other time I should have been utterly incapable of making, I threw myself aside into the bushes just in time to escape his terrible embrace; and, before he had rallied from the confusion caused by striking the ground and missing his prey, I had gained the distance of a dozen rods, and thrown myself behind a large tree. But what was now to be done? I knew, from his trotting about and snuffing to regain the sight and scent of me, which I could now distinctly hear, that he would soon be upon me. If I distrusted the certainty of my aim before this last fright, should I not do it much more now? I felt so; and, as I was now within a mile of the river,—where, if I could reach it, I thought it possible to find a way to baffle, at least, if I did not kill, my ruthless pursuer,—I concluded that my best chance for life was to run for the place. But, in peering out to ascertain the exact whereabouts of the painter before I started, my ear caught the sound of other and different footsteps; and the next moment I had a glimpse of a bear's head, bobbing up and down in his rapid course through the bushes, as he ran at right angles, with all his might, directly through the space between me and the painter, which, I saw, was now just beginning to advance towards me, but which, to my great relief, had seen and was turning in pursuit of the flying and frightened bear.

"But still, fearing he would give up that pursuit, and again take after me, I ran for the river, which I at length reached, and threw myself exhausted down on the bank. As it happened, I had struck the river exactly at the intended point, which was where a small sand-island had been thrown up in the middle of the stream. To this island, in case I kept out of the claws and jaws of the painter till I reached the river, I had calculated to wade; believing, from, what I knew of the repugnance of this class of animals to water, that he would not follow me, or, if he did, I need not fail of shooting him dead while coming through the stream. But I soon found that *I* was not the only one that had thought of this island, in our terrible extremity.

"I had lain but a few minutes on the bank, before I caught the sounds of near and more distant footfalls approaching apace through the forest above me. Starting up, I cocked my rifle, and darted behind a bush near the edge of the water, and had scarcely gained the stand, when the same bear that I had left fleeing before the painter, made his appearance a few rods above me, coming full jump down the bank, plunging into the stream, and swimming and rushing amain for the island. As soon as he could clear the water, he galloped up to the highest part of his new refuge, and commenced digging, in hot haste, a hole in the sand. The instant he had made an excavation large and deep enough to hold his body and sink it below the surface, he threw himself in on his back, hurriedly scratched the sand at the sides a little over his belly and shoulders, and lay still, with his paws stiffly braced upwards.

"The next moment the eagerly-pursuing painter came rushing down the bank to the water, where the bear had entered it; when, after a hesitating pause, he gave an angry yell, and, in two prodigious bounds, landed on the edge of the island. Having raised my rifle for a helping shot, if needed, I awaited, with beating heart and eyes wide open, the coming encounter. With eyes shooting fire, the painter hastily fixed his feet, and, with a long leap, came down on his intrenched opponent. A cloud of dust instantly enveloped the combatants, but through it I could see the ineffectual passes of the painter at the bear's head, and the rapid play of the bear's hind paws under the painter's belly. This bout between them, however, was of but short continuance, and terminated by the painter, which now leaped suddenly aside, and stood for a moment eyeing his opponent askance, as if he had found in those rending hind-claws already much more than he had bargained for. But, quickly rousing himself, he prepared for the final conflict; and, backing to the water's edge, he gave one short bound forward, and, leaping ten feet into the air, came down again, with a wild screech, on his still unmoved antagonist.

"This time, so much more furiously flew up the dust and sand from the spot, that I could see nothing; but the mingling growls and yells of the desperately-grappling brutes were so terrific as to make the hair stand up on my head. Presently, however, I could perceive that the cries of the assailant, which had been becoming less and less fierce, were now turning into howls of pain; and, the next moment, I saw him, rent and bloody, with his entrails out and dragging on the ground behind him, making off till he reached the water on the opposite side of the island, when he staggered through the current, feebly crawled up the bank, and disappeared in the woods, where he must have died miserably within the hour.

"I went home a grateful man; leaving the bear, that had done me such good service, to depart in peace, as I saw him doing before I left, apparently little injured from the conflict."

CHAPTER XIV.

"Ours the wild life the forest still to range,
From toil to rest, and joy in every change."

The low chirping of the wood-birds, the tiny barkings of the out-starting squirrels, the hurrying footsteps of the night-prowling animals, on their way to their coverts, on the land; and the leaping up of fish, the flapping of the wings of ducks, and the far-heard, trumpet-toned cry of the great northern diver, on the water, those unfailing concomitants of approaching day, in the watered wilderness, early aroused the next morning our little band of soundly-sleeping hunters from their woodsmen's feather beds,—the soft, elastic boughs of the health-giving hemlock,—and put them on the stir in building their fire, and making preparations for their breakfast. The business of the day before them was the completion of their camp building; which, being intended, as before mentioned, for their general head-quarters and storehouse, required far more care and labor in the construction than the ordinary structures that are made to serve for shelters for the sojourners of the woods. And, as soon as they had dispatched their morning repast, they rose and prepared themselves to commence the task on hand. As the main part of the company were scattering into the woods, with their hatchets, in search of straight poles to rib out the sides and roof of their structure, which was the first thing in order to be done, Phillips, without explaining his object, quietly intimated to Codman a wish for company, in a short excursion with canoes up the river; and, the latter complying with the intimation, and putting himself under the hunter's lead, the two took to their canoes, with each another canoe in tow, and commenced rowing up the stream; which, having run its rapid and noisy race down to the foot of the mountains, a mile or two above, was here, with gentle pace and seeming reverence, advancing to the lake with its welcome tribute of crystal waters.

"Hillo, there, Mr. Hunter!" sung out the trapper to the other, now some distance ahead, "what may be some of the whys and wherefores of this shine we are cutting, stringing along here with canoes to our tails? What suppose you should be telling, before a great while, lest this end of the fleet might be missing?"

"Soon show you," replied the hunter, without turning his head. "I always liked the Indian fashion of answering questions by deeds instead of words, where the circumstances admit,—it is so much more significant and satisfactory, besides the world of lying it often prevents."

After rowing a short distance farther, in silence, the hunter turned his canoe in shore; and, after the other had followed his example, he said:

"Now, follow me a few rods back into this thicket, up here." And, leading the way, he proceeded to what at first appeared to be an irregular pile of brush, lying by the side of a large fallen tree, but which, when the top brush was removed, and an under-layer of evergreen boughs brushed aside, disclosed a large, compact collection of peeled spruce bark, cut in regular lengths of six or seven feet, and in breadths of about one foot, of exact uniformity, and made so straight and flat by solid packing that a rick of sawed boards would have scarcely presented a more smooth and even appearance.

"Well, I will give in, now, and acknowledge myself beat in wood-craft," said the trapper, comprehending, at once, by whom and for what purpose this acceptable pile of covering material had been cut, and thus nicely cured and stored away for use. "To have done this, you must have come here in June, the peeling month; but how came you to think of this process of preparing the bark, or come here at all to do it, so long beforehand, on the uncertainty of its being needed, this fall, except perhaps by yourself?"

"Well, happening to think, one day, how much better camps might be made from bark peeled, cut, and pressed into the required lengths and shapes, beforehand, as we prepare it for our Indian canoes, than by following our usual bungling method, I concluded to put things in train for trying the experiment this fall; and this fall especially, as I was then calculating, unless you wished to join, to hunt only in company with the two Elwoods, and I was desirous of getting up an extra good camp for them."

"You take an unusual interest in the affairs of this newly-come family, I have noticed."

"If I do, I may have my reasons for it."

"Special reasons, doubtless."

"Ordinary reasons would be enough. In the first place, they are fine people, the son and mother uncommonly so, and the father also I consider a well-disposed man, but who may have some weak points; and this being so, and the son being inexperienced in dealing with designing men, a neighbor, like me, ought, I am sure, to be unwilling to see any advantage taken of them."

"Yes, a fair reason enough for your course, if you had no other; but may be you have other inducements, received, for instance, on your visit to the seaside, the past summer."

"That is all guess-work, remember; but come, let us drop the subject, get this bark into our canoes, and be off down the river with it to camp."

They did so; and, on reaching camp, agreeably surprised their companions with the abundant supply of excellent material which they had brought for covering the cabin, and for which, when the circumstances became known, all were disposed to accord due credit to the provident hunter.

With the material thus obtained, the ribbing of the frame having by this time been completed, all hands now commenced the work of laying on, fitting, and confining the pliant and close-lying strips of bark to the framework of the structure, both above and below. And with so much assiduity and skill did they prosecute their labors, that before night their camp was covered and inclosed on every side, and made to present to the eye, a cabin neat and comely in appearance, and as tight, warm, and secure against storms, as many a dwelling-house in the open country, covered with boards and shingles.

After the company had completed the roof and walls of their camp, constructed a rude door, and made what interior arrangements they deemed necessary for sleeping and storing their provisions, they went out, for the hour or two now remaining before sunset, and scattered for short excursions in their canoes along the neighboring coves of the lake, for the various purposes of fishing, shooting ducks, or inspecting the shores for indications of beaver, otter, and other classes of the smaller fur-animals of amphibious habits. All returning, however, at sunset, they proceeded to cook and eat their suppers, much in the same manner as on the preceding evening; after which, in compliance with the suggestions made by several of the company during the day, they went into a general consultation for the purpose of fixing on the different locations and ranges of river and forest, which each, or each pair of them, should take for their hunting or trapping during the season before them. They soon agreed, in the first place, without any difficulty, in making the shores of the Oquossak, the next lake above, and the last and perhaps largest of the four great lakes forming the chief links of this singular chain of inland waters, the base-line of their operations. Phillips and Codman, having procured a wide strip of the outer bark of the white birch,—ever the woodman's substitute for writing paper, when writing becomes necessary,— then proceeded to draw a map, from personal recollection, of the strangely-irregular lake in question. By this, when completed, it appeared that the main inlet, or the uppermost portion of the Androscoggin river, coming down from the north through a chain of lakelets, or ponds, and running parallel with the eastern shore of the lake, and but a few miles distant from it, entered into a deep, pointed bay, about a third of the way down the eastern shore; where it was joined by another and scarcely lesser river, coming from or through a different chain of these lakelets, scattered along far to the east and northeast of the Oquossak; while a third considerable stream entered the lake at its extreme northwestern termination. These three inlets, that constituted all the rivers of any magnitude running into this lake, would not only afford, it was readily seen, the most desirable hunting-grounds in the sections through which they flowed, but give the greater part of the hunters, if they encamped in pairs, and had their camps at the mouths of these streams, as was expected, an opportunity of locating in near vicinity; while two more of the remaining part of the company would, at the mouth of the northwestern inlet, be less than five miles distant. This arrangement would dispose of six of the company,—two of them on the inlet last mentioned, and four on the two rivers that entered the lake together,—and leave one to remain on the Megantic, to take charge of the head-quarters, or store-camp there, and hunt anywhere he chose in its vicinity. But who the one to be placed in this trust should be, was the next question to be decided. Gaut Gurley, who had been secretly scheming for this post ever since the arrangement which he saw must necessarily create it was agreed on, and who had been insidiously making interest for it, with all the company, except Phillips and Codman, now proposed that the question should be decided by ballot, and without discussion. And, the proposition being seconded by Tomah and assented to by all, each took a small piece of birch bark, marked with a coal the name of the person he would vote for, and deposited it in a hat placed on their stone table for the purpose. After all had voted, the hat was turned and the votes assorted; when it appeared that four votes had been thrown for Gaut Gurley and three for Mark Elwood, making seven in all, and showing that all the company had voted.

"Well, friend Elwood," said Gaut, with a well-assumed air of indifference, when the result was seen, "shall *I* resign in *your* favor, or *you* in *mine*? This thing should be unanimous."

Elwood looked up inquiringly at Gaut, when he read something in the countenance of the latter which gave him to understand what was expected of him, and he accordingly responded: "I should suppose there could not be much question which of the two, a minority or a majority candidate, should ask the other to stand aside,—especially when, as in your case, the majority candidate is clearly chosen. I voted, gentlemen, for Mr. Gurley," he added, turning to the rest of the company; "and I hope those who voted for me will cheerfully acquiesce in the choice of the majority."

"I am a comparative stranger to you all," remarked Carvil, "and, though I voted for Mr. Elwood, I will yet very willingly agree to the selection you have made."

Gaut, knowing well enough who had thrown their votes against him, now glanced at Phillips and Codman; but gathering from their silence and demure and downcast looks that no approving expression was likely to be drawn from either of them, he interrupted the pause that followed Carvil's remarks, by saying:

"Perhaps, then, I ought to accept the post thus assigned me; and on some accounts it will come right all round. I should be compelled, any way, to return once or twice to the settlements during our campaign, on business, and I can attend to that, and procure the fresh supplies of bread and other things we shall need, all under one head. And, besides that, I had already made up my mind I should select this stream, and the coves on this lake, for my trapping and hunting for beaver and other water animals, which I once knew how to take, in preference to going any farther. So I will accept the post, warrant the safe-keeping of the common property, and see what I can do towards contributing my share to the stock of furs."

This point being thus regarded by the company as settled, they next proceeded to the discussion of the more particular duties which should devolve on their chosen camp-keeper; which, at length, resulted in the arrangement that he should go up with his canoe into the Oquossak, once a week, make the circuit of the lake so far as to visit the nearest or lake-shore camps of each or each pair of his companions, bring them fresh provisions, and take back to head-quarters all the furs each had caught in the interim, and be held responsible for the good condition and safe-keeping of all the peltries, and other common property of the company, thus placed in his charge.

After this matter (which was destined to have an important bearing on the fate and fortunes of more than one of the leading personages of our story) was thus disposed of, they then, in conclusion of the business of the evening, proceeded, by mutual agreement, to apportion the different locations for hunting on the upper lake, already fixed on, among the three pairs of hunters the company would now make; decide what individuals should join to form each pair; and what general plan of operations they should adopt, after they had got settled in their respective places. By the amicable arrangement thus made, Phillips and Claud Elwood were to form one of these pairs, and fix their lake-camp at the mouth of the river already named as coming in from the east; Carvil and Mark Elwood to constitute another pair, and encamp at the mouth of the great inlet entering at the same place; while Codman and the young Indian, Tomah, who, from their mutual challenges in beaver-catching, had by this time become friends, and willing to hunt from the same starting-point, were to have their camp at the mouth of the river coming in at the northwest end of the lake. By the plan now adopted, also, each of these three hunting parties, after they had reached their respective destinations and built their camps, were to explore the rivers ten or fifteen miles upward through the forest, and to some suitable and convenient terminus of their proposed trapping and hunting range; there build a camp, in which to lodge on their outward jaunts; and mark off, on their return, by blazing the trees, lines for setting log-traps for sable, marten, stoat, or ermine,—for, whatever may be said to the contrary, the noted ermine of Europe is a native of our northern forests. These marked lines were to diverge from the upper camps along the ridges on each side of the river; sometimes running many miles apart, then turning down to the stream, where indications of beaver and otter had been discovered, so as to afford a chance for setting and tending steel-traps for those animals; then running back again on to the high hills and ridges; but finally converging in, and meeting at the lake camp. And, these preliminary steps being taken, everything would then be in readiness for setting the traps, and for entering on the hopeful business of their expedition.

All these arrangements being now definitely settled and understood, the consultation was broken up, and the company betook themselves once more to their sylvan couches, calculating on an early start the next day for their several destinations on the Oquossak, the nearest of which was at least a dozen miles distant.

Accordingly, with the first crack of dawn the next morning, the loud and startling gallinaceous cachinnation of the droll and wide-awake trapper aroused the woodsmen from their slumbers, and warned them to be up and doing. And soon the whole company were in motion, the kindled fire was crackling and flashing up amidst the dry pine faggots, thrown, on to feed and start it into the steadier blaze and heat of more solid fuel, and the process of cooking was going busily forward. In a short time they were again gathered, in high spirits, round their stone table, unconsciously partaking, as the event proved, the last meal they were ever all to enjoy together in the woods. But let us not anticipate.

As soon as they had dispatched their breakfast, the band about to depart loaded their canoes with traps, guns, camp-kettles, and the provisions needed for immediate use; and, wishing Gaut Gurley a happy and successful time at his solitary station, pushed merrily away into the broad lake, turned their course northward, and sped on their voyage. A few miles rowing brought them to the great inlet, which, like the principal inlets to the lakes below, was another reach of the Androscoggin, flowing directly from the east through a channel, still nearly a hundred yards in width and nearly three miles in length, from its entrance into one lake to the point where it debouches from the other. After a row of an hour up this channel, made interesting and impressive by the magnificent colonnades of princely pines, that, as far as the eye could reach, stood towering away in lessening perspective along its banks, they suddenly emerged into the bright and far-stretching waters of the unmapped Oquossak, which lay nestling and inflected among the dark green cliffs of the boldly intersecting mountains, like some rough, unshapen gem, gleaming out from the rubbish of a mine. And laying their course northeasterly, for the distant bay receiving the waters of the confluent streams before described, they now pulled away through the lake, in as direct a line as its irregular form, would permit. And now, skirting long reaches of its deeply-wooded shores, from which the old forest, never broken by the axe, and rarely ever trod by the foot of the white man, was seen, stretching away back, lift after lift, in pristine grandeur, to the tall summits of the amphitheatric mountains,—now shooting athwart, under some dark headland that stood out boldly disputing the empire with the water, and now threading their way among the clustering green islands that studded the bright and beautiful expanse,—they rowed steadily onward for hours, and at length were gladdened by the sight of the dim but well-remembered outlines of the pointed bay, whose farthest shore was to be the home and haven for most of their number, during their present sojourn in this wild and remote fastness of the wilderness.

To row in, disembark their luggage, select sites for camps, to build those camps, so far as to make them serve for shelters for the night, and to prepare and eat their suppers, occupied the company, who had all decided to remain there that night through the remainder of the day till bed-time. The next morning, after an early breakfast, Codman and Tomah took leave of their companions, and proceeded on further up the lake to their allotted station; leaving the two Elwoods, and their respective hunting companions, to complete their camps, which were situated in near vicinity, get all in readiness, and the next day enter in earnest on the main business of the campaign.

But it is not our intention to follow either of these pairs, or now distinct parties, of adventurous woodsmen, in the general routine of their camp life,—in their solitary and almost daily marches among the tangled wilds, from their inner to outer camps; their toils and fatigues on the way; their pleasant meetings at the ends of their ranges at night, to recount the adventures of the day, and lodge together; their heats and their colds, their dark hours and their bright ones, their curious experiences and startling encounters with wild animals; and finally their varying success in realizing the objects of their expedition, through the successive scenes of the next nine or ten weeks, where

>   —"rifle flashed,
> The grim bear hushed its savage howl,
> In blood and foam, the panther gnashed
> Its fangs with dying howl;
> The fleet deer ceased its flying bound,
> Its snarling wolf-foe bit the ground,
> And, with its moaning cry,
> The beaver sank beneath the wound,
> Its pond-built Venice by."

Suffice it to say, that they were all blest with uninterrupted health and increasing vigor, in realization of the favorite theory of Carvil, in relation to the invigorating and fattening principle of the super-abounding oxygen of the woods. They all highly enjoyed their wild life, and were, even beyond their most sanguine expectations, successful in their aggregate acquisitions of peltries and all kinds of game. Gaut Gurley, whose unremitted attention and apparent faithfulness in the duties of his post soon disarmed the distrusting, came round punctually, every week, supplied them with all they needed, and, while reporting his own good success, in his short ranges in the vicinity of his head-quarters encampment, seemed greatly gratified at the continued successes of all the rest, and exultingly bore off their furs for curing and safe storage with the rich and rapidly-increasing collection at his camp; setting the mark of their collected value, the last time he came round, at upwards of a thousand dollars, and encouraging them with the hope that, probably, before any change would occur in the weather which would compel them to relinquish the business and return to the settlement, a much larger sum would be realized from their exertions. And, in view of this gratifying condition of their affairs, the company at large—as winter at the farthest could not be very distant—now began to anticipate, with much satisfaction, the time when they should return to their families, to gladden them with their welcome presence, and, from the fruits of their enterprise, make such unlooked-for pecuniary additions to the means of domestic comfort and happiness.

CHAPTER XV.

"As the night set in, came hail and snow,
And the air grew sharp and chill,
And the warning roar of a terrible blow
Was heard on the distant hill;
And the norther,—see, on the mountain peak,
In his breath, how the old trees writhe and shriek!
He shouts along o'er the plain, ho, ho!
He drives from his nostrils the blinding snow,
And growls with a savage will."

C. G. EASTMAN.

We will now take the reader to the wild and secluded banks of Dead river, the great southwesterly tributary of the lordly Kennebec, the larger twin brother of the Androscoggin, both of which, after being born of the same parent range of mountains, and wandering off widely apart, at length find, at the end of their courses, like many a pair of long estranged brothers, their final rest in a common estuary at the seaboard. At a point on the banks of the tributary above named, where its long southward sweep brings it nearest, and within twenty miles of the Oquossak, and within a quarter of that distance from the terminating camps of the outward ranges of the hunters, two men in hunting-suits might have been seen, in the fore part of one of the last days of November, in the season of the eventful expedition we have been describing, intently engaged in inspecting some fragments of wrought wood, which, from the clue of some protruding piece, they had kicked up from the leaves and decayed brushwood that had nearly concealed them from view. One of these men was past the middle age, of a hardy but somewhat worn appearance. The other was in the prime of young manhood, of a finely-moulded form and an unusually prepossessing face and countenance. But we may as well let the dialogue that ensued between them disclose their identity; the matter that was now engaging their attention; and their reasons for thus appearing in this remote position.

"This piece," said the elder, closely scanning the fragment he held in his hand, "is evidently oak, and looks mightily as if it was once the stave of an oak keg or half-barrel. Yes, and here is another that will settle the question," he continued, pulling from its concealment a larger and sounder fragment. "There! can't you trace the chine across the end of this?"

"Yes, quite distinctly, and I should not hesitate to pronounce all these fragments the remains of an oak barrel that had once been opened, or left here, if I could conceive how such a thing could come here, in the heart of this extensive wilderness. How do you solve the mystery Mr. Phillips?"

"Well, Claud, I am as much at fault as you. Barrels don't float up stream; and to suppose this came down stream, and still farther from any inhabitants, wouldn't help on the explanation any more; while to suppose it was brought here by hunters through the woods, where they could have no use for it even if they could get it here, is scarcely more probable."

"True; but can't we get a clue from something else about the place? This open space, hereabouts, wears something of the aspect of a place from which the trees have been once cut away, or greatly thinned, out, for some great encampment, for instance. Did you ever hear of any expedition of men through this region, in such numbers as would require the transportation of large quantities of provisions, drawn possibly by oxen, or more probably by men on light sledges?"

"Well, now, come to think of it, I have. And I guess you have blundered right smack on the truth, at the first go off; which is more than I can claim for myself, I admit. Yes, nearly fifty years ago, at the beginning of the old war, as you must have often read, an army *did* pass somewhere through the wilderness of Maine to Quebec. It was under the command of that fiery Satan, Benedict Arnold,—the only man in America, may be, who could have pushed an army, at that time of the year, some weeks later in the season than it is now, through a hundred and fifty miles' reach of such woods as these are, between our last and the first Canadian settlement. My father was one of that army of bold and hardy men. They passed up the Kennebec some distance, and, then, according to his account, left it, and, with the view of getting over the Highlands on to the Great Megantic more easily, turned up a branch, which must have been this very stream. Yes, I see, now. You are right about the appearance of this spot. There *was* once a great encampment here, and doubtless that of Arnold's army, staying over night, and breaking open a barrel of meat, conveyed here in some such way as you suggested."

"It is an interesting discovery; for that was a remarkable expedition, and must have been one of great hardship and suffering."

"Hardship and suffering! Why, they fell short of provisions long before they got out of the wilderness, and, besides the hardships of cold and fatigue, came near starving to death! I have heard my father tell how he was one of a party of thirteen, who, with other like squads, were permitted to scatter forward in search of some inhabitants, for food, lest they all perished together; how, after going two days without putting a morsel into their mouths, except their shoe-strings or the inner bark of trees, they at length were gladdened by the sight of an opening, with a log house, and a cow standing before the door; how, the instant their eyes fell on the cow, they ran like blood-hounds for the spot, seized an axe, brought the animal to the ground, ripped up the hide on one thigh, cut off slices of the quivering flesh, and, by the time the aroused family had got out into the yard, were munching and gobbling them down raw, with the desperate eagerness of ravenous beasts." [Footnote: A historical fact, once related to the author by an old soldier who was one of the party here described.]

"Horrible! but they paid the poor people for their cow, I trust?"

"Yes, twice-over, but that did not reconcile them to the loss of their only cow, where it was so difficult to get another. The children screamed, and even the man and his wife wrung their hands and cried as if their hearts would break."

"That incident is to me a new feature among the horrors of war, which I probably should have never heard of but for coming here and making this curious discovery of one of the relics of that terrible and fruitless campaign of our Revolution. I am glad we concluded to come."

"So am I; for that, and the other reason that I wanted to see the lay of the country, round this river, where, as it happened, I had never been. But my mind misgave me several times, on the way."

"Why so, pray?"

"I can hardly tell, myself, but I began to kinder feel as if something wrong was going on somewhere, and that, though this place could not be more than five miles from our upper camp, where we stayed last night, we had yet better be making our way directly back to the lake. Besides that, I haven't liked the symptoms of the weather, to-day."

"I don't know that I have noticed any thing peculiar in the weather, except a chilliness of the air that I have not felt before this season."

"That's the thing," rejoined the hunter, glancing uneasily up through the treetops, to try to get a view of the sky. "But there are other indications I don't fancy. There is a peculiar raw dampness in the air, and a sort of low, moaning sound heard once in a while murmuring along through the forest, such as I have often noticed before great storms, and sudden changes from fall to winter weather, this time of the year. And hush! hark!" he exclaimed, suddenly cutting short his remark, as the well-known, solemn, and quickly-repeated *konk! konk!* of wild geese, on their passage, greeted their ears.

They ran down to the water's edge to get a view of the open sky, when, looking up, they saw a large flock of these winged, semi-annual voyagers of the air, coming in view over the forest, in their usual widespread, harrow-shaped battalions, and with seemingly hurried flight, pitching down from the British highlands toward the lower regions to the south. And that flock had scarcely receded beyond hearing, when another, and yet another, with the same uneasy cries and rapid flight, passed, in quick succession, over the open reach of sky above them.

"How far do you calculate the nearest shore of the Gulf of St. Lawrence is from here?" asked the hunter, musingly.

"O, not so very great a distance,—three hundred miles, perhaps," replied Claud, looking inquiringly at the other.

"Well," slowly responded the hunter, "those God-taught creatures know more about the coming changes of the weather than all the philosophers in the world. These are but the advanced detachments of armies yet behind them, already, doubtless, on their way from Labrador, and even more northern coasts beyond. In the unusual mild November we have had, they never received their warning till this morning. And these, being on the southern outposts of their summer quarters, the Gulf of St. Lawrence, started at daylight, I presume,—about four hours ago, just about the time I perceived a change in the atmosphere myself. This, at the rapid headway you perceive they are making, would give them time to get here by this hour of the day."

"Then you take this as an indication of the approach of winter weather?"

"I do. And the evident hurriedness of their flight, and the sort of quickened, anxious tone of their cries, show that *they*, at least, think it is not far behind them. But let us put all the signs together. I must get to some place where I can see more of the sky. I noticed, as I was coming in sight of the river, a short way back in the woods, a high, sharp hill, with a bare, open top, rising from the river, about a hundred rods up along here to the left. What suppose we pack up, and go and ascend it? We can, there, besides getting the view we want of the lay of the country, see, probably, the horizon nearly all round. And, all this done, we will then hold a council of war, and decide on our next movement."

This proposal meeting the ready approval of the young man, the two took their rifles, and proceeded to the foot of the eminence in question, which they found to be a steep, conical hill, rising abruptly three or four hundred feet above the general level of the surrounding forest, with a small, pointed apex, from which some tornado had hurled every standing tree except a tall, slender green pine, that shot up eighty or ninety feet, as straight as a flagstaff, from the centre. After a severe scramble up the steeps, in some places almost perpendicular, they at length reached the summit, and commenced leisurely walking round the verge, looking down on the variegated wilderness, which, with its thousand dotted hills and undulating ridges, lay stretched in cold solitude around them. With only a general glance, however, over the surrounding forests, the gaze of the hunter was anxiously lifted upwards, to study the omens of the heavens. The sun, by this time, was scarcely visible beneath the cold, lurid haze which had for some hours been gradually stealing over it; while around the horizon lay piled long, motionless banks of leaden clouds, thick and heavy enough evidently to be dark, but yet of that light, dead, glazed, uncertain hue, which the close observer may have often noted as the precursor of winter-storms. After a long and attentive survey of every visible part of the heavens, the hunter, with an ominous shake of the head, dropped his eyes to the ground, and said:

"I was right, but didn't want to believe it when I got up this morning; and the wild geese are right. We are on the eve of winter, and our best hope is that it may come gently. But even that favor, I greatly fear, we shall not be permitted to realize."

"Well, sir, with that view of the case, in which I am inclined to concur, what do you propose now?" asked Claud.

"Why, I propose, seeing we have all the fur pelts we took from the traps yesterday put up in packs, and have left nothing in our upper camp of any consequence,—I propose, that, instead of going back to our nearest marked line, as we talked of, we strike directly across the woods, by the nearest route, to our lake camp; or, if you are willing to put up with two or three miles additional travel, we will steer so as to take the upper camp of your father and Carvil in our way. We might find them there, perhaps."

"Then let us steer for their camp; I can stand the jaunt. But can you determine the direction to be taken to strike it?"

"Nearly, I think. Their camp, you know, is on the neck or connecting piece of river, between two long ponds, lying about southwest of us. I rather expected to be able to get a glimpse of one of those ponds from the hilltop, but find I can't. I presume I could, however, from the top of this pine tree."

"Yes, but to climb it would be a long, and perhaps dangerous task, would it not?"

"No, neither. We woodsmen are often compelled to resort to such a course, to take our latitude and bearings. And, on the whole, I think in this case it might be the cheapest way. So I will up it, and you may be watching for wild geese, that are still, I perceive, every few minutes, somewhere in sight. Very likely some flock may soon come over us near enough for a shot."

So saying, the resolute and active hunter, casting aside coat, cap, and boots, sprang up several feet on to the clasped trunk of the pine, over whose rough bark he now, by means of the vigorous clenches of his arms and legs, fast made his way upwards. It was a hard struggle for him, however, till he reached the lower limbs, some fifty feet from the ground, when, swinging himself up by a grappled limb, he quickly disappeared among the thick, mantling boughs, on his now doubly-rapid ascent; and, in a few minutes more, he was heard by his companion below, breaking off the obstructing tiptop branches, and, as he gazed abroad from his dizzy height, shouting out the discoveries which were the object of his bold attempt.

"Make ready there, below!" he startlingly exclaimed, all at once, after a long pause, in which he seemed to be silently noting the distant objects in the forest; "make ready there, below, for a famous large flock of wild geese, just heaving in sight over the hills, and coming directly to this spot."

The next moment the expected flock, spread out in columns answering to the two sides of a triangle, each a quarter of a mile in extent, and the nearest nearly in a line with the summit where the young huntsman stood, with raised rifle, awaiting their approach, came in full view, making the forest resound with their multitudinous and mingling cries, and the loud beating of their long wings on the air, as they swept onward in their close proximity to the earth. Singling out the nearest goose of the nearest column, Claud quickly caught his aim, and fired; when the struck bird, with a convulsive start, suddenly clasped its wings, and, in its onward impulse, came down like lightning into the bushes, within five rods from its exulting captor.

"Done like a marksman,—plumped through and through under the wing. You are improving, young man," exclaimed the hunter, who now, rapidly coming down, had reached the foot of the tree, as Claud came forward from the bushes, with his prize. "It is a fine fat one, ain't it?" he continued, glancing at the heavy bird, as he was pulling on his boots. "We will take it along with us for our supper."

"Yes, rather a lucky shot," returned the other, self-complacently. "But what discoveries did you make up there, that will aid us in our course, Mr. Phillips?"

"O, that is all settled," answered the latter, putting on his pack, and buttoning up, preparatory to an immediate start. "I caught glimpses of both the ponds, noted all the hilltops, ridges, and other noticeable landmarks, in the line between here and there, and can lead you as straight as a gun to the spot, for which we will now be off; and the sooner the better, as it is fast growing colder and colder, and the whole heavens are every moment growing more dark and dubious."

They then, after making their way down the precipitous side of the hill to its western foot, struck off, under the lead of the hunter, in a line through the forest, preserving their points of compass, when none of their general landmarks were visible, by noting the peculiar weather-beaten appearance of the mosses on the north sides of the trees, and the usual inclination of the tips of the hemlocks from west to east. And for the next hour and a half, on, on they tramped, in Indian file, and almost unbroken silence, making headway with their long, loping steps, notwithstanding the obstructing fallen trees, brushwood, and constantly occurring inequalities of the ground, with a speed which none but practised woodsmen can attain in the forest, and which is scarcely equalled by the fastest foot-travellers on the smooth and beaten highways of the open country.

At length they were gratified by an indistinct sight of some body of water, gleaming dimly through the trees from some point in front; and the walk of a few hundred yards more brought them out, as it luckily happened, directly to the camp of which they were in search. It was, however, tenantless; their companions had already departed; but the bed of live coals in the usual place, from which the thin vapor was still perceptibly ascending, showed that they could not have left more than an hour before. In glancing into the deserted shanty, they descried a clean strip of white birch bark, lying conspicuously on the ground, a few feet within the entrance. On picking it up, they were soon enabled to read the following words, traced with the charred end of a twig:

"Thinking something unusual to be brewing overhead, we are off for the lake about 10 A. M. CARVIL."

"A very observing, considerate man, that Mr. Carvil," said the hunter, still musingly keeping his eyes on the unique dispatch. "He is one of the few book-learned men I have ever known, who could apply science to the natural philosophy of the woods. I can see how justly he reasoned out this case: knowing that we had some thought of a jaunt to Dead river this trip, he judged we should notice the signs of the weather just as we did, and, as it seems, *he* did; and that, in consequence, when we got there, we should decide on the nearest route back, which would bring us so near their camp that we should be tempted to come to it; and so he left this notice for us that they thought it wisdom to depart."

While the hunter was thus delivering himself, as he stood by the fire before the entrance, spreading out his hands over the coals, Claud went inside, and, returning with two fine, fresh trout, which the late occupants had, for some cause, left behind them, held them up to his musing companion, and exclaimed:

"Look here, Mr. Phillips,—see what they have left for us!"

"Good!" cried the hunter, rousing himself, "for, whether they left them by design or mistake, they come equally well in play at this time. You out with your knife and split them through the back, and I will prepare the coals. We will roast them for a lunch, which will refresh and strengthen us for the ten or twelve miles walk that is still to be accomplished, before reaching the lake."

After dispatching the welcome meal, which in this primitive fashion they had prepared for themselves out of the material thus unexpectedly come to hand, and enjoying the half-hour's rest consequent on the grateful occupation, they again swung on their packs, and, striking into one of the marked lines of their companions, set forth with fresh vigor on their journey. Their walk, however, was a long and dreary one. Contrary to what they had ever before experienced, in jaunts of this length through the woods, not a single hunting adventure occurred, to enliven the tedium of the way. For, although the heavens above were made vocal with the screams of wild geese, still pouring along in their hurried flight to the south, to escape the elemental foe behind, like the rapidly succeeding detachments of some retreating army, yet not a living creature, biped or quadruped, was anywhere to be heard or seen in the forest beneath. All seemed to have instinctively shrunk away and fled, as from the presence of some impending evil, to their dens and coverts, there to await, cowering and silent, the dreaded outbreak. Slowly, but steadily, the lurid storm-clouds were gathering in the heavens, bringing shade after shade over the darkening wilderness. Low, hollow murmurs in the troubled air were now heard, ominously stealing along the wooded hills; and now, in the sharp, momentary rattling of the seared beech-leaves, the whole forest seemed shivering in the dead chill that was settling over the earth. The cold, indeed, was now becoming so intense as to congeal and skim over all the pools and still eddies of the river, and make solid ice along the shores of the rapid currents of the stream; while even the ground was fast becoming so frozen as to clumper and sound beneath the hurrying tread of our anxious travellers. By three in the afternoon, it had become so dark that they could scarcely see the white blazings on the sides of the trees, by which they were guided in their course; and in less than another hour, they were stumbling along almost in utter darkness, uncertain of their way, and nearly despairing of reaching their destination that night. But, while they were on the point of giving up the attempt, the bright glare of an ascending blaze, shooting fiercely through the thickets before them, greeted their gladdened eyes, and put them on exertions that soon brought them rejoicing into the comfortable quarters of their almost equally gratified friends and comrades; where it was at once decided that, instead of proceeding to their own camp, to build a fire and lodge, they should turn in for the night.

After some time passed in the animated and cheery interchange of inquiries and opinions, which usually succeeds on the meeting of anxiously-sought or expected friends, Claud and Phillips, having by this time warmed and measurably rested themselves, took hold with Carvil and Mark Elwood in dressing and cooking for supper and for breakfast the next morning, Claud's goose, and a pair of fine ducks from a flock which the two latter had encountered just before reaching camp that afternoon; and, after completing this process with their good supply of game, and the more agreeable one of eating so much of it as served for a hearty supper, they drew up an extra quantity of fuel for the large fire which they felt it would be necessary to keep up through the night; and then, seating themselves in camp, went into an earnest consultation on the measures and movements next to be taken. When, in view of the lateness of the season, coupled as it was with the alarming portents of an immediate storm, which they had all noticed, it was unanimously determined that they should embark, early next morning, for head-quarters on the Maguntic, where Gaut Gurley, instead of preparing to come round again, as was now nearly his usual time to do, would, under the altered aspect of things, doubtless be awaiting them, and making arrangements for the return of all to the settlement. Then, building up a fire of solid logs, for long burning, the tired woodsmen drew up their bough-pillows towards the entrance of the camp, so as to bring their feet near the fire, closely wrapped their thick blankets around them, lay down, and were soon buried in sound slumber. And it was well for them that they were thus early taking their needed rest; for, soon after midnight, they were awakened by the lively undulations of the piercing cold air that was driving and whistling through the sides of their camp, and by the puffs of suffocating smoke that the eddying winds were ever and anon driving from their fire directly into their faces. One after another they rose, and ran out to see what had caused the, to them, sudden change that had occurred in the air since they went to sleep. And they were not long in ascertaining the truth. The expected storm had set in, with that low, deep commotion of the elements, and that slowly gathering impetus, which, as may often be noted at the commencement of great storms, was but the too certain prelude of its increase and duration. The fine snow was sifting down apace to the already whitened ground, and the rising wind, even in their mountain-hemmed nook, was whirling in fierce and fitful eddies about their camp, and shrilly piping among the strained branches of the vexed forest around; while its loud and awful roar, as it careered along the sides of the distant mountains, told with what strength and fury the storm was commencing over the country at large. In the situation in which the company now found themselves, neither sleep, comfort, nor quiet were to be expected for the remainder of the night. They therefore piled high the wood on their fire, and gathered round the hot blaze, to protect them from the cold, that had now not only grown more intense, but become doubly difficult to withstand, from the force with which it was brought by the driving blasts in contact with their shivering persons. And thus,—in alternately turning their backs and fronts to the fire, while standing in one place, and often shifting places from one side of the fire to the other; in now taking refuge within their camp when the constantly veering gusts bore the smoke and flame outward, and then fleeing out of it when the stifling column was driven inward; but finding no peace nor rest anywhere, among those shifts and commotions of the battling elements,—they wore away the long and comfortless hours of that dreary night, till the return of morning light, which, after many a vain prayer for its speedier appearance, at length gradually broke over the storm-invested wilderness.

As soon as it was light enough to see objects abroad, or see them as well as they can ever be discerned through the fast-falling snow of such a driving storm, Phillips and Carvil sallied out through the snow, already eight inches deep, and made their way down to the nearest shore of the lake, about a quarter of a mile distant, to ascertain the condition of the water before embarking upon it in their canoes, as they had designed to do immediately after breakfast. On reaching the shore, they found the narrow bay, before mentioned as forming the estuary of the two rivers on which they had been located, comparatively calm, though filled with congealing snow and floating ice from the rivers. But all beyond the line of the two points of land inclosing the bay was rolling and tumbling in wild commotion, madly lashing the rocky headlands with the foaming waters, and resounding abroad over the hills with the deep, hoarse roar of the tempest-beaten breakers of the ocean.

"Do you see and hear that?" exclaimed Phillips, pointing to the lake.

"Yes, yes; but what was that I just caught a glimpse of, out there in the offing, to the right?" hastily cried Carvil.

They both peered forward intently; and the next moment they saw a canoe, containing a single rower, low bending to his oar, shoot by the northern headland with the speed of an arrow, strike obliquely out of the white line of rolling waves into the bay, and make towards the point where they stood.

"Who can it be?" inquired Carvil, after watching a while in silence the slow approach of the obstructed canoe.

"In a minute more we shall see," replied the hunter, bending forward to get a view of the man's face, which, being seen the next moment, he added, with a shout: "Hallo, there, Codman, is that you? Why didn't you crow, to let us know who was coming?"

"Crow?" exclaimed the trapper, driving through the ice to the shore; "did you ever hear a rooster crow in a time like this? There! I am safe, at last," he added, leaping out upon the shore, and glancing back with a dubious shake of the head towards the scene from which he had thus escaped. "Yes, safe now, for all my fright; but I would not be out another hour on that terrible lake for all the beaver in the province of Maine! I started at daylight, got out a mile or two, tolerably, but after that, Heaven only knows how I rode on those wild waves without swamping! But no matter,—I am here."

"But where is Tomah, the Indian?" asked the hunter.

"Tomah!" said Codman, in surprise. "Why, haven't you seen him? He went off three days ago, saying he must return to the settlement, to be training his moose to the sledge, so as to start for Boston with him, the first snow. He said he should leave it with Gaut Gurley to see to his share of the furs. I supposed he would call at one of your camps. But come, move on. I suppose you have a fire at camp, and something to eat; I am frozen to death, and starved to death, besides being more than half-dead from the great scaring I've had; but that's all over now, and I'm keen for breakfast. So troop along back to your camp, I say."

To return to camp, take their cold and comfortless breakfast, and decide on the now hard alternatives of remaining where they were, to await the event of the storm, without provisions, and with their imperfect means of protection from the rigor of the elements, or of starting off through the cumbering snow beneath their feet, and the driving tempest above their heads, with the hope of reaching head-quarters by land, before another night should overtake them, was but the work of half an hour. To remain, with the foretaste of the past and the prospects of the future, was a thought so forbidding that none of them could for a moment entertain it; and to set out to travel by land, with such prospects, over the mountains, by the long, winding route on the eastern side of the lake,—which was the only one left to them, and which could not be less than fifteen miles in extent,—was a scarcely less forbidding alternative. But it must be adopted. So, gathering in their steel traps and iron utensils, they buried them all, except their lightest hatchet, under a log, that they should not be encumbered with more weight than was absolutely necessary; snugly packing up the few peltries they had taken since Gaut Gurley had been round, and putting the scanty remains of their food into their pockets, for a lunch on the way, they set forth on their formidable undertaking.

Led on and guided by the calm and resolute hunter,—who at different times had been over the whole way, and in whose skill and discretion, as a woodsman, for conducting them by the nearest and easiest route, they all had undoubting confidence,—they vigorously made their way onwards through the accumulating snows and natural obstructions of the forest; now threading the thickets of the valleys; now skirting the sides of the hills; now crossing deep ravines; and now climbing high mountains in their toilsome march. And, though the storm seemed to rage more and more fiercely with the advancing hours of the day,—whirling clouds of blinding snow in their faces, hurling the decayed limbs and trunks of the older tenants of the wood to the earth around them, in the fury of its blasts, and rattling and creaking through the colliding branches of the writhing green trees, as it swept over the wilderness,—yet, for all these difficulties of the way and commotions of the elements, they faltered not, but continued to move forward in stern and moody silence, hour after hour, in the footsteps of their indomitable leader, until they reached the extreme eastern point of the lake, where their destination required them to turn round it, in a sharp angle to the west. Here, at the suggestion of their leader, who made the encouraging announcement that the worst half of their journey was accomplished, they made a halt, under the lee of a sheltering mountain, for rest and refreshment. And, sitting down on a fallen tree, from whose barkless trunk they brushed off the snow, they took out and commenced chewing their stale and frozen bread, with a few small pieces of duck-meat, remaining from their breakfast, and comprising the last of their provisions. The animal heat, produced by their great and continued exertions in travelling, had thus far prevented them, from suffering much from the cold, or perceiving its actual intensity. But they had been at rest scarcely long enough to finish their meagre repast, when they were driven from their seats by the chill of the invading element, and were eagerly demanding, as a lesser annoyance, again to be led forward on their journey. The snow by this time had accumulated to the depth of a foot and a half, and still came swiftly sifting down aslant to the earth, without the least sign of abatement; while the wind, which was before a gale, had now risen to a hurricane, causing the smitten earth to tremble and shake under the force of the terrible blasts that went shrieking and howling through the bowed, bending, and twisting forests, where

> "The sturdiest birch its strength was feeling,
> And pine trees dark and tall
> To and fro were madly reeling,
> Or dashing headlong in their fall."

But, still undismayed by these manifestations of elemental power around them, or the prospects before them, all terrific and disheartening as they were, and nerved by the consciousness that their only chance of escape from a fearful death depended on their exertions, the bold and hardy woodsmen again started out into the trackless waste, and labored desperately onward, mile after mile, through the impeding snow; sometimes taken to the armpits in its gathering drifts, and sometimes thrown at full length beneath its submerging depths by stepping into some hole or chasm it had concealed from their sight. And thus resolutely did they beat and buffet their rough way through the perplexed and roaring wilderness, and thus stoutly did they bear up against the constantly thickening dangers that environed them during the last part of that dreadful day. But, as night drew on, their strength and spirits began to flag and give way. The cold was increasing in intensity. The tempest howled louder than ever over their heads, and the snow had become so deep and drifted that furlongs became as miles in their progress. And yet, as they supposed, they were miles from their destination. At length, one after another, they faltered and stopped. The strong men quailed at the fate which seemed staring them in the face, and they were on the point of giving up in despair. But hark! that cheery shout which rises above the roaring of the wind, from their more hardy and hopeful leader, who, while all others stopped, had pushed on some thirty rods in advance. It comes again!

"Courage, men! We have struck the river, at whose mouth stands our camp, now not half a mile distant."

Aroused by the glad tidings, that sent a thrill of joy through their sinking hearts, they sprang forward, with the revivified energies which new and suddenly-lighted hope will sometimes so strangely impart, and were soon by the side of the exulting hunter; when together they rushed and floundered along down the banks of the stream towards the place, in joyful excitement at the thought that their troubles were now so nearly over, and with visions of the comfortable quarters, warm fires, and smoking suppers, which they confidently expected were awaiting them at camp, brightly dancing before them. Joy and hope lent wings to their speed; and, in a short time, they could discern the open place and the well-remembered outlines of the locality where the camp was situated. But no bright light greeted their expectant eyes. They were now at the spot, but, to their utter consternation, no camp was to be seen! Could they be mistaken in the place? No; there was the open path leading to the structure; there rose the steep side of the hill; and there, at the foot of it, stood the perpendicular rock against which it was erected! What could it mean? After standing a moment in mute amazement, peering inquiringly at each other, in the fading twilight, they started forward for the rock, and, in so doing, came upon the two front posts, still standing up some feet out of the snow. They were black and charred! The sad truth then flashed over their minds. Their camp had been burnt to the ground, and with it, also, probably, their rich collection of furs,—nearly the whole fruit of all the toils and fatigues of their expedition! O death, death! what shall save the poor trappers, now?

"Great God! I have had a presentiment of this," exclaimed Phillips, the first to find utterance, in a voice trembling with unwonted emotion.

"How could it have happened?" and "Where is Gaut Gurley?" simultaneously burst from the lips of the others.

"Well may you, ask those questions, and well couple them together, I fancy," responded the hunter, with bitter significance. "But away with all speculations about *that*, now. We have something that more nearly concerns us to attend to, in this strait, than forming conjectures about the loss of our property: our lives are at stake! If you will mind me, however, you may all yet be saved."

"Direct us, direct us, and we will obey," eagerly responded one and all.

"Two of you follow me, then, for something dry, if we can find it, for a fire, and the rest go to kicking away and treading down the snow under the rock, with all your might!" sharply commanded the hunter, dashing his way towards the thickets, with hatchet in hand.

With that ready obedience which a superior in energy and experience will always command among his fellows, in emergencies like this, the men went to work in earnest. In a short time the snow was cleared away or beat down compactly over a space some yards in extent along the side of the rock, while the others soon returned with a supply of the driest wood to be found, together with an armfull of hemlock boughs, to strew over the beaten snow. The next thing requiring their attention was the all-important object of starting a fire. But in this they were doomed to sad disappointment. Their punk-wood tinder had been so dampened by the snow sifting into their coat-pockets, where they had deposited it, that it could not be made to catch the sparks of the smitten steel. They then tried the flashing of their guns; but they had no paper, and could find no dry leaves or fleecy bark of the birch, and the finest splinters or shavings they could whittle, in the dark, from the clefts of the imperfectly dry pine, would not take fire from the light, evanescent flash of the powder in their pans. Again and again did they renew the doubtful experiment; but every succeeding trial, from the dampness of their material in the driving snow, and from the unmanageable condition of their benumbed fingers and shivering frames, became more and more hopeless, till at length they were compelled to relinquish wholly the fruitless attempt.

"This is a calamity, indeed!" exclaimed the hunter. "I feared it might be so from the first. Could we have foreseen the want, so as to have been on the lookout for material coming along, or have got here before dark, it might have been averted. But as it is, there is one resort left for us, if we would live in this terrible wind and cold till morning, and that is, to keep in constant and lively motion. Whoever lies down to sleep is a dead man!"

But he found it difficult to impress on the minds of most of them his idea of the danger of ceasing motion. They began to say they felt more comfortable now, and, being very tired, must lay down to take a little rest. Sharply forbidding the indulgence, the hunter sallied out, cut and trimmed two or three green beech switches, and returned with them to his wondering companions; when, finding Mark Elwood, in disregard of his warning, already down and dozing on a bunch of boughs under the rock, he sternly exclaimed:

"Up, there, in an instant!"

"O, let me lie," begged the unconsciously freezing man: "do let me lie a little while. I am almost warm, now, but very, very sleepy," he added, sinking away again into a doze.

Instantly a smart blow from the tough and closely-setting switch of the hunter fell upon the outstretched legs of the dozer, who cringed and groaned, but did not start. Another and another, and yet another, fell with the quickness and force of a pedagogue's rod on the legs of an offending urchin, till the aroused, maddened and enraged victim of the seeming cruelty leaped to his feet, and, with doubled fists, rushed upon the assailant, who darted off into the snow and led his pursuer a doubling race of several hundred yards before he returned to the spot.

"There are some spare switches," resumed the active and stout-hearted hunter, as he came in a little ahead of the puffing, reanimated, and now pacified Elwood; "take them in hand, and do the same by me, if you see me going the same way; it is our only salvation!"

But, notwithstanding all this preaching, and the obvious effects of this wholesome example, others of the company, deceived by the insidious sensation which steals upon the unsuspecting victims of such exposures, as the treacherous herald of their death,—others, in turn, required and promptly received the application of the same strange remedy. But this could not always last. The fatigue of their previously overtasked systems prevented them from keeping up their exertions many hours more; and, declaring they could bear up no longer, one after another sunk down under the rock; and even their hitherto indomitable leader himself now visibly relaxed, and at length threw himself down with the rest, feebly murmuring:

"I know what this feeling means; but it is so sweet! let us all die together!"

At that instant a shock, quickly followed by the loud, gathering rumblings of an earthquake, somewhere above them, suddenly aroused and brought every man to his feet. And the next moment an avalanche of snow, sweeping down the steep side of the rock-faced declivity above, shot obliquely over their heads to the level below, leaving them unharmed, but buried twenty feet beneath the outward surface.

"Now, God be praised!" cried the hunter, at once comprehending what had happened, and starting forward to feel out what space was left them between their shielding rock in the rear and the wedged and compact slant snow-wall in front, which, with the no less deeply blocked ends, formed the roof and sides of their new and thus strangely built prison-house. "This is the work of Providence! We are now, at least, safe from the cold, as you will all, I think, soon have the pleasure of perceiving."

"You are right, Mr. Phillips," responded Carvil; "and it is strange some of us did not think of building a snow-house at the outset. Even the wild partridges, that in coldest weather protect themselves by burrowing in the snow, might have taught us the lesson."

"Yes, but it has been far better done in the way God has provided for us. And we have only now to get our blood into full circulation to insure us safety and rest through the night; and let us do this by shaking out our boughs, and treading down the snow, as smooth as a floor, to receive them for our bedding."

"It may be as you say about its being mild here, Mr. Phillips," doubtingly observed Mark Elwood; "but it seems strange philosophy to me, that being inclosed in snow, the coldest substance in nature, should make us warmer than in the open air."

"And still I suspect it is a fact, father," said Claud. "The Esquimaux, and other nations of the extreme north, it is known, live in snow-houses, without fire, the whole of their long and rigorous winters."

"O, Phillips is right enough about *that*," added Codman, now evidently fast regaining his usual buoyancy of spirits; "yes, right enough about *that*, whether he was about that plaguey switching he gave us, or not. Why, I can feel a great change in the air here already! warm enough, soon; safe, at any rate; so, hurra for life and home, which, being once so honestly lost, will now be clear gain. Hurra! whoo-rah! whoo-rah-ee! Kuk-kuk-ke-o-ho!"

And the hunter *was* right, and the trapper was right. Their perils and physical sufferings were over. They were not only safe, but fast becoming comfortable. And, by the time they had trod down the snow as hard and smooth as had been proposed, and shaken out the boughs and distributed them for their respective beds, the air seemed as warm as that of a mild day in October. Their clothes were smoking and becoming dry by the evaporation of the dampness caused by the snow. Their limbs had become pliant, and their whole systems restored to their wonted warmth and circulation. And, wrapping themselves in their blankets, they laid down—as they knew they could now safely do—and were soon lost in refreshing slumber, from which they did not awake till a late hour the next morning.

When they awoke, after their deep slumbers, they at once concluded, from the altered and lighter hue of all around them, as well as by their own feelings, that it must be day without; and with one accord commenced, with their hatchets, cutting and digging a hole through the wall of their snowy prison-house, in the place where they judged it most likely to be thinnest. After working by turns some thirty or forty minutes, and cutting or beating out an upward passage eight or ten yards in extent, they suddenly broke through into the open air. The roaring of the storm no longer greeted their ears. The terrible conflict of the elements, which yesterday kept the heavens and earth in such hideous commotion, was over and gone. Though it was as cold as in the depths of winter, the sky was almost cloudless; and the sun, already far on his diurnal circuit, was glimmering brightly over the dreary wastes of the snow-covered wilderness. By common consent, they then packed up, and immediately commenced beating their slow and toilsome way towards the nearest habitation, which was that of the old chief, now only about five miles distant, over land, on the shore of the lake below. With far less fatigue and other suffering, save that of hunger, than they had anticipated, they reached the hospitable cabin of Wenongonet before night. Here their wants were supplied; here an earnest discussion—in which they were aided by the shrewd surmises of the chief—was held, respecting the burning of their camp and the probable loss of their common property; and, finally, here, though the "*Light of the Lodge*" was absent at her city home, they were agreeably entertained through the night and succeeding day,—when, the lakes having become frozen over sufficiently strong to make travelling on the ice as safe as it was convenient and easy, they, on the second morning after their arrival at his house, bade their entertainer good-by, and set out for their homes in the settlement, which they respectively reached by daylight, to the great relief of their anxious and now overjoyed families and friends.

CHAPTER XVI.

"There was a laughing devil in his sneer,
That rais'd emotions both of hate and fear."

In the early part of an appointed day, about a fortnight after the return of the imperilled and unfortunate trappers to their homes, as described in the preceding chapter, an unusual gathering of men was to be seen within and around a building whose barn, open shed, watering-trough, and sign-post, showed its aspirations to be a tavern, occupying a central position among a small, scattering group of primitive-looking houses, situated on the banks of the Androscoggin, five miles below that lake, and where it might be considered as fairly under way, as an uninterrupted river, in its devious course to the ocean.

In the yard and around the door stood men, gathered in small knots, engaged in low, earnest conversation; while, every few minutes, some were seen issuing from the house and hastily departing, as if dispatched on special messages,—the company in the mean time being continually augmented by fresh arrivals of the settlers, who came straggling in from both directions of the great road, which, leading from the more thickly-settled parts of Maine to the Connecticut, here passed over the Androscoggin.

Within the house, in the largest room, and behind a table, drawn up near the wall at the farther end, sat a magistrate, in all the grave dignity of a court, with pen in hand and paper before him, as if in readiness to take such testimony in the case on hand as should be presented for his consideration. On his right sat Mark Elwood, Phillips, and Codman, appearing as the representatives of the injured trappers or hunters, who were the prosecutors in the case; while on his left sat Gaut Gurley, in custody of the sheriff and his assistant, who had arrested and brought him there to answer to the complaint of the former. Gaut appeared perfectly unconcerned, glancing boldly about him with an air of proud defiance; while his former companions, the trappers just named, sat looking down at their feet, compressing their lips and knitting their brows in moody and indignant silence.

But, before proceeding with any further description of the court, its parties or doings, let us briefly recur to what had happened in the interim between the return of the trappers and their present appearance in court, for redress for the outrages that they supposed had been designedly committed upon them, or at least for bringing to punishment the man who, they felt morally certain, must be the perpetrator.

After the trappers had reached their homes, become fully restored from the chill and fatigues they had undergone during the terrible storm with which their expedition so disastrously terminated, and attended to such domestic wants as demanded their immediate care, they met at the house of Phillips, in accordance with an appointment they made when they parted, to report what evidence each might be able to collect relative to the burning of their camp, and the suspected previous abstraction of their furs; and thereupon to decide what measures should be taken in the premises. Finding that Gaut Gurley had been seen at home, or in the vicinity, some days previous to the storm, and that he was not likely to come to *them*, they dispatched a disinterested person to *him*, to notify him of their arrival, and the condition in which they found matters at the store-camp, left in his charge, and also of their wish that he would attend their proposed meeting, and account for the catastrophe which had so unexpectedly occurred. He pretended to know nothing of the affair, and feigned great surprise at the news; said he had left the camp and its stores, all safe, two days before the storm, to come to the settlement for more provisions; believing that his companions would remain a fortnight longer; that, having procured his supplies, he was intending to return to camp the day the storm came on; and finally that it devolved on those last at the camp, and not on *him*, to account for what had taken place. He therefore declined meeting them on the business. As soon as they ascertained that Gaut had taken this stand, which only added to their previous convictions of his guilt, the different members of the company made journeys to the nearest villages or trading-places in Maine and New Hampshire, to see if any furs, answering in description to their collection, had recently been sold in any of those towns. And at length they found, in one of the frontier villages in Maine, a small collection of peltries, which they thought they could identify, and which the trader said he had lately purchased of an unknown travelling pedlar, who, out of a large lot of peltries, would sell only these at prices that would warrant the purchasing. This small lot of furs they prevailed on the trader to let them take home with them, for the purpose of making proof in court. This was all the direct evidence they could find to implicate Gaut; but they believed it would be sufficient. For, at the meeting they then held, Mark Elwood found among the furs a beaver-skin, that he could swear was of his own taking, from a careless slit he remembered to have made in the skinning. Codman found another, which he could safely identify by a mangled ear which was caught in one end of the trap, while the tail was caught in the other. And Phillips found an otter skin, with a bullet-hole on each side, made, as he well remembered, by shooting the animal through and through in the region of the heart. On this proof they unanimously decided on a prosecution; and accordingly Phillips and Mark Elwood set off the next day for Lancaster, the shire-town on the Connecticut, for legal advice, warrants, and a sheriff to serve them. On reaching the place, they were told by the attorney they consulted that they could not make out larceny or theft against Gurley for taking the furs placed in his trust, but for their private redress must resort to a civil action of trover, or unlawful conversion of the common property. A criminal process for arson, or the burning of the camp, would probably be sustained. And the result of the consultation was, that a complaint and warrant for arson should be issued, and the arrest made by the sheriff, who should also have in his hands a civil process returnable to the court of Common Pleas, to serve on Gurley and his property, provided the proof elicited at the court of inquiry on the criminal charge should be such as to afford them any prospect of a recovery.

It was under these circumstances that Gaut Gurley had been arrested for the burning of the camp, and brought before the magistrate, who, with the lawyers employed on both sides, had come to this place, as before described, for the hearing of the case.

The magistrate now declared the court open, and directed the parties to proceed with the case. The attorney for the prosecution then rose, read the complaint, and briefly stated what they expected to prove, to substantiate the allegations it contained. Mark Elwood, Phillips, Codman, and the trader who had purchased the furs of the pedlar, and who had been summoned for the purpose, were then called to the stand, and sworn, as witnesses on the part of the prosecution.

The trader, being first called on, testified to the identity of the furs which had been produced in court with the lot he had bought of the pedlar, as before mentioned; and he further stated that the man had a large lot, which well answered the general description given by the complainants of the lot they had in camp; but where or how he obtained the lot, or who he was, or where he went to when he left town, he did not learn, and had no means of ascertaining. All he could say, was, that these were the furs he purchased, and the only ones of the whole lot on the prices of which he and the fellow could agree, so as to effect a trade.

Phillips, next called, swore plumply that the bullet-pierced otter-skin before him was taken by his own hand from the animal he shot. He also added that there were several strings of sable-skins in the lot before him, which he felt confident he had seen among the furs of the company, and he especially pointed out one strung together by a braid of wickape bark. And in this last statement he was confirmed by Codman, who, besides identifying one beaver-skin, had the same impression in relation to the string of sable; but neither of them would swear positively in the matter of the smaller furs.

Mark Elwood, the last of the witnesses to be examined, then took the stand; and, contrary to what might have been expected from one of his wavering disposition, and particularly from one who had been so strangely kept under the influence and fear of the man on trial, bore himself resolutely under the menacing looks which the latter fixed upon him by way of intimidation. For some time he had utterly refused to harbor the idea of Gaut's guilt. He believed the burning of the camp was accidental; that Gaut, in anticipation of the storm, had taken all the furs home with him, and would soon call the company together for the distribution. But when he heard of the course Gaut was taking, and coupled it with the other circumstances, he suddenly changed his tone, fell into the belief of his companions, and more loudly and openly than any of them denounced the crime and its author,— seemingly throwing off, at once and forever, the mysterious spell which had so long bound him. Accordingly he now swore confidently to the beaverskin in question, as one of his own taking, and, facing him boldly, even went so far as to declare his full belief in Gaut's guilt, not only in the burning of the camp, but in the stealing of the furs.

This gratuitous assertion of a mere matter of belief in the respondent's guilt, which was no legal evidence in the case, at once aroused, as might have been expected, the ire of Gaut's lawyer, who, with, fierce denunciations of the conduct of the witness, subjected him to a severe cross-examination.

"What reason, then," asked the somewhat mollified lawyer, now himself incautiously venturing on ground which, with a better knowledge of the parties, he would have seen might injure his cause, and on which his client evidently wished him not to push inquiries. "What reason, then, could you have for your extraordinary conduct in trying, against all rule, to lug in here your mere ungrounded conjectures, to prejudice the court and spectators against an innocent man?"

"Innocent?" here broke in Phillips, provoked by what, in his exasperated state of feeling, he viewed as the cool impudence and hypocrisy of the lawyer. "Innocent, hey? Well, well, there are various ways of lying in this world, I see plainly."

"What do *you* know about my client, whom you are all conspiring to ruin?" exclaimed the excited lawyer, turning fiercely on the interposing hunter.

"Know about him?" retorted the other. "I know enough, besides this outrageous affair; I know enough to—"

"Beware!" suddenly exclaimed Gaut Gurley, with a look that brought the speaker to a stand.

"I don't fear you, sir," said the hunter, confronting the other with an unflinching countenance. "But you may be right; it may be *I had* better forbear; it may be your time is not yet come," he added, in a low, significant tone.

"Now, I will finish with you, sir," resumed Gaut's lawyer, turning again sternly to Elwood, from whom he—like many other over-acting attorneys, who cannot see where they should stop in examinations of this kind—seemed to think he could draw something more that would make for his client. "When that fellow interrupted me, just now, I was asking what reason, besides some grudge or malice, you had for your unwarrantable course in pronouncing the respondent guilty, without proof; for, allowing the furs you swear to *were* once yours, you don't show, by a single particle of proof, that he had any thing to do with it more than yourselves, who were quite as likely to have taken them as he. Yes, what reasons,—facts, facts, I mean; no more guess-work here; so speak out, sir, like an honest man, if you can."

"I will, then," promptly responded Elwood. "You shall have facts, to your heart's content; I said what I did because I am convinced he *is* guilty."

"Convinced!" sneeringly interrupted the other; "there it is again; thrusting in sheer conjectures for evidence! I must call on the court to interpose with the stubborn and wilful fellow. Didn't I tell you, sir, I'd have no more of your guess-work? Facts, sir, facts, or nothing."

"Well, you shall have them, then," replied the other, in a determined tone, "for I know enough facts to convince *me*, at least, of his guilt. Both before and after we started on our expedition, he threw out hints to me which I did not then quite understand, but which, since this affair, I have recalled, and now know what they meant. He hinted, if I would fall into his plan and keep council, we might—"

"Might what?" sharply demanded the excited and alarmed attorney. "Do you know you are under oath, sir? Might what, I say?"

"Might get all the furs into our hands, and—"

"Traitor! liar! scoundrel!" exclaimed Gaut Gurley, in a tone that sounded like the hiss of a serpent, as he bent forward and glared upon Elwood, with an expression so absolutely fiendish as to make every one in the room pause and shudder, and as to be remembered and recounted, months afterwards, in connection with events which seemed destined to spring from this worse than fruitless trial.

"You was going to say," said the attorney for the prosecution, here eagerly pricking up and turning to the interrupted and now evidently discomposed witness,—"you was going to say, he proposed that he and you should take all the furs to yourselves, and so rob the rest of the company!"

"I can't tell the words; but I think he meant that," replied Elwood, in more subdued tones.

"O ho," exclaimed Gaut's lawyer; "you *now* think, that is, you guess, he meant something that you didn't dream of his meaning at the time he uttered it. Pretty evidence this; make the most of it!"

"We will," said the opposite counsel; "and I request the court to take it all down, together with the prisoner's exclamations of *traitor*, etc., which involves, indirectly, an admission that I shall remark on in the argument. Yes, let all this be noted carefully. It is important. It goes to show the previous design, which, coupled with the identified furs, is, I trust the court will see, sufficient to fix the crime on the respondent, beyond all doubt or question."

"We will soon show you how much you will make out of your identified furs," rejoined the other lawyer, with a confident and defiant air.

"Have you witnesses to introduce on the part of the defence?" asked the court.

"Yes, your honor; but our most important one has not yet arrived. We are expecting him every minute."

At that moment, a shout of surprise and laughter, together with an unusual commotion in the yard, arrested the attention of all in the court-room; and they mostly rushed to the door or windows to ascertain the cause, when they were amused to behold the young Indian, Tomah, driving into the yard, with his moose harnessed to a pung or sledge, of his own rigging up, on which--with reins and whip in hand—he sat as jauntily as a coachman, and almost with, the same ease, apparently, brought his strange steed to a stand before the door.

"Our witness has come!" exclaimed Gaut's lawyer, exultingly. "Mr. Sheriff, send out and bring him in. We will now dispose of this miserable prosecution, in short metre."

In a few minutes Tomah entered the room, and, readily comprehending,—from a knowledge of the usages of courts he had obtained during his residence in the villages of the whites,—what was expected of him, now demurely advanced in front of the magistrate, raised his hand, and received the oath of a witness. He was then shown the lot of furs that had been identified by the hunters present, his attention directed to the peculiar marks by which part of them had been distinguished, and he was asked if he had ever seen these furs, and noticed the marks on them, before.

"Yes, think so," replied Tomah, quietly, as he rapidly handled every large skin, and each parcel of the smaller ones, keenly noting the palpable marks shown him on the former, and every tie confining together the latter. "Yes; here bullet-holes on otter; slit on this beaver; cropt ear on that; little fat back of fore-legs on rest of beaver; wickape strings on that bunch sable; elm-bark tie on that; and beech twigs on that. Yes, seen 'em all."

"Where? And how do you know the furs? Tell the court all about it," said Gaut's lawyer, as an exultant smile played over his sardonic features.

"Well, now," calmly and with his usual passionless cast of countenance replied Tomah, after a considerable pause; "well, this lot of skins all taken from the great lot taken by our company up round the great lakes, this fall. I come back to settlement, three, four, five days, may be, 'fore the rest; to see to moose, train him for Boston, and make sled; wanted my part of furs to sell right off, to bear expenses, and get off on journey soon. Mr. Gurley, then, after while, said he venture to divide off to me greater part of what I would get for my share of skins then got into the great camp. So he do it; and I take my part, just this lot you show me here, and steer off with them to Bethel; but, 'fore got quite there, come cross pedlar and sold them cheap, for money, and go right back to Mr. Gurley's, where moose was. Found Mr. Gurley home, too; said he left all furs safe in camp; come for provisions to carry back, to hunt one, two weeks longer; but storm come, and he stayed to home, and soon heard all the men got home, too; big storm, bad; I no start for Boston yet, but most ready; go soon, get heap of money for moose, certain."

The counsel for the prosecution and his clients—on hearing such a piece of testimony from a witness whom they themselves would have summoned, but for the belief that he would be so much under the influence and training of Gaut, that little could be drawn from him making against the latter—were taken so completely by surprise, by the unexpected *denouement*, that they all sat mute and dumb-founded for some moments; both lawyer and clients being scarcely able to credit their own senses, and each hoping that the other had discovered some flaw in the testimony, by which it could be picked to pieces. But no such flaw or discrepancy could be discovered; and the testimony, after the severe and prolonged cross-examination to which it was subjected by the rallying and desperate attorney, remained wholly unshaken, in every material part, standing out, in all its decisive force and effect, for the exclusive benefit of the respondent. Every person in the room, indeed, at length became convinced that the young Indian had told the truth, and that he could know nothing of Gaut's guilt, though unconciously made a witness in his favor; with the view, probably, of meeting just such an exigency as had occurred in the present prosecution.

The attorney for the prosecution, then, it being agreed to submit the case on the testimony now in, made a long and ingenious speech, abandoning the matter of the identified furs; dwelling largely on Gaut's dimly-hinted proposals to Elwood to join in the crime; and, on the ground that he was the only person in a situation to burn and rob the camp, raising the violent presumption that he must have perpetrated the double crime.

Gaut's lawyer then rose, with a confident and exultant air, and said he might, with the best reason in the world, make a plea to the jurisdiction of the court, since he had discovered that the camp which was alleged to have been burnt was situated some miles within the boundary of Maine; that no New Hampshire magistrate, of course, could take jurisdiction of the case; and, that the respondent, on that ground alone, must be at once discharged, if he wished it. But he did not wish it. He courted a trial and decision, on the merits of the cases which, after briefly urging the strong points of the defence, he submitted to the court.

Tomah's testimony had settled the case; and, though nearly every one in the room, probably, were deeply impressed with suspicions of Gaut's guilt, yet all felt that the evidence was not sufficient for a legal conviction. And they were not surprised, therefore, when the court, after briefly commenting on the testimony, pronounced the full discharge of the prisoner.

"Ha, ha!" exclaimed Gaut, with a laugh so inconceivably devilish that his own lawyer, even, recoiled at the sound. "Ha, ha!" he repeated, with a smile on his lips, made ghastly by the fires of concentrated malice that shot from his eyes. "Wouldn't my good friends, here, like to try this game again?"

"Yes," boldly retorted the hunter. "Yes, and we shall, with evidence Heaven will direct us where to find. Your time hasn't come. But it *will* come! God ain't dead yet!"

CHAPTER XVII.

"Be still the unimaginable lodge
For solitary thinkings; such as dodge
Conception to the very bourn of Heaven,
Then leave the naked brain; be still the leaven
That, spreading in this dull and clodded earth,
Gives it a touch ethereal, a new birth." KEATS.

It is not to be supposed that a lawsuit, or prosecution, in so new and remote a settlement, especially one that involved so many interests, and whose result must have so many and complicated bearings, as the one described in the last chapter, would be suffered to pass away like any ordinary occurrence and be forgotten. With the settlers, besides the novelty of having a court held among them, for any cause, it was an extraordinary occurrence that there should be any grounds for a prosecution or lawsuit of this character,—extraordinary that any one should be found base enough to violate the common faith and honesty which the trappers and hunters had, up to that time, so implicitly reposed in, and observed with each other,—and doubly extraordinary that the perpetrator could not be detected and brought to punishment. To them, such a flagitious betrayal of trust was a new and startling event. They felt it deeply concerned them all; and the sensation it produced was accordingly as profound as it was general, in all that region of the country.

But, if such was the effect of the unfortunate occurrence in question, on the community at large, how much more deeply would the effect be naturally felt by the parties immediately concerned? By the loss of their stock of furs, three families, at least, were deprived of the means on which they had relied for supplying them, with a large part of the necessaries of life, through the ensuing winter; while, besides this, many a wife and child were doomed to sad disappointment, in being thus deprived of the fondly-anticipated purchases of articles of dress, books, and various other little comforts, which had been promised them on the division and sale of the peltries. Nor were these the only interests and feelings affected by the event and its concomitants. Friendships were broken, and even more tender relations were disturbed, if, indeed, their further existence were not to be terminated. By the open, and as was supposed irreconcilable, quarrel between Mark Elwood and the terribly vindictive Gaut Gurley, their children, Claud and Avis, who were understood to be under mutual engagement of marriage, were placed in a position at once painful and embarrassing in the extreme. And Claud, especially, although he had carefully abstained from all accusations of Gaut, had taken no part in getting up the prosecution, and purposely absented himself from the trial, yet felt very keenly the perplexing dilemma into which he would be thrown, by continuing the connecting link between two such deadly foes as he now found his father, whom he could not desert, and Gaut Gurley, whom he felt conscious he could not defend. And for this reason he had, from time to time, deferred the visit to Avis, which he had designed, and which she would naturally expect on his return from the expedition. But still he could not see how a quarrel between the fathers discharged him from his obligations to her; and he grew more and more doubtful and uneasy in the position he found himself occupying. He was soon, however, to be relieved. One day, a short time after the trial, while he was anxiously revolving the subject in mind, a boy, who had come as a special messenger from the Magalloway settlement (for the purpose, as it appeared), brought him the following letter:

"DEAR CLAUD,—You do not know, you cannot know, what the effort costs me to write this. You do not know, you cannot know, what I have felt, what I have suffered since I became fully apprised of the painful circumstances under which your late expedition was brought to a close; and especially since I became apprised of the lamentable scenes that occurred in the court, growing out of that unfortunate—O how unfortunate, expedition! Before that court was held, and during the doubtful days which intervened between it and your escape from the terrible perils that attended your return, the hope that all would, all *must* turn out right, in some measure relieved my harrowing fears and anxieties; though even then the latter was to the former as days of cloud to minutes of sunshine. But, when I heard what occurred at the trial,—the bitter crimination and recrimination, the open rupture, the menaces exchanged, and the angry parting,—and, more alarming than all, when I saw my father return in that fearful mood, from which he still refuses to be diverted, the last gleam of hope faded, and all became cloud, all gloom,—dark, impenetrable, and forbidding. My nights, when sleep at length comes to close my weeping eyes, are passed in troubled dreams; my days in more troubled thoughts, which I would fain believe were dreams also. O, why need this be? I have done nothing,—you have done nothing; and I have no doubt of your faith and honor for performing all I shall ever require at your hands. But, Claud, I love you, and all

'Know love is woman's happiness;'

and all know, likewise, that the ties of love are but gossamer threads, which a word may rupture, a breath shake, and even the power of unpleasant associations destroy. Still, is there not one hope,—the hope that this thread, hitherto so blissfully uniting our hearts, subtle and attenuated as it is, may yet be preserved unbroken, if we suffer no opinion, no word, no syllable to escape our lips, respecting the unfortunate affair that is embroiling our parents; if we wholly deny ourselves the pleasure of that social intercourse which, to *me*, at least, has thus far made this wilderness an Eden of delight?

But can it be thus preserved, if we keep up that intercourse, as in the sunshine of our love,—those pleasant, fleeting, rosy months, when I was so happy, O so very happy, in the feelings of the present and the prospects of the future? No, no, it is not possible, it is not possible for you to come here, and encounter my father in such a mood, and then return and receive the upbraidings of your own, that you are joining or upholding the house of his foes. It is not possible for you to do this, and your heart receive no jar, and mine no fears or suspicions of its continued fealty. I dare not risk it. Then do not, dearest Claud, O do not come here, at least for the present. Perhaps my dark forebodings, that our connection is not to be blessed for our future happiness, may be groundless. Perhaps the storm that now so darkly hangs over us may pass harmlessly away. Perhaps this painful and perplexing misunderstanding—as I trust in Heaven's mercy it only is—may yet be placed in a light which will admit of a full reconciliation between our respective families. But, till then, let our relations to each other stand, if you feel disposed to let them, precisely as we left them at our last mournfully happy parting; for, till then, though it break my heart, I could never, never consent to a renewal of our intercourse. Have I said enough, and not too much? I could not, under the almost insupportable weight of grief, fear, and anxiety, that is distracting my brain, and crushing my poor heart,—I could not say less, I dare not say more. O Claud, Claud, why has this dreadful cloud come over us? O, pray that it may be speedily removed, and once more let in, on our pained and perplexed hearts, the sunshine of their former happiness. Dearest Claud, good-by; don't come, but don't forget.

"AVIS."

Claud felt greatly relieved, in some respects, by this unexpected missive; in others, the contents caused him uneasiness and self-condemnation. It relieved him from the sense of obligation he had entertained, to make the dreaded visit to the house of Gaut Gurley,—who, with every desire to arrive at a different conclusion, he could no longer believe guiltless of the basest of frauds, and the basest of means to conceal it. It relieved him, indeed, on this point; but, as we have said, made him sad and thoughtful on others. The great grief and distress under which the fair writer was so evidently laboring, and the deep-rooted love for him which was revealed in almost every line, but which her pride, in the bright hours of their courtship, had never permitted her to disclose, keenly touched his feelings, and rose in condemnation of the comparative indifference, which, in spite of all his efforts to correct its waywardness, he felt conscious had been gradually stealing over his heart, since his admiration, to say the least, had been raised by a rival vision of loveliness. In the newly-awakened feeling of the moment, however, he bitterly upbraided himself for his tergiversations in suffering his thoughts to vacillate between the Star of the Magalloway, who had his plighted faith, and

Flower of the Lakes, who had no claims to his special consideration. But still, when his thoughts wandered over the scenes of the past summer, which now, since trial and hardship had brought his mind back within the dominion of reason and judgment, seemed much more like dreams than realities,—when he thought of the manner in which he became acquainted with Avis Gurley; how he persisted in gaining her affections, and kindling into an overmastering flame his own fancy-lit love; and finally, how, against the known wishes of his family, and the dictates of his own sober judgment, he had urged her into an engagement of marriage, which he could now see had, as his mother predicted, in all probability led to a renewal of the intimacy between his father and Gaut Gurley, and that last intimacy to the present disaster, and a new quarrel, whose consequences might yet well be looked for with uneasiness and apprehension,—when he thought of all this, he deeply condemned his own indiscretion, and could not help wishing himself clear from an engagement, which, like every thing connected with the schemes of that dark and dreaded man, who was now an object of suspicion through the whole settlement, seemed destined to lead only to trouble and disaster. Such was the maze of perplexity by which the young man, now too late for an honorable retreat, found himself on every side thickly environed. Yet, for all this, and in despite of all these perplexities and misgivings, he resolved he would not cease to play the man, but honorably fulfil all his obligations in such manner as should be required of him.

So much for the love and its hapless entanglements, which had been so deeply but so unsatisfactorily occupying, for the last few weeks, the thoughts of Claud Elwood, who then little suspected that there was another heart, besides that of the pure, proud, and impassioned Avis Gurley, whose every pulse, in the great unseen system of intermingling sympathies, beat in trembling vibration to his own,—a heart that had been won uncourted and unknown,—a heart that had secretly nursed, in the favoring solitudes of these wild lakes, and brooded over, a passion more deep and intense than words could well be found to describe. There *was* such a heart; and that heart was now wildly beating, in the agonizing uncertainties of a hoped reciprocation, in the bosom of that peerless child of the forest, the beautiful Fluella; and all the more intense were its workings, because confined to its own deep recesses, where the hidden flame was laboring constantly for an outlet to its pride-walled prison, but as constantly shrinking in terror from the disclosure. She had once, however, through the violence of emotions which she could not control, accidentally betrayed the state of her feelings; but it was to one in whose discretion and friendship she was soon made to repose undoubting confidence, and with whom, therefore, she at length became reconciled to let her secret remain. The person, who had thus become the depositary of that secret was, as the reader may remember, Mrs. Elwood. The consciousness that this lady knew all, coupled as it was with the thought of the relation in which the latter stood to the object of her secret idolatry, had irresistibly drawn to her the yearning heart of the guileless maiden. She had longed for another interview, but dare not seek it; longed for some excuse for opening a communication with her, but could not find one. At length, however, fortune opened the desired avenue; and, after much hesitation and trembling, she summoned up the courage to avail herself of the offered opportunity. Phillips, in his determination to ferret out the outrage which had been committed on him and his companions, and of the author of which he still entertained no doubt, had, immediately after the trial, commenced a series of rapid journeys to all the nearest villages or trading towns in Maine and New Hampshire, to ascertain if any lot of furs, answering to those caught by his company, had been sold in those places. And one of these journeys, for that and other purposes, he had extended to the seaboard. On his return home, he immediately repaired to his neighbor Elwood's, and, unperceived, slipped into the hands of Mrs. Elwood a letter, which the wondering matron soon took to a private room, curiously opened, and, with a deep, undefined interest and varying emotions, commenced reading. It ran thus:

"MRS. ELWOOD, MY FRIEND,—Our Mr. Phillips has been here, and told us all that has happened in your settlement. Mrs. Elwood, I am greatly troubled at the loss your family suffer, with the rest of the hunters, but still more troubled and fearful for your husband and your noble son, about what may grow out of the quarrel with that dark man. My father knew him, time long past, and said there would be mischief done the company, when we heard he was going with them. I hope Mr. Elwood will keep out of his way; and I hope, Claud,—O, I cannot write the thought. Mrs. Elwood, I am very unhappy. I sometimes wish your brave and noble son had suffered me to go down and be lost in the dark, wild waters of those fearful rapids. By the goodness of my white father, whom I am proud to hope you may some time see with me in your settlement, I have all the comforts and indulgences that a heart at ease could desire; warm, carpeted rooms, dress, books, company, smooth flatterers, who mean little, it may be, together with *real* friends, who mean much, and prove it by actions, which do not, like words, ever deceive. And yet, Mrs. Elwood, they are all now without any charms for me. My heart is in your settlement. The grand old forest, and the bright lake, were always things of beauty for me, before I saw *him*; but now, when associated *with* him,—O, Mrs. Elwood, if I did not know you had something of what I meant should forever be kept secret from all but the Great Eye, in your keeping, and if you had not made me feel you would be my discreet friend, and keep it as safe from all as an unspoken thought, I would not for worlds write what I have, and what I every moment find my pen on the point of writing more fully. O, how I wish I could make you understand, without words, what I feel,—how I grieve over what I almost know must be vain hopes, and vainer visions of happiness! You have sometimes had, it may be, very bright, delightful dreams, which seemed to bring you all your heart desired; and then you suddenly awoke, and found all had vanished, leaving you dark and sad with disappointment and regret. If you have, you may fancy what my thoughts are undergoing every hour of the day. O, how my heart is drawn away towards you! I often feel that I must fly up, like a bird, to be there. I should come now, but for what might be thought. I shall certainly be there in early spring. I can't stay away, though I may come only to see what I could bear less easy than these haunting, troubled fancies. Mrs. Elwood, adieu. You won't show this, or breathe a word about it,—I know you won't; you could not be so cruel as that. Mrs. Elwood, may I not sign myself your friend? FLUELLA."

On perusing this unexpected communication, Mrs. Elwood felt—she scarcely knew herself what she felt, except a keenly appreciating sense of the writer's embarrassed feelings, and except, also, the pleasurable emotions which this timid and tender outpouring of an unsophisticated heart somehow afforded her. Ever since her singular interview with this remarkable girl, as described in a former chapter, Mrs. Elwood had not ceased to think of her as of some good angel, sent by an interposing Providence, in answer to the agonizing supplications which immediately preceded her unexpected appearance at the time,—sent to be the means, in some unforeseen way, of extricating her family from the fatal influences, as she viewed them, under which they had insidiously been brought by their different connections with the Gurleys. Especially had she been impressed that this would prove the case, in all that related to her idolized son, Claud; whom, in her disregard to all considerations of lineage, when relieved by such excellence of beauty and character, she would a thousand times rather have seen united to the Indian girl than to the one he appeared to have chosen. She was, therefore, besides being touched by the broken pathos of the letter, gratified by its reception; for it seemed to come as a sort of confirmation of her grateful presentiment, that her son, at least, was to be happily disenthralled. Nor was she, at this time, without the evidence which led her to hope that her husband, also, had now finally escaped from the toils that had, once and again, caused him such calamity and suffering. The sudden and terrible outbreak of indignation, which, with equal surprise and gratification, she had seen him exhibit against Gaut, and the quarrel in court, which followed in consequence, must, she thought, now forever keep them separate. If so, poorly as her family could afford to suffer their part of the loss of the avails of the fall's work, she would cheerfully bear it, and even look upon the event in the light of a Heaven-sent mercy. But even of this poor comfort she was destined soon to be deprived. After the trial, Mark Elwood—who, however bravely he bore himself at first, on that occasion, was finally seen to quail under the terrible glances of Gaut—soon became strangely silent respecting the prosecution and supposed perpetration of the offence about which he had before manifested so much zeal and indignation. And, in the active exertions which Phillips and Codman, in the vain search for evidence or some clue to the robbery of the furs, perseveringly kept up during the whole of the long and dreary winter that followed, he could not be induced to take any decided part. Nor would he, when they met him at his own house, or that of Phillips, as they several times did, that winter, to compare the discoveries and observations they had made, and discuss the subject, any longer maintain the position he at first so boldly took, respecting Gaut's guilt, or say any thing in aid of their deliberations. *He*, indeed, as *they* grew more decided and convinced, seemed to grow more wavering and doubtful. Such was his demeanor and conduct in company of his late companions; while, with his own family, he appeared moody, irresolute, and restless, and even, at length, he began to throw out occasional hints tending to defend or extenuate the conduct of the very man whom, a few weeks before, he had so confidently denounced as a thief and a robber. Alarmed at these indications of returning weakness and fatuity in her husband, Mrs. Elwood soon put herself on inquiry, to ascertain the cause; and she was not long in making discoveries that more than justified her worst fears and suspicions.

It appeared that Gaut Gurley, after his arrest, and after his escape from the punishment of the law, through the means, as was now generally believed, which he had cunningly provided before he entered on the commission of the offence charged, remained almost constantly at home, during nearly the whole winter, brooding, in savage mood, over his own dark thoughts and varying schemes for advantage and revenge, keeping his family in continual awe of him, and causing all who approached him to recoil, shuddering, from his presence, and mark him as a dangerous man in the community. Towards spring, however, he appeared suddenly to change his tactics, or, at least, to undergo a great change in his deportment and conduct. All at once, he came round in his usual manner. The dark cloud had been banished from his brow. He civilly accosted every acquaintance he met, appeared cheerful and good-humored, and desirous of prolonging the conversation with all with whom he came in contact, without seeming to notice, in the least, the evident inclination of most of the settlers to avoid his company. He came down, every few days, to the little village before named as the place where the court was held, and lounged for hours about the tavern; which, during the winter season, was the common resort of the settlers. Here he soon encountered his old companions, Phillips, Codman, and the Elwoods, all of whom, notwithstanding the cold and demure manner with which the two former, at least, turned away from him, he saluted with careless ease, and as if nothing had happened to disturb their former social relations. And, having thus surmounted the somewhat difficult task of breaking the ice with them, without receiving the open and absolute repulse which, however disposed, they did not deem it wise to give him, he, at the next meeting, ventured to broach the subject of their late quarrel, affecting to laugh at their mutual exhibitions of folly in getting so angry with each other in court, under the belief, on his part, that *they* had got the furs, and, on their part, that *he* had made way with them; when neither of them were guilty, and ought not to be charged with the offence. For himself, he said, he was now satisfied, on thinking the matter over, who were the real culprits. They were a couple of "cussed runagate Indians," that had strolled over from Canada, and, having discovered his camp, had laid in wait for his absence. He had seen the tracks of two different-sized moccasins in the sand on the lake-shore, but two days before he left; but the circumstance was forgotten, or he should not have left the camp unguarded. It was a great loss for them all; but it would not help the matter to mourn now. It must be borne; and he knew of no way to make it up but to try their luck in another expedition. He should, for his part; for he had no notion of giving up so.

Such was the drift of his conversation at this interview; and, seeming to think he had ventured far enough for one experiment on their credulity, he dropped that subject and struck off on to others. But the next time he met them he contrived to turn the conversation upon the same theme; when, telling them with a confidential air that, a few days before he left camp, he discovered, on a stream coming in at the upper end of the Megantic, a succession of freshly-constructed beaver dams, which, from the number of houses and other indications around each, he thought must be occupied by one of the largest colonies of beavers ever collected on one stream in that part of the country, he directly proposed to them to join him, when the spring opened, in an expedition to secure this extraordinary collection of the valuable animals that were, unquestionably, still all there, and as unquestionably might be captured.

This story, with the accompanying proposal, presented, as Gaut well knew, the most tempting inducement that could be offered, to trappers. But it made no impression on Phillips and Codman. They deeply distrusted the man, his whole story, and the motives which they believed moved him to concoct it. Spurning in their hearts, therefore, the bait that had been so artfully laid for them, they would have nothing to do with *him* or his proposal. And, both then and thereafter, they remained unmoved, and stood proof against all the arguments his taxed ingenuity and devilish cunning could invent and bring to bear upon them.

With the infatuated Mark Elwood, however, the case seemed to be almost wholly reversed. He again listened,—was again lost. He, restless, uneasy, and evidently apprehensive of something he did not disclose, from continuing under the terrible displeasure which Gaut had so significantly manifested towards him,—he had appeared, from the first, to hail with pleasure the indications of the relenting mood of the other, and seemed but too glad to be again noticed with favor. He could see no reason to distrust the man's sincerity, he said, when others raised the question; and he was much inclined to adopt his version of the robbery and burning of their camp. When, therefore, the proposal of a new expedition was made, under the circumstances we have named, the blinded Elwood seemed fully prepared to accept it; and he would have openly and without reserve done so, but for the restraining presence of his companions, who, he felt conscious, would disapprove and deprecate his conduct. Gaut had noticed all this, and was not long in bringing about a private interview with his dupe and victim, which resulted, as might be supposed, in settling the matter in just the way he intended.

From that time, the conduct of Mark Elwood became wholly inexplicable to all his friends and acquaintances in the settlement. He commenced with defending Gaut Gurley, thus giving the lie to all he had said, and ended with declaring an intention of accompanying him in another trapping expedition to the upper lakes, to be entered upon on a given day in April, then near at hand. And, in spite of all the advice and warnings of his late associates in the former disastrous campaign; the remonstrances of his son, who shared in the apprehensions of the others; and the agonizing tears and entreaties of his wife, he strangely persisted in his purpose, and, like the fated one of the Scriptures, steadily "set his face" towards his contemplated destination.

"The man is *hurried!*" said Phillips to Codman, as they left Elwood's on a second and last visit, made with the sole object of dissuading him from a step which they shrank from themselves,—that of going into the distant forest with such a desperate fellow as they now deeply suspected Gaut Gurley to be,—"the man is evidently *hurried*. When I saw that look Gaut gave Elwood in court, I knew he was marked for destruction, more especially than the rest of us, who are doubtless both placed on the same list. And Elwood would see it himself, if he was right-minded. Yes, he is *hurried*, and can't help it. He will go, and God grant my fears may not be realized."

And he did go, but not alone. As soon as Claud became fully satisfied that his father's purpose was not to be shaken, he began earnestly to debate in mind the question whether he himself should not, as a filial duty, become a participant in the expedition, with the view of making his presence instrumental in averting the apprehended danger. And, although he perceived that his mother's distress, all troubled and doubtful as she was in deciding between her conflicting duties of affection, would be enhanced by the step; and, although his mind had been still more staggered by a brief confidential note from Avis Gurley, advising him, if not too late, to find means to break up the project of the expedition entirely, yet he finally made up his mind in the affirmative. And, accordingly, on the morning of the appointed day, both father and son, after a leave-taking with the despondent wife and mother, more ominously sad and mournful than had ever before marked their family trials, set forth again for the wild wastes of the lakes, with their now doubly questionable companion.

CHAPTER XVIII.

"But there was weeping far away;
And gentle eyes, for him,
With watching many an anxious day,
Were sorrowful and dim."
BRYANT'S MURDERED TRAVELLER.

It was the second week in May; and spring, delightful spring, sweet herald of happiness to all the living creatures that have undergone the almost literal imprisonment of one of the long and dreary winters of our hyperborean clime, was beginning to sprinkle the green glories of approaching summer over the reanimated wilderness. In the physical world, all seemed light and laughing around:

—"the green soil with joyous living things Swarm'd, the wide air was full of joyous wings."

The sun, no longer feebly struggling through the dark, obstructed medium of a northern winter's atmosphere, was throwing abroad his clear, unstinted floods of living light, bathing with soft radiance the diversified face of the basking forest, and gleaming far and brightly over the soothed waters of the sleeping lake. The mild and genial zephyrs were discoursing the low, sweet, melancholy music of their aeolian harps, among the gently-wavering tops of the whispering pines. The choral throng of feathered songsters were filling every grove, glade, or glen, of field and forest, with the glad strains of their merry melodies. And all nature seemed crying aloud, in the fulness of her happiness,

"The summer is coming; rejoice ye, rejoice!"

So smiled every thing, animate and inanimate, in the visible physical world, as circumscribed to this secluded settlement, on the morning when opened the first scene in the closing act of our story's changeful drama. But in the moral world, so far as the interests and feelings of most of our leading personages were involved, the skies were overcast with contrasted clouds of doubt and darkness.

On that morning, at the Elwood Landing, on the western shore of Umbagog, stood a collected group of excited people, of different ages and sexes, gazing anxiously across the lake in the direction of the great inlet, as if expecting the appearance of some object or person from that quarter. But, before naming the cause of their assembling and the objects of their present solicitude, we will leave them a moment for a brief—but, for the understanding of the reader, necessary—recurrence to what had transpired, in the interim between the departure of the two Elwoods and Gaut Gurley, and the present occasion.

For nearly a month after her husband and son left home, Mrs. Elwood had been wholly unable to obtain any tidings of them, or any information even of their locality on the upper lakes. And gloomily, O how gloomily, with her, passed the long and dreary days and sleepless nights of that dismal period! Little had occurred to vary the monotony of her harrowing anxieties; and that little tended rather to increase than relieve them. For, even from the limited intercourse she had with families of the settlers,—although their conversation, out of regard to her feelings, was restrained and guarded, when the subject nearest her heart was introduced,—she gathered the fact that she was not alone in her fears and anxieties, but that they were shared, to a greater or less extent, by the people of the whole settlement; among whom the subject was being daily discussed, at every fireside, with avowed apprehensions that some fearful fate was awaiting one or both of the Elwoods, in their sojourn in the forest, in whose dark recesses there would be no witnesses to restrain the evil-doer from the purposes of robbery and revenge which they generally believed he secretly entertained. But, among all the settlers, no one had exhibited so much anxiety and restlessness as the hunter, Phillips. He had been almost continually absent from home, evidently to distant places, but where and with what objects he declined to make known. The direction and object of one of these secret journeys, however, was inferred from the unexpectedly early return of Fluella, the lovely maid of the forest, who had no sooner reached her old home than she flew to the Elwood cottage, to mingle her tears and sympathies with those of the anxious and troubled matron; who, in the circumstances, could have received no more acceptable visit. With the opening of the season, also, other absentees had returned to the settlement. Carvil had come back, to ascertain what had been effected in relation to the supposed robbery of the furs, the fall before, having intrusted his interests to the care of Phillips; and now feeling, with the others, apprehensive for the result of the new expedition, he was anxiously awaiting the return of the absent trappers. Tomah, the eccentric young Indian, likewise had surprised the settlers by his sudden reappearance among them, in a suit of superfine broadcloth, hat and boots to match, gold watch, showy seals, and all the gewgaw *etceteras* that go to make up the animal they call a city dandy. He had sold his moose, it appeared, for four hundred dollars, and brought nearly the whole of it home on his bedizened person,— with the object, as he soon admitted, of dazzling the hitherto obdurate Fluella.

"Yes,—catch her sartain, now," he said, with a complaisant glance over his dashing rig, on departing for the chief's, as soon as he ascertained the fair object of his pursuit had returned to her father's. But he soon came back, in a great miff, and offered to sell the whole of his fine new outfit for just one half what it cost him. Contrary to expectation, he declared he would have nothing more to do with Gaut Gurley; concerning whom he had seen something, about the time of the trial, to awaken his suspicions, and against whom he now evidently stood ready to array himself, with the rest, on the next occasion.

With these few incidents, April passed away, and the first day of May, the usual limit of the fur season, had arrived; but with it the absent trappers had failed to make their appearance. Another week passed, and still they came not. "What could it mean?" was on every tongue. Men ominously shook their heads, and women and children began, in the connection, to talk in suppressed voices of the dark character of Gaut Gurley.

At this juncture, word came that Gaut had returned, and had several times been seen about his home. A man was immediately dispatched to Gaut's residence, for inquiries about the Elwoods; but the messenger returned and reported that Gaut said he parted with them on the Maguntic,—he to go over the mountains to his home, on the Magalloway, and they, in their canoe, that had been frozen up in Oquossak, the fall before, to go to Bethel to sell their furs. Further than this, he knew nothing about them.

"I don't believe a word of it!" exclaimed the hunter, who with many others had anxiously awaited, at the tavern, the messenger's return: "not one word of it! They would not have gone off to Bethel after such an absence, before returning home; or, if they had, they would have been here before this time. But the story shall be investigated without twelve hours delay. It is time we were moving in the business. Who will furnish me with a good saddle-horse?"

The horse was furnished; and within half an hour the excited hunter was speeding his way to Bethel.

He returned early the next morning, in a state of still greater excitement and concern than before; having ridden all night, in his anxiety to reach the settlement by the time people were up, so that immediate measures might be put afoot to scour the country in search of the missing Elwoods, whose continued absence had now become doubly mysterious and alarming, by the discovery he had made, as he feared he should, that they had not gone to Bethel at all, nor been seen or heard of anywhere in that direction.

The news of Gaut's return alone, his improbable story, and the discovery of its almost certain falsity, spread like wild-fire over the settlement; and the people, already prepared to believe the worst by their previous suspicions of Gaut's evil designs, rose up as one man, instinctively shuddering at the thought of the apprehended crime, and feeling irresistibly impelled to attempt something to bring about that fearful atonement which Heaven demands of every man who wilfully sheds the blood of his fellow-man. So deep and absorbing was this feeling, indeed, in the present instance, that men dropped their hoes in the field, left their axes sticking in the trees, and threw aside all other kinds of business, and, with excited and troubled looks, hurried off to the scene of action, to see, hear, and join in whatever movement the exigencies of the case might require to be made. And before night nearly the whole of the settlers, residing within a circuit of a dozen miles of the surrounding country, had assembled at the tavern in the rustic hamlet, which, as before mentioned, they made, on all extraordinary occasions, the place of their common rendezvous. Here, after conversing a while in scattered groups, exchanging in low, hurried tones, and with many an apprehensive glance around them, their various opinions and conjectures, they gradually gathered in one room in the tavern, formed themselves into something like an organized meeting, and began their deliberations. But, before they had settled on any definite course of action, their attention was suddenly turned from the channel their minds were all evidently taking, by a new and unexpected occurrence.

Two young men, who had that day been across the lake to the Great Rapids, for the purpose of fishing, returned to the village about sunset, with the news that they had discovered, at the foot of the most dangerous pass of the rapids, wedged in among the projecting flood-wood of the place, a partially-wrecked and stove canoe, which they both recognized as the one kept by the Elwoods at their landing last summer, and, of course, the one they took away with them in their succeeding fall expedition. This fact, all at once readily perceived, might throw an entirely new aspect over the whole of the mysterious affair; and they soon decided on dispatching the same young men, at daybreak the next morning, across the lake, to examine carefully both shores of the inlet up to, and some distance beyond, the place where they found the canoe, to see if they could find any thing else, or discover any indications going to show that anybody had been wrecked and drowned there; then to return, as quickly as possible, with the wrecked canoe in tow, and whatever else they might find, to the Elwood landing; where the company would assemble, by the middle of the forenoon, to receive them, hear their report, examine the canoe, and take action according to the circumstances.

It was done; and this was the occasion of the assembling at the landing of the mingled and anxious group which we began to describe near the commencement of this chapter, and to which we will now return.

Foremost in the mingled group of people which we have thus brought to view, was the agonized wife and mother of the missing or lost men; whose doubtful fate was also engrossing, though less intensely, every thought and feeling of the sympathizing company around her. She had gradually worked herself down to the extremest verge of the low shore, and had unconsciously placed one foot in the edge of the water, as if irresistibly drawn to the farthest possible limit in the supposed direction of those two objects of her affection, who, alive or dead, were still her all-in-all of this world; and there she stood, slightly inclined forward, but motionless, mute, and pale as a marble statue, with lips painfully compressed, and eyes, glazed and watery, intently fixed on the opposite shore of the lake to which she was looking for relief, at least from the terrible suspense under which she was suffering. By her side, a little back, stood the wife of the hunter, and two or three other women of the vicinity, who had more particularly interested themselves in her troubles,— some shedding sympathetic tears, and some offering an occasional word, which they hoped might in a slight degree divert her sorrows or console her in her anguish. But, alike regardless of their falling tears and soothing remarks, she gazed on, in unbroken silence, hour after hour, taking no note of time, or any object around her, in the all-absorbing intensity of her feelings. Little, indeed, was said by *any* of the company. The younger portion stood in hushed awe at the sight of grief in the older, and at the thought of what might the next hour befall. And the men, though visibly exercised by strong emotions, and occasionally revealing a trembling lip or starting tear, as they glanced at the face of the chief sufferer, yet offered scarce a remark to relieve the pervading gloom of the sad and anxious hour. The whole group, indeed, might have been taken for a funeral cortege, awaiting on the shore the expected remains of some deceased friend.

After standing in this manner till nearly noon, the company caught sight of a scarcely-perceptible object on the water, in the direction of the great inlet. And, although for some time it appeared like a speck, as seen against the low, green fringe of the opposite and far-distant shore, yet it at length so enlarged on the vision that the form of a canoe and the gleam of flashing oars became distinctly discernible. Soon a little variation in the line of approach brought not only the canoe and the rowers, but another canoe in tow, plainly in view; and then all knew that their painful suspense was about to be ended. Another half-hour had to be passed by the company, who still stood there in trembling expectation, awaiting the approach of the canoes; when, as the latter now came within hailing distance, the impatient hunter stepped down to the water's edge, and called out:

"What news do you bring?"

"None! but we have brought the canoe."

"I see; but have you made no discoveries?"

"None whatever."

"No caps, packs, or bunches of furs washed up anywhere?"

"No, nothing. We examined thoroughly both shores of the rapids, and found nothing, and no mark or sign of any thing about which any conclusion could be formed respecting the manner the canoe got there."

"But the oars?"

"We found them in the same flood-wood with the boat, and they appeared as if they were thrown out of the canoe when it struck."

The canoe, which was the object of scrutiny, and which had been injured much less than had been supposed, a break in the upper part of the bow being the only ruptured part, was now drawn up on the shore; when Phillips, Codman, and Tomah took upon themselves to go into a minute and careful inspection of every part of its outer and inner surface, together with every appearance from which any inference having the least bearing on the question at issue could be drawn by these experienced and observing canoe-men.

"Men no leave oars in canoe, when go over falls," at length observed the Indian, standing back with the air of one who has satisfied himself with an examination,—"no leave oars that way; have them out to use; and then, when upset, drop 'em in the river; where get scattered, go down, wash up different places, mile apart, may be,—not together, right close side of canoe, likely. Don't believe so much story, like that come to."

"Spoke like a man who knows something," said the trapper, the next to offer comments. "And here is a loosened slip-knot in the end of this bark boat-rope, which I have been looking at. See! it has been drawn into a fixed knot, that hasn't been altered since it has had considerable use and steady pulling through it, as I see by the chafed bark inside the small hole within the knot. The hole is too small to have been brought into this shape by hitching it to a stake or projecting limb of a tree on shore. It looks exactly as if a tie attached to some other canoe had been passed through it, to draw this canoe along by; and here is a slight mark of a knife, where that tie has been cut out, owing to the difficulty of untying. This canoe must have been hitched behind some other canoe, and towed down to the head of the rapids, and there sent adrift."

"Yes," responded the hunter, who had been particularly confining his attention to the outer and top edges along the sides of the boat; "yes; and here is the moss or scurf that had gathered on these upper edges, on both sides, during the snows and thaws of winter, still remaining entire and unbroken, in every part of this delicate weather coating, which even a thumbnail, as you see, can't pass over without marring it or leaving a mark. No man could have rowed this canoe twenty rods without grazing these edges and leaving marks on them. Yes, you are both right. This canoe, which

I suppose you all agree was Mr. Elwood's, has not been rowed since he left it hauled up on the shore of the Oquossak last fall, to be buried by the great snow-storm; and the Elwoods are both safe, for all being wrecked and drowned from *that* boat, or any other, I presume."

The countenance of Mrs. Elwood, who stood at some little distance from the spot where the examination of the canoe had been going on, but near enough to hear most of what was said, visibly brightened at this announcement. The hunter saw the expression, and a shade of anguish passed over his face, as, turning to those immediately around him, and speaking in a low, subdued, and commiserating tone, he resumed:

"I cannot find it in my heart to dampen the new-lighted hope which this turn of the affair seems to give that poor, wretched wife and mother. But, to my mind, all this makes it doubly certain that the Elwoods have met with foul play. It looks exactly like one of Gaut's devilish schemes of finesse, to cause this canoe to be sent down the rapids, and be so found as to lead folks to suppose the owners were drowned, and to put the public on a false scent. Yes, friends, you may depend there has been foul play,—I dare not guess how foul. I have felt it the last fortnight, as if same unseen hand was writing the dreadful secret on my heart. I feel it still, now stronger than ever. And I call God to witness my resolution, that I will know no rest or relaxing till I see the dark deed laid open to day, and its infernal author brought to justice. Will you all join me in the work, without flinching or flagging?"

The low but firmly-responded "Yes, yes, all of us," told the hunter that he would know no lack of efficient aid in carrying out his resolution.

"Let us, then," he said, "leave the women and boys, a few minutes, and retire back here a few rods, out of their hearing, to determine on the first steps to be taken."

In accordance with this suggestion, the men withdrew, by themselves, to a convenient place on the site of an old camping-ground, within the forest, a few rods farther up the lake, leaving Mrs. Elwood and her female attendants slowly retracing their steps back to her house, from which they had accompanied her to this spot, and the boys amusing themselves in seeing who could throw a stone farthest into the lake. The men, now relieved from the fear of causing Mrs. Elwood needless alarm, and of having their remarks reported by others of the mingled company,—to the injury, perhaps, of the investigation on hand,—at once gave vent to their smothered convictions, and feelings of indignation and horror, in an exciting debate; which soon resulted in the determination to dispatch, the next morning, four men in two canoes up the lakes, in search of the missing, or such traces of them as might lead to a discovery of their fate; while the rest should remain in the settlement, to watch for new indications there and keep a vigilant eye on the movements of the bold but wary villain, whom they all believed to be the perpetrator of the supposed outrage. But, before they had fully settled the details of their plan, their attention was arrested by a shouting from the boys, who announced that a strange canoe was approaching them from the other part of the lake. Hearing this, and thinking the new-comer might have perhaps arrived from the upper lakes, and could give them important information, the men immediately suspended their consultation, and came out to the landing to hail him, or to await his approach. They soon discovered that the rower was an Indian, and it was not long before the trapper began to recognize the canoe, from some peculiarity about the bow, to be his own, and the one he had left with the boats of his companions on the Oquossak the season before. This, if true, might lead to important developments; and the company kept their eyes keenly fixed on the rower, to see if he would manifest any disposition to avoid them. But he kept steadily on towards the landing, and, in another minute, was within near hailing distance.

"Hillo! my red friend, where did you get that canoe?" cried the trapper.

"Tell you soon,—you make me believe you right to know," quietly replied the native, without appearing to be in the least disturbed by the question, or any inference which might naturally be drawn from it.

"Well, I *can* make you believe I have a right to know, if you are *willing* to believe; for I can swear the canoe is my own, and prove it, too, by some of these gentlemen," returned the trapper, with warmth.

"Maybe,—we see soon," responded the other, an intelligent, good-looking, middle-aged Indian, now slipping ashore and firmly confronting the company.

"Now tell us where you got it, sir," again sharply demanded the trapper. "I have offered to swear to my ownership, and prove it; so tell how you came by it, unless you would have us believe you stole it."

"Stole it?" reproachfully said the Indian. "Ask that man," he added, pointing to Carvil, whom he appeared to have previously recognized,—"ask him, if me do thing like that?"

"Moose-killer, is this you?" exclaimed Carvil, who had been eying the stranger Indian with a hesitating air. "I thought, from the first, I knew you, but couldn't quite decide. Moose-killer, I am glad you have come. We are just at this time trying to search out a dark affair, which we fear has happened, and with which this boat you came in may possibly be connected. We should be glad to make a few inquiries of you, when you are ready to hear them. There need," he added, turning to the trapper and the others, "there need be no fear but this man will tell a true story; I have met him on the Great

Megantic, where he goes by the name I have called him, on account of his well-known expertness in moose-killing."

The Indian started at the significant allusion which had been made to the subject that was then engaging the attention of those present, and its possible connection with his canoe; and, with unusual promptness for one of his demure and slow-speaking race, announced himself ready to tell his story.

"Moose-killer is about to speak," said Carvil, looking round on the eagerly expectant company. "We will all listen. What he will say will be true."

"Hear, in my country," thereupon began Moose-killer, in the abbreviated, broken, and sententious language peculiar to the Red Man,—"hear, in my country, beaver bring more this side the mountains; so come over, and been to Bethel-town to sell 'em. Come over mountains, down piece, the river you call Magalloway,—then strike off down to big lake, Megantic. Then follow shore long way; but stop sudden,—start back! See much blood on the leaves,—trail all along down to the water. Then go back, look again,—find where man fall, bleed much,—die,—lay there till dead quite. Man, because see where hands catch hold of moss, leaves,—feet kick in ground. All dead, because feet limber and no catch in brush dragging to shore,—find where canoe hitch to shore,—dead man put in, rowed away, sunk in lake, likely. Look all over ground again, much time,—then come on long way, and find that canoe, hid in bushes,—take it, go sell beaver,—then come here quick to tell story, see who missing."

We will not undertake to describe the intense excitement which this brief but pregnant story of the Indian produced on the company, who; though hoping to gather something from him that might be of use in the inquiry on hand, were yet little expecting a development so startling as this. They— especially those but little acquainted with the Indian character—could, at first, hardly believe that a story of such horrors, if true, could be told so quietly, and with so little apparent feeling, as the narrator had exhibited during his recital; and they immediately subjected him to a long and close cross-examination. Nothing, however, was elicited to weaken his story, but some things to confirm it. Among these was a faint stain of blood, which Moose-killer pointed out to the company, in the bow of the canoe, and which was evidently but lately made; while the size and height of the man, supposed to be murdered, which the Indian judged of by a similar curious process with that by which he reached his other conclusions, were seen to correspond with the dimensions of the elder Elwood; who was believed to be the man thus indicated, though it left the fate of Claud still shrouded in mystery.

"Poor Mark Elwood!" exclaimed the hunter, with a sigh, as they closed their examination of the Indian. "He is dead; whatever may have become of his son, for whom there is still some hope, *he*, at least, is dead! murdered in cold blood! and who need doubt the identity of the accursed author of the deed?"

"This is, certainly, something like tangible evidence," responded Carvil, whose former studies enabled him to speak more understandingly, in the matter of legal evidence, than his companions. "And, though it is still only circumstantial, yet, when taken in connection with Gaut's false story, and all other of the attending circumstances, it stands out most remarkably significant against the man; and, even without any additional proof, it would, I think, warrant us in arresting him."

"In God's name, then, let it be done, before he escapes from the country!" cried the hunter, with startling emphasis. "But we must all keep the discoveries we have made to-day, as well as the movements we may now make, as secret as death, lest he hear of them and take the alarm."

An earnest consultation was then held, and a plan of operations soon adopted. By this it was arranged that Moose-killer—who, when he had gathered what was known of Gaut Gurley, and obtained a description of his person, entered into the arrangements with an unexpected alacrity—it was arranged that Moose-killer, Carvil, Tomah, and two of the settlers, should start immediately up the lakes, in further search for the body of Mark Elwood (whose fate was now treated as settled), and, also, for a more general search round the two upper lakes for his son, Claud; who, it was hoped, had by some means been separated from his father, and suffered to escape, despite the improbability that he would remain so long absent, if nothing had befallen him. Phillips also concluded to accompany them as far as the next lake above, to see the chief and his daughter, to confide to them the discoveries of the day, and put them on the lookout for further indications. The rest of the company were to return quietly and separately, as far as could conveniently be done, to the village, and there remain till after dark; when two of their number were to ride, as fast as horses could carry them, to Lancaster, for warrants, a sheriff, and his posse, to be on the ground as early as possible the next morning; while others were to proceed up the Magalloway, and lurk round in the woods within sight of the house of Gaut Gurley, as spies on his movements.

The company then separated on their several destinations; and, during the remainder of the afternoon, nothing occurred in the settlement which need here be mentioned, except the secret and cautiously-made preparations for the proposed action of the night, that, though imperceptible to the uninitiated, were yet actively going on at the village. About sunset, however, the hunter returned from his visit to the chief's; but in a state of no little perplexity and concern, at an event which he unexpectedly found had there occurred. This was the unaccountable absence of Fluella, who, without apprising her father of her intentions, had secretly left home several days before. As the hunter had depended considerably on the girl's acuteness and means of observation at the commanding point of her residence, he was both disappointed and puzzled at her absence. And, as he had been debating with himself, on his way across the lake, whether he had not better call on Mrs. Elwood, and take the first step towards gradually preparing her mind for the worst, in regard to her husband, he now resolved to do so, with the further object of getting her version of Fluella's absence at such a juncture. Accordingly, he called at the house; and, seeing the afflicted woman's entreatingly expectant looks, he at once entered on his painful task by hinting his fears for the fate of her husband; when, somewhat to his surprise, she cut him short by sadly remarking:

"I know it all."

"How?—what have you heard?" eagerly asked the hunter.

"I don't know it by what I have heard," she replied, in the same sad accents; "for I have heard less, perhaps, than you; but I knew it would be so, from the hour he departed. And, a few days ago, my heart received a shock. It was from the same blow that killed him. Yes, poor Mr. Elwood is dead! I have buried him! But my son Claud—O, my son Claud!" The astonished hunter then told her of the singular absence of Fluella; when, again to his surprise, she started up, and joyfully exclaimed, "He lives!—though in danger, perhaps, he lives, and I shall see him again!"

Wondering whether her reason was not unsettled, the hunter departed, and hurried on to the village.

CHAPTER XIX.

"What justice ever other judgment taught,
But he should die who merits not to live."
SPENSER.

About the middle of the afternoon, on the day next succeeding the eventful one which was marked by the occurrences narrated in the last chapter, a cavalcade of about a dozen men on horseback, followed by a single wagon, containing some fire-arms, two or three pairs of iron handcuffs, and a few other articles of luggage, came clattering down the road from the west, towards the tavern with which the reader has already been made familiar. The men, who had been dispatched for the shire-town of the county, had ridden hard all night, reached the place at daylight, drummed up the officers of justice, got them started at an early hour, and urged them on with such speed that, within twenty hours, they had arrived at the scene of action. After the halt of an hour at the tavern, for rest and refreshment, and a brief consultation with the settlers, the sheriff, and his posse, now swelled by volunteers from the settlement, set forth, under the guidance of Phillips, for the residence of the supposed criminal, calculating to reach there about dusk,—the hour they deemed most favorable for making the arrest. After proceeding in silence about two-thirds of the way to their destination, they halted, to make their final preparations and arrangements for the onset; when, knowing the great strength and desperate character of the man with whom they would have to deal, they first carefully prepared their fire-arms, and then detailed a half-dozen of their number, most conversant with the locality, to go forward, spread themselves around the borders of Gaut's clearing, and cautiously advance to the house, so as to head off any attempt he might make to escape, when the main body made their appearance. All the time spent in these precautions, however, as well as this whole jaunt thus far up the river, was destined to be mostly lost; for, as the company were again beginning to move forward, they were met by the scouts, dispatched the night before, hurrying back, most of them in a disabled condition, and with the report that Gaut had escaped about an hour before. They had lain in their coverts all day, and in the fore part of it nothing had been seen to excite their suspicions; but, towards night, they noticed him cleaning his rifle and pistols, as near as they could judge, and then, soon after, bringing out a pack and placing it by the side of his rifle at the door; and scarcely had they time to concentrate before he came out, shouldered his pack, took his arms, and proceeded towards a canoe moored on the bank of the river. They then instantly resolved to intercept him; and, running for the spot, came up to him just as he had laid his rifle in the boat; when he turned upon them with the suddenness and fury of a pursued tiger; seized the foremost, who had laid his hands on the canoe, and, with giant strength, threw him headlong into the river; hurled the second with stunning effect on the ground; knocked down a third with his fist; leaped into his canoe, sent it swiftly across the stream, ran up the opposite bank, and disappeared in the woods, before they had recovered from their confusion, or thought of having recourse to their rifles to stop him.

"Slipped through our fingers and gone!" said the sheriff with an air of chagrin and disappointment.

"Yes, for this onset," said Codman, the next to volunteer remarks in the provoking nonplus in which they now all found themselves. "Yes, but I should like mightily to know how he got wind of our movements? If the devil didn't tell him, I don't think he done as well by his friend as he ought."

"Perhaps," rejoined the sheriff, after the laugh of some and the approving glances of others, which had followed the characteristic remark of the trapper, had passed away,—"perhaps he, or some of his family, caught a glimpse of these scouts round their clearing during the day; or perhaps he has an accomplice, or tool, whom he had engaged to watch public movements, and bring him word."

"I have thought of some such thing, myself," remarked Phillips. "In the case of his robbing our camp, last fall, I felt quite confident he must have had some accomplice, or some secret agent, to take off the furs for him. If he has such an one now, I think it must be a Jesuit priest, as I have heard that such a looking personage has, once or twice, been seen at Gaut's house since he moved into the settlement."

"Well, if the villain has such a character as that in tow, he would be devil enough for all common purposes," responded the sheriff. "But, however all that may be, I fear he has struck a line for Canada, and this is the last we shall ever see of him in this country."

"Not for Canada," confidently said the hunter; "for I know enough about him to make me feel quite sure that he will never again trust his head within reach of British authority."

"Ah!" exclaimed the sheriff, "what is it you know?"

"I think it had better not be told just yet," answered the other, decisively. "Let us first see whether he can't be caught and hung here, for his last crying offence."

"But do you think he can yet be overtaken, and arrested?" asked the former.

"Certainly I do," returned the hunter, with earnest confidence. "He must, and *shall*, be taken! God's curse is on the man; and he will never, I tell you, *never* be suffered to escape us."

"Well, then," resumed the sheriff, thoughtfully, "what course do you think he will take, and where secrete himself, so that he can be found? I, on my part, stand ready to do every thing in my power to bring the miscreant, of whose guilt I think there can now be but little doubt, to immediate justice. Now, as you are said to be a man of observation and energy, Mr. Phillips, let us have the benefit of your opinion and advice in the matter."

"It is my opinion," said the hunter, in response, after dropping his head a moment in study, "it is very clearly my opinion that the fellow will now aim to reach some of the eastern cities,—over the Umbagog, most likely, in a canoe that he keeps concealed somewhere on the western shore, which is only a mile or two over this ridge, that rises from the other bank of the river, here against us. He will not be likely to come back to his house, or the river, where he will still suppose we are on the watch; nor will he start out on the lake till after dark, lest he be seen, and his course traced; but lie concealed till that time in some of the difficult rocky steeps that shut down to the lake."

"Your ideas of his probable aims and movements appear reasonable, Mr. Phillips. Now, what are the steps you would advise to be taken for his apprehension?" asked the sheriff.

"Well, my plan would be something like this," replied the hunter, musingly. "I would post half a dozen men, for the night,—to be relieved in the morning,—a half mile or so apart, along this river, above and below here, to be walking back and forth, and occasionally firing a gun. The others go back, and a sufficient number get on to the lake before dark to have canoes in station every quarter of a mile along the western shore. Codman, you will be a good hand to manage this company. As for myself, I will wade the river somewhere hereabouts, go over through the woods to the lake-shore, be mousing round the shore a little, in search of his canoe, and, if I find it, be out on the water by the time you get there; if not, I will be within call of some of you, and give, for a signal, the cry of a raccoon, which I can imitate tolerably, I believe."

"But you don't propose to go alone?" asked several, anxiously. "It might be dangerous business, if you should happen to encounter him with no help within call."

"Yes, I think I will go alone," quietly replied the hunter. "If he can see me before I do him, he will do better than I think he can. And, if I *do* get my eye on him first, he will stop and yield, or die, as sure as my rifle is true to its old trust; for I should feel it my bounden duty to stop him by bullet, if need be, in case he should attempt to flee, as much as I should to shoot a painter carrying off one of my own children."

By the approval of the sheriff, and the concurrence of all, the hunter's plan of operations was immediately adopted. And, accordingly, the designated numbers were told off to man the river, and at once set in motion to perform the duty; while the rest retraced their way to the village, except the hunter, who, seeking a shoal place, waded the river, and was soon out of sight among the thickets of the opposite bank.

On the return of the company to the tavern, every boat to be found on the river, from that place to the lake, was immediately put in requisition, for the service of the night. And by early twilight, eight canoes, each containing two or three well-armed men, led on by the trapper, in a single canoe, were seen emerging from the outlet into the broad lake, and slowly filing off along its western border. Coasting in closely to the shore, so as to keep within the shadow of the woods, they pursued their noiseless way up the lake, to a point where the low, marshy land lying between the lower part of the Umbagog and the Magalloway rises into the gradually-swelling ridge, which, a mile or two farther on, becomes a rocky, precipitous mountain, whose beetling cliffs, overhanging the deep, dark waters beneath, were crowned with their primeval growth of towering pines. Here they paused long enough to station one of their canoes, near a small point, commanding a view across the corresponding coves on either side; and then cautiously proceeded onward, dropping a canoe, in like manner, every five or six hundred yards, till the extremity of the western coast was reached, the line efficiently manned, and the trapper left to cruise alone over the cordon of boats thus stretched along the shore, to carry any needed intelligence, and make independent observations. It was now dark, and, being a moonless night, all within the shade of the mountains, especially, was wrapt in almost impenetrable gloom; so that the ear, rather than the eye, must now be depended on for whatever discoveries were to be made. Nothing as yet, to the disappointment and increasing anxiety of the company, had been seen or heard of the hunter.

"He cannot have been killed, so soon, can he?" whispered the sheriff, in one of the last-stationed canoes, as the trapper glided alongside, to hold communication with the officer.

"No," was the low-toned reply; "that could not have happened, if there were any *fear* of such a thing, without one or more rifle-shots, which, in this calm evening, and this favorable locality for conveying sounds to a great distance, we must have heard, even down to the tavern. No, I will risk him. I think he must have got on to the fellow's trail, and, if near the lake, lies in some spot where he can't move away without danger of alarming the game.

We have nothing to do but wait patiently. Phillips knows we are here in waiting, and he will report himself as soon as he can."

They did not, however, have to wait long. In a few minutes, a small, shrill, quavering cry, which few could have distinguished from that of a raccoon, rose from a thicket on the shore, a short distance below.

"Ah! that is he," softly cried the trapper; "I know the thicket he is hailing from. If you will remain just where you are, I will scull my canoe down to the spot, take him in with me, if he has not found a boat,—or at any rate bring him here to make his report."

Like the gliding of a fish, shrinking away from sight, the light canoe, under the invisible impulse of the dexterously handled oar of the trapper, passed noiselessly away, and disappeared in the darkness. But, long before the expectant officer, who had been vainly listening for some sound, either of the going or the coming of the absent canoe, had thought of its return, it was again at his side, with the anticipated addition to its occupants.

"Here is the man, to speak for himself," said the trapper, putting out a hand to guard off and prevent the canoes from grazing.

"Well, Mr. Phillips," said the sheriff, in the same cautious under-tone by which all their communications had been graduated, "we are all looking to you,—what is your report?"

"In the first place, that he is here."

"Where?"

"Sixty or seventy rods to the north of us, in a secure retreat up among the rocks, about a dozen rods from the shore."

"Are you sure of that?"

"Yes."

"How did you make the discovery?"

"I will tell you. When I came over, I struck down to the lake, nearly abreast the lower end of the ridge, and cautiously moved along the shore, upwards, in search of the suspected boat; without discovering it, however, till I came to the rocky pass I have alluded to, a short distance above here; when, peering out into the approaching darkness, I caught sight of it run under a treetop lying partly in the water. Your boats had not got on there; and thinking, if I took the boat out on to the water, as I had proposed, he might discover the loss too soon, take the alarm, and conclude to escape through the woods round the upper lakes, I varied my plan, and stationed myself back a few rods, to see if he would not come down to escape by his canoe. I had trailed him to the top of this rocky eastern slope, before I struck down to the lake, and knew he must be somewhere near; so I cocked my rifle, for instant use, and stood ready for his approach. And in a short time I caught the sound of his movements, sliding cautiously down the rocky steeps from the spot above, where I suspected he had housed himself. But, before he reached the bottom of the short ravine he must come down, or could be seen where I stood, a dry stick unluckily broke under my foot, and the sound, as I perceived at once, brought him to a stand. And, though he did not know, and don't know yet, whether the sound was caused by the step of man or beast, yet he soon seemed to think it safest to retreat; and my ear could distinctly trace his movements, as he clambered and pulled himself along back up the ledges to his retreat. I then went down to the shore; and perceiving, from the slight agitation of the water and the faint sound of its gurgling under oars, that you had got on to the ground, I stole down the shore a piece, and gave the signal, as you heard."

"Are you familiar with the place where you think he lies concealed?"

"Yes, nearly as much so as with my own door-yard."

"What sort of a place is it, and how many ways are there to reach it or to escape from it?"

"It is the most curious place in all these parts, and there is but one way, I ever could find, to get to it; and that is, by climbing up the ledgy shelf of the face of the hill, through a sort of ravine that opens from it down to the lake, where there is scarce room, enough, on either side, to pass along the shore between the perpendicular cliffs and the water. It is an old bear's den, in fact, passing horizontally into the rocks twelve or fifteen feet, of varying breadth, and, after you get in, from three to six feet in height. I have taken at least a half-dozen fine bears from it, in my day, and supposed I was the only one knowing of it; but Gaut must have discovered it before this; for I at once found by his trail that he steered directly for the spot, on leaving the Magalloway."

"He did?" interposed the trapper; "*he* find it, when he has been here in the settlement less than a year, and knows little about the woods; and *I*, who have been here a dozen years, knew nothing about it? He never found it without *help*, and that, too, from the same character that let him know we were coming to his house, to-day. I tell you, the Old Boy is in that man!"

"Then we will hang him and the Old Boy with one rope," resumed the hunter, "for we are now sure of him."

"I hope so," said the sheriff; "but can he be taken to-night?"

"He might, possibly, if we were willing to run risks enough," replied the hunter, doubtfully. "But I should hardly think it advisable to make the attempt. He could not be drawn from the cave, if we made the onset; while, if we entered it, he could easily kill several of us before he could be secured."

"What shall be done, then?"

"I have been studying on that, and the best thing I can think of, is, to post men enough to guard him securely through the night; and then have on force enough in the morning to unburrow him, by some means or other, which we will contrive when the time comes."

"But will he not come down, to escape in his boat, to-night?"

"I rather expect not. After hearing the noise I made, and, then coupling it with my signal, which he will then be suspicious of, as well as of the sounds that most likely have reached or will reach his ears from some of our boats; after all this, he will, probably, be afraid of falling into a trap, and would prefer taking his chances of escape by daylight. But, if he should come down, I will arrange things so that we will have him, to a dead certainty."

The suggestions of the hunter were again adopted; and he was again requested to take the lead in putting the proposed plan into execution.

Accordingly, after directing the trapper to concentrate those stationed in their canoes above with those in one or two below, he entered the boat with the sheriff and his associate; and, taking an oar, slowly rowed along towards the place he had designated as the retreat of the desperate outlaw, on whose seizure they were so resolutely determined.

After reaching the spot, and waiting till the expected boat-crews arrived, the hunter quietly landed, and stationed two of the men in the narrow pass north of the gorge, with orders to keep a sharp lookout through the night, hail whoever might approach, and shoot him down before suffering him to escape. He next led two more up round the nearest approaches of the cave, and posted one on each side, a little above it, to prevent all possibility of escape over the rocks and ledges in that direction; and then, returning down to the shore, selected the trapper to occupy with him the southern pass to the gorge, thus reserving for himself, and the man on whom he believed he could best rely in an emergency, the post where an encounter would be most likely to occur. After completing these arrangements, and landing a pair of handcuffs from the sheriff's boat, he dismissed the officer to collect all the rest of the company, not thus retained, and return to the village for the night, and for a fresh rally the next morning.

It was now ten o'clock at night; and from that time, for the next six hours, the stillness and darkness of death brooded over the slumbering waters of the lake. The mute men on guard,—to whom the slowly-passing hours seemed doubly long and gloomy, from the oppressive sense of the duty of silence,—stood immovably at their posts, alternately employing themselves in guessing at the hour of the night, and intently listening to catch some sound which should indicate the presence of the dreaded object of their watch. But, through the whole night, no such sound or indication reached their strained senses; and most of them, at length, were brought to the belief that either he had never been there, or that he had, by some unknown means, effected his escape. The hunter, however, never for a moment permitted his faith to waver. He not only felt confident that Gaut was still in his dark cage in the rocks, but that, the next day, safe means would be found to uncage him, and deliver him over to hands of justice, to undergo the penalties of his crimes. And, as soon as the anxiously-awaited daylight began to make its appearance in the east, he began gradually to work his noiseless way into the mouth of the gorge, and then up over the steeps and ragged ledges, till he had gained a stand under cover of a tuft of clinging evergreens, where he could obtain an unobstructed view of the mouth of the cavern, some six rods above. Here, low crouched behind his bushy screen, with rifle cocked and levelled at the entrance, he lay, silently awaiting the approach of daylight, expecting that Gaut would then, at least, be peering out to ascertain the state of affairs on the shore below. And the event soon showed the correctness of his reasoning. As the brightening flushes of morning fell on the water, and began to throw the reflected light on the face of the mountain, so as to bring its darker recesses to view, the hunter's practised ear soon detected a movement within the cave; and presently the head, and then the shoulders, of the wary outlaw rose gradually in sight against the rocks, immediately over the low entrance.

"Yield yourself a prisoner, or die!" suddenly broke from the lips of the concealed hunter.

Gaut cast a startled glance around him, and then instantly threw himself to the ground, but barely in time to escape the bullet of the exploding rifle below, which struck the rock in the exact spot that a half-second before was darkened by the shade of his head and shoulders.

"Went through the hair on top of his head, I think, but missed his skull by something like an inch, probably," said the hunter, quickly gliding down a few feet over the edge of the shelf, where he lay so as to put a rock between him and the mouth of the cave. "But, on the whole, I am glad of it; for I had rather see him go by the hand of the hangman than my own."

The hunter then quietly reloaded his rifle, and went down among his excited companions; who, the ban of silence being now removed by his example, came forward to talk over this unexpected and startling incident of the morning, which had served the double purpose of demonstrating to the former that Gaut would never surrender himself a prisoner, and to the latter, the doubted fact that the object of their search was there, as represented to them the evening before. With the whole of them, indeed, the affair had now assumed a new aspect. Phillips and Codman put their heads together, and began to start and discuss various expedients for dislodging the intrenched fugitive; while the others, in their excitement and agitation, walked hurriedly about in their confined positions speaking or thinking of the desperate and dangerous struggle now likely soon to ensue in the attempted capture, and anxiously awaiting the arrival of the sheriff and the additional force, which, it was understood, he would rally and bring on with him.

"They are coming!" at length cried one of the men from the cliff above; "they are coming in troops, and in all directions."

The men on shore now eagerly ran down to the farthest projecting rocks, or on fallen trees extending into the water, to obtain unobstructed views of the company thus announced to be approaching in the distance; when, instead of the few they had expected, they beheld a whole fleet of canoes emerging from the distant outlet below, and rowing with all speed towards them; while, at the same time, another company of boats was seen approaching from the settlement around the upper end of the lake.

It appeared that, when the sheriff with his attendants reached the village the evening before, and announced the exciting tidings that the desperate man, whom all were so intent on hunting down, had been driven to a stronghold among the rocks of the mountain up the lake, where it might require a large force to take him, men started off in all directions, and rode all night with the news; which, flying like wind over this and the adjoining settlements, threw the whole country, for thirty or forty miles around, into commotion, and put scores of bold men immediately on the march for the scene of action. And the upshot was that, by sunrise the next morning, more than fifty men, hurrying in from all quarters, had assembled at the village, and having appropriated all the boats on the rivers, for many miles above and below, had joined the company of the sheriff, and under his lead were now on their way to the great point of attraction; together with many others entering the lake from other quarters.

In a short time the long retinue of canoes came clustering to the shore; when the motley company, preceded by the sheriff and his immediate attendants, all landed, and, crowding around the hunter and his associates, listened, with many a half-suppressed exclamation, indicative of the deep excitement that agitated the mass, to the recital of the discoveries and incidents of the morning.

"I cannot believe," said the sheriff who had been listening with keen interest to the hunter's account of his bold but fruitless attempt to compel the submission of the desperado, "I cannot believe, after all, that the fellow will be so foolhardy as to persist in his refusal to surrender, when he knows there is now no longer any chance for him to escape. I will try him faithfully before resorting to extreme measures."

"That may be well enough, perhaps," remarked the hunter, demurely, feeling a little rebuked for his own hastiness in firing on the man, by some of the expressions of the officer; "yes, that will be well enough. But, if you succeed in drawing him out to be taken by means of words alone, I will try the experiment on the very next wolf or painter I drive into his den."

"Nevertheless, it shall be tried," returned the officer.

And accordingly, having called to his side a small band of well-armed assistants, he proceeded with them up the gorge, till he had gained the shelf which afforded the hunter a covert in the previous assault; when he stepped fearlessly out in full view of the mouth of the cavern, and, with a loud voice, calling the name of Gaut Gurley, "commanded him, in the name and by the authority of the State of New Hampshire, to come out and surrender himself a prisoner, to answer, in court, to the charges set forth in a warrant then ready to be produced."

The officer now paused; and all listened; but no sound came from the cave. The summons was then repeated, in a still louder and more determined tone of voice. And this time a sound, resembling the growl of a chafed tiger, was heard within, belching out a volley of muttered curses, and ending with the distinguishable words of defiance:

"If you want me, come and take me; and we will see who dies first."

"Your blood be on your own head, then, obstinate wretch!" exclaimed the excited officer. "Men, prepare to throw a volley of bullets into that cavern. Ready—aim—fire!"

The single report of a half-dozen exploding muskets instantly followed the word, ringing out and reverberating along the mountain like the shock of a field-piece; while, with the dying sound, a hoarse shout of derisive laughter from the cave greeted the ears of the awe-struck and shuddering company around.

"There is no use in that," said the hunter, who had followed and posted himself a little in the rear of the besieging party, under the apprehension that the besieged might make a rush out of his retreat, in the smoke and confusion consequent on the firing,—"there is no use in any thing of that kind. The entrance, after the first four or five feet, suddenly expands into quite a large space, into one of the corners of which he could easily step, as he doubtless did just now, and be safe against a regiment of rifles from without."

"Then we will smoke him out!" fiercely exclaimed the sheriff, recovering from his astonishment at finding the culprit had not been annihilated, and beginning to be enraged at seeing himself and his authority thus alike despised; "we will smoke him out, like a burrowed wild beast, and soon convince the scoffing villain that we are not to be foiled in this manner. Hillo, there, below! gather and bring up here at least a cartload of dry and green boughs."

With eager alacrity the throng below sprang to do the bidding of the officer; and, in a short time, they came clambering up the steeps, with their shouldered loads of mingled material, to the post occupied by the advanced party; who took, and, keeping as much as possible out of the range of the entrance, carried them up, and threw them over the next shelf on to the little level space lying around the mouth of the cavern. This process was briskly continued, till a pile as large as a haycock was raised against the upright ledge through which the cave opened by a low narrow mouth at the bottom. A fire was then struck, a pine knot kindled, and held ready for the intended application; when the sheriff, proclaiming to the desperate object of these fearful preparations what was in store for him, commanded him once more, and for the last time, to surrender. But, receiving no reply, he then, ordering the men to stand ready with poles to scatter the material the moment the victim should cry for mercy, seized the flaming brand and hurled it into the most combustible part of the pile before him.

Within the space of a minute the appearance of the quickly-catching blaze, now seen leaping in a thousand dimly-sparkling tongues of flame, from layer to layer and from, side to side, through the crevices of the loosely-packed mass, gave proof that the whole pile was becoming thoroughly ignited. And the next moment the cave, and the whole visible range of rocks above, were lost to sight in the dense cloud of smoke that deeply wrapt and rolled over them. Expecting every instant to hear the agonized cries of the victim, now seemingly enfolded in the very embrace of the terrible element, calling aloud for mercy and offering submission, the whole company, crowding the gorge below, or peering over from the surrounding cliffs, climbed for the purpose, stood for some time mute and appalled at the spectacle, and the thought of the fearful issue it involved. No sound or sight, however, except the crackling of the consuming fagots and the flaring sheet of the ascending flames, greeted their expectant senses.

"Pretty much as I have long thought it would turn out, in the end," said the trapper, the first to break the silence, as the fire was seen to be slacking away, without any thing yet being heard from the dreaded inmate of the cave.

"His master is taking him off in a winding-sheet of smoke and flame. I shouldn't be surprised at a clap of thunder or an earthquake to wind up with."

"At any rate," observed another of the crowd, "he must be suffocated by this time."

"Yes," responded a third, "dead, dead as a door-nail; so, there is an end of the incarnate Beelzebub that we have known by the name of Gaut Gurley."

"I am not so clear about that," now interposed the hunter, who had stood intently watching the varying aspects of the fire and smoke about the cave. "I thought, myself, that this operation must put him on begging terms, if any thing would; and the question is, whether it wouldn't now, before he found himself in any danger of smothering. I don't understand it; but stay,—what is that rising from the top of the rocks, some distance back from the front of the den? Mr. Sheriff, do you see it?"

"See what, sir?"

"Why, that slender column of smoke rising gently out of the top of the rocks, directly over the cave, and growing more visible every moment, as the smoke from the fire down here in front becomes light and thin in the clear blaze."

"I do see what appears, here, to be something of the kind not proceeding directly from the fire;—yes, plainly, now. What does it mean, Mr. Phillips?"

"It means that the rascal has a chimney to his house, or what, for his safety, is the same. The rocks forming the top of the cavern are piled up so loosely that the smoke rises through them almost as easy and natural as from a chimney. He had nothing to do but to throw himself on the bottom, to be out of its way, and breathe as good air as the best of us."

"By Heavens, Phillips, I believe you are right! And that is not all there is to it, either: if our smoking-out experiment has failed, it has shown a better one. The same looseness of the rocks that permitted the escape of the smoke so freely, will permit, also, their being removed or torn away. We will now uncage him by digging down into his den. Ho there! my merry men below, go to cutting heavy pry-poles, and look up your crow-bars, picks, sledge-hammers, and shovels. There is work for you all."

As soon as the unexpected discoveries which had led to these new orders, and consequent change of the whole plan of attack, were understood and fully comprehended by all, the solemn and revolting character of the scene was instantly converted into one of bustle and animation. As the plan thus indicated by the sheriff required the scene, of operations to be transferred to the top of the rocks above the cave, to which there was no means of access from the gorge in front, he, leaving a strong guard in the pass now occupied, took the hunter and came down to the shore; when the latter, followed by the officer and a score of resolute, strong-armed men with their various implements, led the devious way back through the woods, and up round the ledgy and precipitous face of the mountain, till they reached a point a little above the level of the cave. Here they paused, and sent the hunter out along a lateral shelf of the declivity, to search for the most accessible path to their destination. While the company were pausing here for this purpose, their attention was suddenly arrested by the heralding shouts of another company of men, evidently approaching from the other side of the mountain. And, soon after, a band of a dozen well-armed, hardy-looking fellows, headed by a tall, powerfully-framed man, made their appearance, pushing their way down the brush-tangled steeps from above.

"Turner!" exclaimed the sheriff, addressing the leader of the approaching band, who was at once recognized to be an ex-sheriff of the county, and one of the most daring and successful felon-hunters ever known in northern New-Hampshire; "General Turner, of all men you are the one I should have most wished to see, just at this time. We have a tough case on hand; but how did you get here?"

"The only way left for us. When we reached the tavern down here on the river, not a boat was to be had; and so we steered up the Magalloway, and came over by land, as you see. I had heard of this desperate character, and your dealings with him, before the present outrage, and have now come to help you put him through. Now tell us the state of the siege,—some idea of which we got from a man we met, a mile back on our way."

The sheriff then related all that had transpired, and named the new plan of operations, of which they were then proceeding to test the feasibility.

"We will have him!" said Turner, with a determined look. "If we can't tear away the rocks with bars and sledges, we will send off for a barrel of gunpowder to blow them open; and if that fails, I will go into the cave, myself, and if I don't snake him out before I've done with him, he must be a harder customer than it has ever yet been my lot to encounter."

By this time the hunter had returned, and now pointed out the best way to the place of which they were in quest; when the sheriff, ex-sheriff, and their respective followers, preceded by their guide, commenced forcing their passage along the craggy cliffs; and, within ten minutes, they found themselves standing on the off-set forming the rocky roofing of the cavern. The appearance of the place was much more favorable for the proposed attempt at excavation than any of them had anticipated. From the front face of the rock, which was pierced by the mouth of the cave at the bottom, and which presented a perpendicular of about fifteen feet, the topmost stones rapidly fell off to a depression over the centre of the cave, which, it was at once seen, must greatly reduce the depth of rock to be removed or broken up, before reaching the interior. And, in addition to this encouraging discovery, the rocks in and around this depression, through which the smoke was yet visibly oozing, appeared to be detached from the main ledge, and, though heavy, such as might be removed by appliances at command. Still, there was a formidable mass to be disrupted and removed before an entrance could be effected in that direction. But the men, impatient of inaction, and eager to be doing something to forward the common object,—like all bodies of excited people anxious to cooperate, but unable to decide on a course of action,—scarcely waited to be told what was wanted, before they all sprang to the work with that resistless union of faith and exertions which requires no intervention of miracles to remove mountains. The moss, earth, decayed wood, and all else of the loose covering of rocks, quickly disappeared under their busy hands or rapidly-plied implements. The smaller stones and broken fragments, as soon as loosened or beat off by the bars and sledges, were seized and hurled in showers over the surrounding ledges; the larger ones, when started from their beds by the long heavy prys, were grappled with the united strength of all that could get to them, rolled up, pitched over the precipice in front, and sent bounding and crashing down the gorge below. And the whole forest resounded with the din of their heavy blows and the mingling sounds of their varied labors.

While all who could find room to work on the excavation were thus briskly pushing forward their operations, a smaller party were engaged in beating down the rocky battlement in front; and so vigorously and successfully were the efforts of these also directed, that, in a short time, the top was so lowered, and the seamy rocks so split down, that, with the mass of stones thrown over, a path of easy descent was formed from the top, down to the shelf below, on one side of the mouth of the cave; which was now securely blocked up, and closely invested by the party previously stationed in near vicinity to guard it.

Thus bravely, and with no token of faltering at the obstacles which they frequently encountered, and which sometimes required their greatest exertions to overcome, did these strong-armed and determined men push on their herculean labors, for the space of nearly two hours; when suddenly a shout of exultation rose from those at work lowest down in the excavation, and the next moment the voice of the ex-sheriff was heard exclaiming to those around him:

"Courage, men! the game is nearly unkenneled. I have driven my bar through, and the hole is so large that the bar has slipped from my hands and gone to the bottom!"

The excitement now became intense; and all crowded round the rim of the excavation, and, with uneasy looks and hushed voices, eagerly peered down into the dimly-visible perforation at the bottom; while those already within the excavated basin began, with beating hearts, carefully loosening and pulling out the shivered and detached stones, lying around the small aperture just effected, and continued the process until all the outer edges of the broad, thin rock, which the crow-bar had perforated, and which appeared to form the lower or interior layer of the roofing of the cavern, were fully laid bare, and brought within the reach of the outstretched arms of those bending down to grasp them. A dozen brawny hands were then seen securing their gripe on one side of the rock; when, at the word of the sheriff, a sudden pull was made with a force that raised the whole mass nearly a foot from its bed.

"It comes bravely!" said the sheriff. "Now fix yourselves for another pull; while two or three of you above there come forward with your rifles, and stand with them levelled at the hole, as we open it, lest the desperate dog make a rush before we are prepared. Now altogether,—there, now!"

The effort was made, and the sheeted rock was brought to a perpendicular; when it was grappled by the men with might and main, lifted clear from its bed, and thrust aside, letting the sunlight down upon the bottom of the cave through a chasm nearly large enough to permit two men to jump in abreast. There was now a dead pause; and all eyes were turned on the chasm in silent and trembling expectation. But nothing appearing, the hunter and ex-sheriff crept down prostrate to the brink of the chasm, and worked their heads cautiously below, to get a fuller view of the interior. After looking, with slightly varied positions, about a minute, they both rose and came up on the bank; when the ex-sheriff, turning to the hunter, softly said:

"He is there. I caught sight of his legs standing in a corner near the mouth of the cave. Did *you* get a view?"

"Yes, a better one than that; I saw his legs, and as much of his body as I could without bringing my *own* head within the line of his eyes. He stands there on the watch, with cocked rifle pointing to this opening, while he has a dirk within his left hand grasping the rifle, and I think a pistol within his other hand, held in a similar manner. I can read his plan."

"What is it, as *you* read it?"

"To take the first that enters with his rifle, pistol the second, make a rush through the rest, and stab as he goes."

"About the truth, probably. But what is to be done? Shall you and I leap down, make a spring upon him, and stand our chance?"

"Why,—yes," replied the hunter, with a little hesitation; "yes, if we can't do better than throw away one good life, at least, for a bad one. But if we could contrive to divert his attention suddenly to the mouth of the cave—"

"You are right! Stay here a moment, and I will put matters in train to carry out your suggestion," eagerly interrupted Turner, taking the sheriff confidentially aside.

In a few minutes the determined ex-sheriff followed by four or five stout, resolute men, whose special assistance he had bespoken for the occasion, returned to the side of the hunter, and said:

"Get down there in your old position, where you can watch his movements. They have gone down to unblock the mouth of the cave outside, and make a feint of entering. If they succeed in drawing his fire, I will take that as a signal,—if not, then you give me the word, at the right moment, when his head, and with it naturally his rifle, is turned to the supposed new point of attack, and I will leap down and make a spring to get within the line of the muzzle before he can fire; and, the instant I disappear, you and these men follow, and be close on my heels for the grapple."

The hunter then edged down to his former place of observation, where he lay, while Turner sat crouching on the brink ready for the leap, narrowly watching the movements of the dreaded foe within, who was seen to be still standing motionless in the same position as before. Presently the movements of those outside the old entrance of the cavern, as they began cautiously to remove the blockading stones, became clearly audible, and soon a few straggling rays of light began to gleam into the interior from that direction. On perceiving these indications, the wary desperado began, for the first time, to exhibit signs of uneasiness. Slightly changing his position, he glanced rapidly from the already half-cleared entrance in front to the chasm just opened through the top in the rear. But neither seeing or hearing any thing that led him to expect any assault, except from the front, and evidently supposing it was now the intention of his assailants to drive him up through the top opening, to be seized as he came out, he drew back a step, and, turning the muzzle of his rifle towards the mouth of the cave, stood ready to fire upon the first who should make his appearance. This movement was not lost on the keenly-watching, hunter, who saw that it afforded a fair chance for a successful surprise; and he once parted his lips to give the signal for the onset. But, perceiving from the incoming light that the mouth of the cave was cleared from its obstructions, he ventured to await the effect of the feint now momentarily expected from that quarter. He had judged wisely. The delay was not in vain. A rustling sound, seeming to come from some one squeezing through the entrance, was now heard; and soon a dark object, resembling the head and shoulders of a man, making slow and cautious advances, was fully protruded into the cavern; when, suddenly, the whole ledge shook with the stunning report of a rifle, and the next moment, Turner, Phillips, and their chosen backers, had all disappeared in the cloud of smoke that came pouring up through the chasm. Quick, heavy, muffled sounds, as of fiercely-grappling tigers, instantly came from within. And within another minute, the stentorian voice of the daring leader of the onset was heard, shouting for the hand-cuffs and fetters.

The fierce siege was over. The desperate intentions and giant strength of the besieged, after a brief but terrible struggle, had been thwarted and overcome by the intrepidity and equal strength of the ex-sheriff; and he, now firmly clenched round the body, and held down, with every limb in the vise-like grasp of his iron-fisted captors, lay disarmed, helpless, and panting on the ground.

"There!" sternly cried the victorious leader of the hazardous assault, as he rose to his feet, after he had seen the heavy irons securely locked on the wrists and ankles of the silent and sullen prisoner,—"there! drag him out, feet foremost, into the open light of day, where he and his dark deeds have all now got to come, to meet the vengeance of an outraged community!"

It was done, and with no gentle hand; when a long, wild shout of exultation fiercely broke from the closely-encircling throng, thrilling the trembling forest around with the din, and rolling away to the farthest shores of the lake, to proclaim that the first murderer of the settlement—the black-hearted Gaut Gurley—was now a prisoner, and in the uncompromising hands of public justice.

The animated spectacle which now ensued, of trundling, pushing, and tumbling the chafed and growling prisoner down to the shore, amid the unrestrained demonstrations of the exulting multitude; the noisy and bustling embarkation, on the lake; the ostentatious display of mimic banners, formed by raising on tall poles, handkerchiefs, hats, coats, and whatever would make a show in the distance, as the long line of canoes, with the closely guarded prisoner in the centre, filed off in gorgeous array, through the glitter of the sun-lit lake, on their way to the great outlet; the pause and concentration there; the rapid descent down the river to the village, where a board of magistrates were waiting to sit on the case of the expected prisoner; and, finally, the loudly heralding *kuk-kuk-ke-o-hos* of the overflowing trapper, to announce, over a two-mile reach of the stream, the triumphant approach,— this animated and here extraordinary spectacle, we must leave to the delineation of the reader's imagination. Our attention is more strongly demanded in a different direction, to bring up other important incidents of our story, before proceeding any farther with the actors who have figured in this part of the narrative, or taking note of the examination to which they were now hurrying the prisoner.

CHAPTER XX.

"By thine infinite of woe,
All we know not, all we know;
If there be what dieth not,
Thine, affection, is its lot."

Deep in the wilderness of woods and waters encircling the mouth of a small inlet, at the extreme northwestern end of the picturesque Maguntic, there lay encamped, at the point of a low headland, on one of the first nights of May, the three trappers, whose expedition had been the subject of so many gloomy speculations, and whose unexpectedly prolonged absence had caused, as we have seen, so much anxiety in the settlement to which they belonged. They had extended their outward journey more than double the distance contemplated by the Elwoods, at least when they left home; the mover of the expedition, Gaut Gurley, having proposed to make the shores of the Maguntic, and its feeding streams only, the range of their operations. But when they arrived there, as they did, on the ice, which was still firm and solid on the lakes, Gaut pretended to believe that the rich beaver-haunts, to which he had promised to lead them, could not be identified, much less reached, until the ice had broken up in the streams and lake. He, therefore, now proposed that they should first proceed over to the chief inlet of the Oquossak, stay one night in the camp, which was left in the great snowstorm of the fall before, dig out the steel-traps buried there, and, the next day, slide over the boats, also left there, on the glare ice,—as all agreed could easily be done on some light and simple contrivance,—and land them on the west shore of the Maguntic, where they could be concealed, and found ready for use when the lake opened. He would then, he said, lead them to a place among the head-water streams of the Magalloway, only a day's journey distant, where he once "trapped it" himself, and where, as the rivers there broke up early, he could promise them immediate success.

All this had been done; and the party, having spent nearly three weeks among the lakelets and interweaving streams going to make up the sources of the Magalloway and Connecticut rivers, with occasional recourse to the nearest habitations on the upper Magalloway, for provisions, but with very indifferent success in taking furs, had now, on the urging of young Elwood, returned to the Maguntic,—which, after a hard day's journey, they had reached, at the point where we have introduced them, about sunset the day but one preceding, thrown up a temporary shanty, and encamped for the night. On rising the next morning, Gaut had proposed that Claud remain at camp that day, to build a better shanty, and hunt in the near vicinity; while he and Mark Elwood should explore the stream, to a pond some miles above, where his previously discovered beaver-haunts, he said, were mostly to be found, and where, the snow and ice having wholly disappeared, they could now operate to good advantage. With this arrangement, however, the young man, whose secret suspicions had been aroused by one or two previous attempts made by Gaut to separate him from his father, plausibly refused to comply; and the consequence was, that they had all made the proposed explorations together, returned to camp without discovering any indications of the promised beaver, and laid down for the night, with the understanding, reluctantly agreed to by the moody and morose Gaut, that they should proceed down the lake to their boats the next morning, and embark for an immediate return to their homes, where the Elwoods felt conscious they must, by this time, be anxiously expected.

Such were the circumstances under which we have brought this singularly-assorted party of trappers to the notice of the reader, as they lay sleeping in their bough-constructed tents,—Gaut and Mark Elwood under one cover, and Claud under another, which he had fixed up for himself on the opposite side of their fire,—on the ominous night which was destined to prelude the most tragic and melancholy scene of our variously eventful story.

It was the hour of nature's deepest repose, and the bright midnight moon, stealing through the gently-swaying boughs of the dark pines that rose heavenward, like pinnacles, along the silent shores around, was throwing her broken beams fitfully down upon the faces of the unconscious sleepers, faintly revealing the impress which the thoughts and purposes of the last waking hours had left on the countenance of each. And these impresses were as variant as the characters of those on whose features they rested: that lingering on the sternly-compressed lips and dark, beetling brows of Gaut Gurley, ever sinister, was doubly so now; that on the face of Mark Elwood, whose vacillations of thought and feeling, through life, had exempted his features from any stamp betokening fixed peculiarity of character, was one of fatuous security; and that resting on the intellectual and guileless face of Claud Elwood was one of simple care and inquietude.

But what is that light, shadowy form, hovering near the sylvan couch of Claud, like some unsubstantial being of the air; now advancing, now shrinking away, and now again flitting forward to the head of the youthful sleeper, and there pausing and preventing the light from longer revealing his features? Yes, what is it? would ask a doubting spectator of this singular night-scene. A passing cloud come over the moon? No, there is none in the heavens. But why the useless speculation? for it is gone now, leaving the sleeper's face again visible, and wearing a more unquiet and disturbed air than before. His features twitch nervously, and expressions of terror and surprise flit over them. He dreams, and his dream is a troubled one. Let the novelist's license be invoked to interpret it.

He was alone with his father on a boundless plain, when suddenly a dark, whirlwind tempest-cloud fell upon the earth around them, and soon separated him from the object of his care. As he was anxiously pressing on through the thickly-enveloping vapors, in the direction in which the latter had disappeared, he was suddenly confronted by a monstrous, black, and fearful living apparition, who stood before him in all the horrid paraphernalia ascribed to the prince of darkness, apparently ready to crush him to the earth, when a bright angel form swiftly interposed. Starting back, with the rapidly-chasing sensations of terror and surprise, he looked again, and the fiend stood stript of his infernal guise, and suddenly transformed into the person of Gaut Gurley, who, with a howl of dismay, quickly turned and fled in confusion. The amazed dreamer then turned to his deliverer, who had been transformed into the beauteous Fluella, whose image, he was conscious, was no longer a stranger among the lurking inmates of his heart. A sweet, benignant smile was breaking over her lovely features; and, under the sudden impulse of the grateful surprise, he eagerly stretched out his arms towards her, and, in the effort, awoke.

"Where, where is she?" he exclaimed, springing to his feet, and glaring wildly around him. "Why!" he continued, after a pause, in which he appeared to be rallying his bewildered senses,—"why! what is this? a dream, nothing but a dream? It must be so. But what a strange one! and what could have caused it? Was there not some one standing over me, just now, darkening my face like a shadow? I feel a dim consciousness of something like it. But that, probably, was part of the same dream. Yes, yes, all a mere dream; all nothing; so, begone with you, miserable phantoms! I will not suffer—"

But, as if not satisfied with his own reasoning, he stopped short, and, for many minutes, stood motionless, with his head dropped in deep thought; when, arousing himself, he returned to his rude resting-place, and laid down again, but only to toss and turn, in the restless excitement which he obviously found himself unable to allay. After a while spent in this tantalizing unrest, he rose and slowly made his way down to the edge of the lake, a few rods distant, where, scooping up water with his hands, he first drank eagerly, then, bathed his fevered brow, and then, rising, he stood some time silent on the shore,—now pensively gazing out on the darkly-bright expanse of the moon-lit lake; and now listening to the mysterious voices of night in the wilderness, which, in low, soft, whispering undulations of sound, came, at varied intervals, gently murmuring along the wooded shores, to die away into silence in the remote recesses of the forest. These phenomena of the wilds he had once or twice before noted, and tried to account for, without, however, attaching much consequence to them. But now they became invested with a strange significance, and seemed to him, in his present excited and apprehensive state of mind, portentous of impending evil. While his thoughts were taking this channel, the possibility of what might be done in his absence suddenly appeared to occur to him; and he hastened back to camp, where he slightly replenished the fire, and, taking a recumbent position, with his loaded rifle within reach, kept awake, and on the watch, till morning.

After daylight Claud arose, as if nothing unusual had occurred to disturb him, bustled about, built a good fire, and began to prepare a morning meal from the fine string of trout he had taken during yesterday's excursion. The noise of these preparations soon awoke the two sleepers; who, complimenting him on his early rising, also arose, and soon joined him in partaking the repast, which, by this time, he had in readiness.

As soon as they had finished their meal, which was enlivened by no other than an occasional brief, commonplace remark, the thoughts of each of them being evidently engrossed by his own peculiar schemes and anxieties, the trappers, by common consent, set about their preparations to depart; and, having completed them, leisurely took their way down the western shore of the lake towards the spot at which they had hauled up and concealed their canoe, and which, if they followed the deep indentures of the shore in this part of the lake, must be four or five miles distant.

For the first mile or two of their progress nothing noticeable to an indifferent observer occurred to vary the monotony of their walk, as they tramped steadily and silently forward, in the usual, and, indeed, almost the only practicable mode of travelling in the forest, appropriately denominated Indian file. But young Elwood, whose feelings had been deeply stirred by the fancies of the night, which, to say the least, had the effect to make him more keenly apprehensive and vigilant, had noted several little circumstances, that, to him, wore a questionable appearance. Gaut, who at first led the way, soon manoeuvred to get Mark Elwood, the next in the order of their march, in front; and then urged him forward at a much faster pace than before, at the same time often casting furtive glances behind him, as if to see whether Claud, who seemed inclined to walk more slowly than the rest, would not fall behind, and soon be out of sight. And, when the latter quickened his pace, he showed signs of vexation, which had not passed unnoticed. All this Claud had noted, together with the singular expression which Gaut's countenance assumed, and which filled him with an undefinable dread, and a lively suspicion that the man was on the eve of attempting the execution of foul purposes. Consequently he resolved to follow up closely, having no fears for himself, and believing his presence would prevent any attempt that might be meditated against his father. This precaution, for some time, the young man was careful to observe; but, as he was passing over a small brook that crossed his path, his eye caught the appearance of a slight trail, a few rods up the stream, and curiosity prompted him to turn aside to examine it. When he reached the place, he soon detected indications which convinced him that some person had recently been there; and, forgetful of his resolution, in the interest the circumstance excited, he commenced a closer inspection, which resulted in discovering a fresh imprint, in the soft mud on one side of the brook, of a small moccasined foot. This curious and unexpected discovery, uncertain as were its indications of any identity of the person, or even of the age or sex of the person, by whom that delicate footprint was made, at once diverted his attention, from the particular care by which it had been engrossed, and started that other of the two trains of thought, which, for the last month, but especially since his singular awakening the past night, had constituted the chief burden of his mind,—his increasing apprehensions for his father's safety, and his lurking but irrepressible regard for the chief's beautiful daughter, whose image, since his dream, had haunted him with a pertinacity for which a resort to reason alone would fail to account.

"If music be the food of love,"

dreams, we apprehend, whatever the immortal bard might have thought of the matter, have often proved the more exciting stimulus of the tender passion; many of whose happiest consummations might be traced back to an origin in some peopled scene of a dreaming fancy, whose peculiar effect on the sympathies has frequently been felt by the sternest and most sceptical, though never very clearly explained in any of our written systems of the philosophy of the soul and its affections.

In the pleasing indulgence of the feelings and fancies which had been thus freshly kindled, Claud stood, for some minutes, quite unconscious of the lapse of time, though it had been long enough to place his companions far out of sight and hearing. From this reverie he was suddenly aroused by the sharp report of a rifle, bursting on his ear from the woods, about a quarter of a mile off, in the direction just taken by his companions. Starting at the sound, which sent a boding chill through his heart, and bitterly taxing himself for his inadvertent loitering, he sprang back to the trail he had left, and made his way along over it towards the place indicated by the firing, with all the speed which excited nerves and agonizing anxiety could bring to his aid. But, before reaching the spot at which he was aiming, and just as he was beginning to slacken his pace, to look around for it, Gaut Gurley burst through the bushes, a few rods ahead, and, running towards him with all the manifestations of a man in hasty retreat before a pursuing foe, eagerly exclaimed:

"Run, Claud! run for your life! We have just been beset by hostile Indians, who fired on us, and, I fear, have killed your father. I have misled them a little; but they will soon be on our trail. Run! run!" he added, seizing the other by the arm to start him into instant flight.

"What!" exclaimed the astonished young man, hanging back, and by degrees recovering from the surprise with which he was at first overwhelmed by the strange and startling announcement. "What! hostile Indians?—hostile to whom, to my father, or to me, that I should run from them? Gaut Gurley, what, O what does this mean?"

"Why, it means," said the other, keeping up all the motions and flourishes naturally used by one urging another to flee,—"it means, as I say, our lives are in danger. Let us escape while we can. Come, come, there's not a moment to lose!"

"I will *know*," said Claud, with a quick, searching glance at the face of the other,—"yes, I *will know* for myself what has happened," he sternly added, suddenly breaking from the grasp on his arm, and bounding forward to execute his purpose with a quickness and rapidity that made pursuit useless.

"Hold!" cried Gaut, in an increasingly fierce and angry tone, "hold, instantly,—on your life, hold! I warn you, sir, to stop, instantly to stop!"

But, heeding neither the entreaties nor the threats which, his ear told him, were strangely mingled in the tones of the words thus thundered after him, Claud, in his agony of apprehension, eagerly rushed on towards the forbidden scene, which could not now be thirty rods distant, and had proceeded, perhaps, forty yards; when, just as he was straightening up, after stooping to pass under an obstructing limb of a tree, extending across his path, he became conscious of the sound of the sudden hitting of the limb, and partly so of the concussion of a shot, still farther in his rear. But he neither heard nor knew more; and, the next moment, lay stretched senseless on the ground.

When he awoke to consciousness, after, he knew not what lapse of time, he found himself in a different place; lying, as he felt conscious, badly wounded, on a soft, elastic bed of boughs, within a dense thicket of low evergreens, through which his opening eye caught the gleams of widely-surrounding waters. A ministering angel, in the shape of the peerless daughter of the wilds, who had lately so much occupied his thoughts, was wistfully bending over him, with a countenance in which commiseration and woe had found an impersonation which no artist's pencil could have equalled.

"Fluella!" he feebly murmured,—"how came you here, Fluella?"

She saw that the effort to speak caused him a pang, and, without replying to the question, motioned him to silence; when, being no longer able to master her emotions, she sat down by his side, and, covering her face with both hands, began to grieve and sob like a child. Poor girl! who could measure the depth of her heart's anguish? She could not answer, had she deemed it best. We must answer the question for her. But, to do so, to the full understanding of the reader, we must again recur to the events of the past,—her troubled past, at least,—during the three or four days preceding the time of her appearance as an actor in the sad scene before us.

She had learned from Mrs. Elwood that Claud had pledged himself to her that he would return from his expedition within the month of April; and to Fluella, with her undoubting confidence in his word, a failure to redeem that pledge would be but little less than certain intelligence that some evil had befallen either him or his father, in their unknown place of sojourn in the wilderness. Consequently her solicitude—growing out of her secretly nourished but overmastering love for him—became, as the time approached which was to relieve or realize her fears for the result of an expedition undertaken under such dreadful auspices, each day more deep and absorbing. And, the last morning but one of the expiring month, she went out early on to the rock-bound shore of the lake, on which her father's cabin was situated, and commenced her watch from the most commanding points, for the appearance of the expected party, on their way homeward from the upper lakes. And during that anxious day, and the still more anxious one that followed, she kept up her vigils, with no other cessation than what her brief absences for her hastily-snatched meals at the house required; sometimes standing, for an hour at a time, in one spot, intently gazing out into the lake, and sometimes moving restlessly about, and hurrying from cliff to cliff along the beetling shore, to obtain a better observation. But, no appearance or indications of their coming rewarding her vigils during all that time, she retired from the shore, at the approach of night, on the last day of April, sad and sick at heart from disappointment, and painfully oppressed with apprehension for the fate of one for whose safety she felt she would have given her own worthless life as a willing sacrifice. But, her feelings still allowing her neither peace nor quietude, she left the house after supper; and, in the light of the nearly full moon, that was now throwing its mellow beams over the wild landscape, unconsciously took her way to the lake-shore, where she had already spent so many weary hours in her fruitless vigils. Here, climbing a tall rock on the bluff shore, she resumed her watch, and long stood, straining both eye and ear to catch sight of some moving thing, or the sound of some plashing oar, out on the lake, that might indicate the coming, even at this late hour, of the objects of her solicitude. But no such sight or sound came up from the sleeping waters, to greet and gladden her aching senses. All there was as motionless and silent as the plains of the dead.

"The time is past!" she at length despairingly muttered, slowly withdrawing her gaze, and standing as if to collect her thoughts and ponder. "Yes, passed by, now. He will not come!"

And her ideas immediately reverted to the other alternative for which she had before made up her mind, in case the party did not return within the month; but which, having been kept in the background of her thoughts, by her hope of their coming, now occurred to her with startling effect. She fancied Claud the victim of outrage or misfortune,—perhaps wounded and dying, by the same hand that might have previously struck down his father,—perhaps taken sick on his way home alone, and now lying helpless in the woods, where none could witness his sufferings or hear his cries for assistance. The thought sent a pang through her bosom, the more painful because, being something like a legitimate conclusion of her previous reasoning, she could not divest herself of it. She stood bewildered in the woes of her thick-coming fancies. The images thus conjured up from her distracting anxieties and excited brain, all heightened by the natural inspirations of the place and the hour, soon became to her vivid realities. And her burning thoughts at once insensibly ran into the form and spirit of one of the many beautiful plaints of England's gifted poetess:

"I heard a song upon the wandering wind,
A song of many tones, though one full soul
Breathed through them all imploringly; and made
All nature, as they pass'd,—all quivering leaves,
And low responsive reeds and waters,—thrill,
As with the consciousness of human prayer.
　　　　　——the tones
Were of a suppliant. '*Leave me not*' was still
The burden of their music."

"I will *not* leave you!" she exclaimed, startling the silent glens and grottos around by the wild energy of her tones, and eagerly stretching out her hands towards the imagined scene, and the suppliant for her ministering services, "O Claud, I will come to you. My love, my life, my more than life, I will soon be with you! Go after him?" she resumed, after a sudden pause, to which she seemed to be brought by recalling her thoughts to their wonted channel, and being startled at the sober import of her own words. "Go in search of him in the woods! Yes," she added, after another long and thoughtful pause,—"yes, why not? I cannot, O, I *cannot* stay here another day, with these but too prophetic words, I fear, ringing in my ears. To be in the same wilderness with him were a pleasure, to the insupportable suspense I must suffer here. If I discover all to be well, I need not show myself; but, if it be as I fear, O, what happiness to be near him! Yes, it is decided; I will start in the morning."

And, hastily descending from her stand, with the firm, quick step and decisive air of one whose purpose is fixed, she struck off directly for the house; where, after a few hasty preparations, she retired to her bed, and, happily, after the exhausting cares of the day, was soon quieted into sound and refreshing slumber.

In accordance with her still unaltered resolution, she rose early the next morning; and with an indefinite intimation to her family of her intention to be absent among friends a day or two, swung to her side a small square basket of nutritious provisions, took a thick shawl to protect her from the damps of the night, proceeded directly to her canoe at the landing, embarked, and struck out vigorously along the winding shore, on her way to the next upper lake. A steady but quiet row of a couple of hours took her out of the great lake on which she had embarked, up the principal inlet, and into the Maguntic, whose western shores, she had understood, were to be the base of the operations of the absent party. Here she turned short to the left, and, drawing in close to land, rowed slowly and cautiously along the western shore, following round all the numerous indentations, and continually sending her searching glances up its wooded shores, that no appearance of the trail of human beings might escape her observation.

After rowing two or three miles in this manner, and without noticing any thing that particularly attracted her attention, she reached the first of the three headlands, making out from this side a considerable distance into the lake, beyond the average line of the shore. As she was rounding this point, her eye fell on a dark protuberance, in a dense thicket a few rods in-shore, which appeared of a more oblong and regular form than is usual in such places. And, scanning the appearance more closely, she soon discerned a small piece of wrought wood, resembling a part of the blade of an oar, slightly projecting from one side of the apparent brush-heap. Starting at the sight, she immediately ran her canoe ashore, and proceeded at once to the spot; when, closely peering under the brush-wood, she discovered three canoes, with their oars, concealed beneath a deep covering of boughs, surmounted by a scraggy treetop lying carelessly over them, as if blown from some neighboring tree.

This, to her, was an important discovery; for it told her—after she had carefully examined the place, and found that no one had been to the boats since they were concealed, which she thought must have been done several weeks before—it told her, at once, that the trappers had gone to some distant locality among the streams and mountains, to the west or north, from which they had not yet returned to the lake; but doubtless would so return before proceeding homeward, provided the Elwoods had not both been slain or disabled by their suspected companion. The discovery, notwithstanding the light it had thrown on the first movements of the trappers, and much as it narrowed the range of her search for them, but little relieved her harrowing apprehensions; and she resolved to proceed up the lake with her observations, which might now as well be confined to this side of it, and the larger streams which should here be found entering it, and down some of which the company, if they came at all, would probably now soon come, on their way to the canoes. And, accordingly, she again set forth on her solitary journey. But, being conscious that the trappers might now at any time suddenly make their appearance, she proceeded more cautiously, keeping as far as possible out of the views that might be taken from distant points of the lake, and from time to time turning a watchful eye and ear on the shores around and before her. Thus, slowly and timidly advancing, she at length reached and rounded the second headland in her course, where another and still more interesting discovery was in store for her. As she came out from the overhanging trees beneath which she had shot along the point, she unexpectedly gained a clear view of the extreme end of the lake, with what appeared to be the mouth of a considerable stream, and suddenly backed her oar, to pause and reconnoitre; when she soon noticed one spot, near the supposed inlet, which wore a different hue from the rest, and which, a closer inspection told her, must be imparted by the lingering of undissipated smoke, from a fire kindled there as late, at least, as that morning. Her heart beat violently at the discovery; for she felt assured that the trappers had reached the lake, had encamped there the night before, and could not now be many miles distant. Fearing she should be seen, if she remained longer on the water, she at once resolved to conceal her canoe in some place near by, and proceed by land through the woods to the spot of the supposed encampment, or near enough to ascertain how far her conjectures were true, and how far her new-lit hopes were to be realized. All this—after many a misgiving and many an alarm, from the sudden movements of the smaller animals of the forest, started out from their coverts by her stealthy advance—had been by her, at length, successfully accomplished; the camp detected from a neighboring thicket; cautiously approached, finally entered, and the joyful discovery made that three persons had slept there the night before. Hieing back, like a frighted bird, into the screening forest, she selected a covert in a dense thicket on an elevation about an hundred yards distant, where, unseen by the most searching eye, she could look down into the camp; and there she lay down and anxiously awaited the approach of night, and, with it, the expected return of the party, who, she felt confident, could be no others than those of whom she was in search. And it was not all a dream with Claud, when he fancied some one standing by his couch of repose. A flitting form had, that night, indeed, for a moment hovered over him, looking down, with the sleepless eye of love, on his broken slumbers, and trying to divine, perhaps, the very dreams which, through some mysterious agency of the mental sympathies, her presence was inciting.

Although the maiden had now the unspeakable satisfaction of knowing that none of her fears had thus far been realized, yet she felt keenly sensible that the danger was not over; and she therefore determined that she would not lose sight of the objects of her vigilance and anxiety, at least until she had seen them embarked for home on the open lake, where deeds of darkness would be less likely to be attempted than in the screening forest. She had, therefore, started from her uneasy slumbers, the next morning, at daybreak; watched from her covert, with lively concern, the movements in the camp; and no sooner seen them packed up for a start, and headed towards their boats, then she shrank noiselessly away from her concealment, which was situated so as to give her considerably the start of them; and fled rapidly down the lake, in a line parallel to the one along the shore which the trappers would naturally take, and so near it that, from chosen stands, she could see them as they came along. And thus, for miles, like the timid antelope, she hovered on their flank,—now pausing to get a glance of them through the trees as they came in sight, and now fleeing forward again, for a new position, to repeat the observation. Up to this time she had kept considerably in advance of the moving party; but now, suddenly missing Claud, she sought a covert, and stood watching for him, till Mark Elwood, followed by Gaut Gurley, came abreast of the spot she occupied; when, suddenly, the forest shook and trembled from the report of a gun, bursting from the bushes, seemingly, almost beneath her feet. A single wild glance revealed to her appalled senses Gaut Gurley, clenching his smoking rifle, and, with the look of an exulting fiend, glaring out from behind a tree, towards his prostrate, convulsed, and dying victim. On recovering from the deeply paralyzing effect of the horrid spectacle, her first thought was for Claud; and, with the distracting thought, her eye involuntarily sought for the murderer of his father, who had shrunk back from his position, but whom she soon detected hastily reloading his rifle, and then starting, with a quick step, along back the path in which he had just come,—in search, as her alarmed heart suggested, of another victim for his infernal malice. With a sharp, smothered cry of anguish, she bounded out from her covert, and flew back, in a line parallel with that of the retreating murderer, till she saw him meet the alarmed young man hurrying forward to the rescue; when she suddenly paused, and listened with breathless interest to the dialogue we have already related as occurring between them. She heard—and her heart bounded with pride as she did so—she heard the manly and determined language of the young man; she saw him rush by the wretch who was trying to mislead him, to conceal his own crime. But she saw, also, the next moment, with a dismay that transfixed her to the spot, the murderous rifle raised, and the retreating, unconscious object of its aim stumble forward to the ground; then the monster, as if uncertain of the execution of his bullet, rush forward, with gleaming knife, apparently to finish his work; and then disappear in the direction of the concealed canoes, now less than a half-mile beyond. All this she had witnessed, with an agony which no pen can describe; and then, with the last glimpse of the retiring assassin, flown, to the side of his second victim, badly but not fatally wounded; staunched, as she best could, the blood pouring from his wounds; hurried off for her canoe, luckily hid near by; brought it up to the shore, within a few yards of the spot where he had fallen; drawn him gently down to it, and got him into it, she knew not how; and then, after obliterating the trail, entered herself, and rowed off to the thickly wooded little island, a furlong to the northeast, but hid by an intervening point from the view of the foe, now supposed to be on his way to the boats. Here she had contrived to draw Claud up, in the light canoe, on the farthest shore, and, by degrees, got both him and the boat on the dry, mossy ground, safely within a thicket wholly impervious to outward view. Still fearful of Gaut's return, she crept to the south end of the island, which she had scarcely reached when she saw him come round the point, land, drag down the body of Mark Elwood, take it out some distance from the shore, and sink it, by steel-traps and stones tied to it, deep in the lake. She then, with lively concern, saw him return and proceed towards the spot where Claud had fallen, but soon reappear, evidently much disturbed at not finding the body, yet not seeming to suspect how it had been disposed of, though several times coming down to the edge of the water and peering anxiously up and down the lake; but she was soon relieved from her fears by seeing him take to his boat, row rapidly round the point, there take in tow two other canoes,—which, it appeared, he had brought up and left there,—and then row down the lake, in the direction of the great outlet; under the belief, doubtless, that Claud had revived, struck down through the woods for the upper end of the lake below, where, if he had not before sunk down and died of his wounds, he might be waylaid and finished. Thus relieved of this pressing apprehension, she hurried back to her charge, and carefully examined his wounds; when she found that the bullet, whose greatest force had been broken by the obstructing limb, had struck near the top of his head, and ploughed over the skull without breaking it; that, of the two stabs inflicted, one had been turned by the collar-bone, making only a long, surface wound, the other had passed through the fleshy part of the arm and terminated on a rib beneath, producing a flow of blood, which, but for the timely and plentiful application of beaver-fur, pulled from a skin which she saw protruding from his pack, must have soon terminated his life. With the drinking-cup she found slung to his side, she brought water, washed the wounds, laid the ruptured parts in place, and, with plasters of cloth cut from her handkerchief, and made adhesive by balsam taken from a tree at hand, covered and protected them; and thus, by the application of a skill she learned from her father, placed them in a situation where nature, with proper care, would, of herself, complete the sanatory operation. She then resumed the process of bathing his head and face, and, within another hour, was thrilled with joy in witnessing his return to consciousness, in the manner we described before leaving him for this long but necessary, digression.

After giving vent to her painfully laboring emotions a while, the maiden softly arose, and, creeping down under the overhanging boughs to the edge of the water, sat down on a stone and bathed her throbbing brow, for some time, in the limpid wave; after which, having in a good measure regained her usual firmness and tranquillity, she returned to the side of her wounded friend, whom she found wrapt in the deep slumber generally produced by exhaustion from loss of blood. After gazing a while on his face, with the sad and yearning look of a mother on a disease-smitten child, a new thought seemed suddenly to occur to her, and she noiselessly stole away to her former lookout, at the south end of the island, where, with a brightening eye, she caught sight of the loathed and dreaded homicide, just entering the distant outlet. Waiting no longer than to feel assured that he had disappeared with the real intention of descending the stream, she returned to her still sleeping charge, slowly and carefully slid the canoe down into the water, headed it round with her hands, gained her seat in the stern, and pushed out into the lake, shaping her course obliquely down it towards the mouth of a small river entering from the eastern side, at the lower end of the lake, but still nearly a mile distant from the outlet in which the murderer had disappeared. Softly and smoothly as a gently-rocking cradle, the light canoe, under the skillfully plied oar of the careful maiden, glided through the waveless waters on her destined course, and, for more than an hour, steadily kept on its noiseless way, without once appearing to disturb the repose of the slumbering invalid. But, as the hitherto low-looking forest bordering the eastern shore began to loom up, and thus apprise the fair rower that she was now nearing the point to which she had been directing her course, she noticed, with concern, that the lake was beginning to be agitated, even where she then was, from a gathering breeze; while a long, light, advancing line, extending across the lake in the distance behind her, plainly told of the rapid approach of wind, which must soon greatly increase the disturbance of the waters, and the consequent rocking of the canoe. Knowing how injuriously such motion of the boat might affect the invalid, she put forth her utmost strength in propelling the canoe forward to reach the quiet haven before her, in season to escape the threatened roughness of the water. But her best exertions could secure only a partial immunity from the trouble she thus sought to avoid. The wind struck her long before gaining the place; when, in spite of all her endeavors to steady it, the canoe began to lurch and toss among the gathering waves; while the almost immediate awakening of the disturbed invalid, his twinges of pain and suppressed groans, told her, as they sent responsive thrills of anguish through her bosom, how much he was suffering from the motion. To her great relief, however, she now soon reached and shot into the still waters of the stream, and this trouble, at least, was over. Here, after passing in out of sight of the lake, she drew up her oar, and paused to reflect and conclude what should be her next movement; when Claud, whose head was pillowed in the bow of the boat, and whose eye was resting tenderly on her downcast countenance, soon read her perplexity, and again asked to be informed of all that had happened, and the object of her present movement. She told him,—with such reservations as maidenly modesty and pride suggested,—she told him all she had seen, and in conclusion proposed, as their enemy might ambush them, and as it was now drawing towards night, and the lake would not be quiet enough for some hours, at least, to permit them to proceed, that they should row up the river till they found an eligible spot, and encamp for the night. To this Claud readily assented; and they again set forth up the gentle stream, that, as before intimated, here came in from the southeast; and, after proceeding some distance, the anxious eye of the maiden fell on a place on the left bank, where a temporary shelter could easily be rigged up, under the wide-spreading and low-set limbs of a thick-topped evergreen, which, of itself, would be ample protection against the dews of heaven. Drawing up the canoe on land near the tree, in the same manner as at the island, she proceeded to gather large quantities of fine hemlock boughs, and dry, elastic mosses, arrange them under the tree, in the form of bed and pillow, and over the whole to spread Claud's blanket; thus making a couch as safe and comfortable as ever received the limbs of a suffering invalid. Upon this, partly by his own exertions and partly by her assistance, he was then, without much difficulty, soon transferred from the canoe; when, with his light hatchet (she having brought all his implements along with him in the boat), she soon erected neat, closely-woven wicker walls of boughs, from the ground to the limbs above, on both sides, providing within one of them a space for herself. She then brought fuel, kindled a small fire in front, and took her position at his side, to be ready for such ministering offices as his case might seem to require. She found that he had again fallen into a profound slumber, which she at first regarded as a favorable omen; and, in the conscious security of the spot, in the belief that he had received none of the injuries she had apprehended from the motion of the boat, and, above all, in the indulgence of that overweening pride of affection which covets all pains and sacrifices for the loved one, she felt a satisfaction which was almost happiness, in her situation. But it was not destined to be of very long duration. She at length began to perceive a gradual reddening of his cheeks, and then, soon after, an increasing shortness of respiration, and a general restlessness of the system. Alarmed at these symptoms, she felt his pulse, and at once discovered that he was in a high fever, supervening from his wounds, and caused, or much aggravated, doubtless, by the jostling of the boat on his way hither. Starting back, as if some unexpected calamity had suddenly fallen upon her, she stood some minutes absorbed in earnest self-consultation. What should she do? She could not, dare not, even were it daytime, leave him to go miles away for her father, or others, for aid or advice. No; she must stay by him. And, having seen the alleviating effects of cold water in fevers and inflammations, and knowing that there were no other remedies within reach, she at once decided on its application. Accordingly, with her cup of water at her side, and a piece of soft, clean moss in her hand, she began sponging his face, neck, and the flesh around his wounds; and repeating this process at short intervals, she continued the tender assiduities, with only occasional snatches of repose, till the welcome morning light broke over the forest. She then rose, and, with a miniature camp-kettle found among her patient's effects, prepared some gruel from the pounded parched corn which she had brought with her. This he mechanically took from her hand, when aroused for the purpose, but immediately relapsed again into the same state of unconsciousness and stupor in which he had lain through the night. Through the day and night that followed, but little variation was discernible in his condition, and as little was made in his treatment, by his fair, anxious nurse. Through the next day and night it was still the same; but towards night, on the third day after his attack, he began to show signs of amendment, and before dark his fever had entirely subsided. Perceiving this, the rejoiced maiden prepared him some more stimulating nourishment, in the shape of broth made from jerked venison. Having partaken freely of this, he then, with a whispered "*I am much better, Fluella,*" sank back on his couch, and was soon buried in a sweet and tranquil slumber. Having carefully adjusted his blanket around him, and added her own shawl to the covering, and being now once more relieved of her most pressing fears for his fate, the exhausted girl laid down on her own rude couch, and, before she was aware, fell into a slumber so deep and absorbing that she never once awoke till the sun was peering over the eastern mountains the next morning. Her first waking glance was directed to the couch of the invalid. It was empty. Starting to her feet, with a countenance almost wild with concern, she hurriedly ran her eye through the forest around her; when, with a suppressed exclamation of joyful surprise, she soon caught sight of his form, slowly making his way back from a short walk, which he had, on awakening, an hour before, found himself able to take, along a smooth and level path on the bank of the river.

But we have not the space, nor even the ability, to portray adequately the restrained but lively emotions of joy and the charming embarrassment that thrilled the tumultuously-beating bosom of the one, and the deep gratitude and silent admiration that took possession of the other, of this singularly situated young couple, during the succeeding scenes of Claud's now rapid convalescence. Suffice it to say, that, on the afternoon of the second day but one from this auspicious morning, they were on their happy way down through the lakes and the connecting river, to the chief's residence, where they safely arrived some hours before night, and where they were greeted with demonstrations of delight which told what anxieties had been suffered on their account. Here, for the first time, they learned that the murderer had been taken and carried to the village for his preliminary trial; that the examination had been postponed, to allow the prisoner time to send for his counsel; and that the hearing was to commence that very evening, though the hunter, who had that day made a hurried journey to the chief's, to see if Fluella had returned or Claud been heard from, had expressed great fears that the evidence yet discovered might not be deemed sufficient to convict him of murder, and perhaps not to imprison him for a final trial. Claud, perceiving at once the importance of Fluella's testimony, as well as of his own, proposed that they should immediately proceed that evening down the lakes to the place of trial. But neither the chief nor his daughter would suffer him to undertake the journey that night. At her earnest suggestion, however, it was at length arranged that she, accompanied by her half-brother, a lad of fifteen, should go down that evening, and that the chief, with Claud, should follow early the next morning.

In pursuance of this arrangement, the resolute girl and her attendant, as soon as she had changed her dress and refreshed herself with a meal, embarked on the lake, and, at the end of the next hour, they reached the Great Rapids, leading, as before described, down into the Umbagog. Here her brother, whose eye and ear, ever since they started, had often been turned suspiciously to a dark, heavy cloud, which, seeming to hang over the upper portions of the Magalloway, had been continually sending forth peals of heavy thunder, hesitated about proceeding any farther, and warned his unheeding sister of their liability of being overtaken by the thunder-storm. But, finding her determined to proceed, if she was compelled to do so alone, he yielded, and, landing their canoe at the usual carrying places, they shot rapidly down the stream, and in less than another hour came out on the broad Umbagog, just as darkness was beginning to enshroud its waters, and cut off their view of the distant shores for which they were destined. But for the light of day they found an ample substitute in the electric displays, which, lighting up the lake to the blaze of noonday, were every instant leaping from, the black, angry clouds, now evidently passing off, with one almost continued roar of reverberating thunders, but a few miles to the north of them. A rapid row of about three miles now brought them to the foot of the lake, where the maiden had proposed to enter the river, and row down it to the swift water, a short distance above the village, and then proceed by land. Here, however, her course was unexpectedly impeded by one of those paradoxical occurrences which is peculiar to the spot, and which often happens on great and sudden rises of the Magalloway, that, though entering the Androscoggin a mile down its course, thus becomes higher than the level of the Umbagog, and pours its surplus waters along up its stream in the channel of the river last named, with a strong, rushing current into the lake. And our adventurers now found that masses of tangled trees, mill-logs, and all sorts of floodwood, were driving so strongly and thickly up this channel that it would be in vain for them to attempt to proceed in that direction. But the purpose of the heroic girl to reach the village, by some means or other, was not to be thus shaken. She directed the boat to be rowed back to the Elwood Landing, where, leaving it, she with her attendant took the path to the cottage; and reaching this, and finding all dark within she boldly led the way down the long road to the bridge, miles below, with no other light than the still lingering flashes of lightning afforded to her hurrying footsteps. But it was not till after an exhausting walk, and some time past midnight, that she reached the bridge leading over the river to the tavern, where the trial was proceeding; and then only to encounter another great obstacle to her progress. On coming up to the bridge, she perceived, with astonishment and dismay, that one-half of the structure, with the exception of a single string-piece, the only connection now remaining between the two sides of the river, had been swept away by the sudden flood, or the revolving trees it bore on its rushing surface. She also ascertained, from a woman still up, watching with a sick child, in a house near by, that every boat on that side the river had been either carried off by the unexpected freshet, or taken since the bridge went off, by persons still coming in, to get over to the exciting trial, which, it was understood, would occupy the whole night. After pausing a moment, the still unshaken maiden borrowed and lighted a lantern, when, without disclosing her purpose, she left the house and proceeded directly to the end of the string-piece. She first examined it carefully, and finding it broad, level, and fixed in its bed, she then mounted the dizzy beam, and stood for a moment glancing down on the wild rush of roaring waters beneath. Her movements, to which the light she carried had attracted attention, were by this time seen and comprehended by the crowd around the tavern, on the opposite side, who now came rushing to the other end of the bridge, to deter her from the bold attempt. But she heeded them not; and in a moment more was seen, with a quick, firm step, gliding over the awful chasm; in another, she had reached the end, and stood in safety on the planks beyond,—where she was greeted by the throng, who had witnessed with amazement the perilous passage, in a shout of exultation at her escape, that rose loud and wild above the roar of the waters around them.

CHAPTER XXI.

"So those two voices met; so Joy and Death
Mingled their accents; and, amidst the rush
Of many thoughts, the listening poet cried,
O! thou art mighty, thou art wonderful,
Mysterious Nature! Not in thy free range
Of woods and wilds alone, thou blendest thus
The dirge note and the song of festival;
But in one *heart*, one changeful human heart,—
Ay, and within one hour of that strange world,—
Thou call'st their music forth, with all its tones
To startle and to pierce!—the dying Swan's,
And the glad Sky-lark's,—Triumph and Despair!"

Our tale is running rapidly to a close, and we must no more loiter to gather flowers by the wayside, but depict the events which now come thickly crowding together to make up the mingled catastrophe.

When the sheriff and his scores of exulting assistants reached the village with their prisoner,—the desperate villain, whom they had, with so much difficulty and danger, dislodged and seized in his rocky den in the mountains,—the latter requested a postponement of his examination till the afternoon of the next day, that he might have time to send for, and obtain, his lawyer. This request was the more readily granted, as the party sent up the lakes with Moose-killer, for more evidence, had not yet returned, and as their expected discoveries, or at least their presence with those already made, might and would be required to fasten the crime, in law, on the undoubted criminal. The court, therefore, was adjourned to an indefinite hour the next afternoon; and the crowd, except the court, its officers, and those from a distance, dispersed to assemble, the next day, with increased numbers, to witness the final disposal of one who had now become, in the minds of all, the monster outlaw of the settlement. The prisoner was then taken to an adjoining old and empty log-house, a straw-bed laid on the floor for him, and a strong guard placed over him, both within and around the house without; so that, being constantly under the eyes of vigilant, well-armed men, there should be no possibility of his escape, either by his own exertions, or by the aid of secret accomplices. And these precautions being faithfully observed, the night wore away without alarm, or any kind of disturbance. The fore part of the succeeding day also passed, though people soon began to pour into the village from all quarters, with singular quietness,—all seeming to be oppressed with that deep feeling of hushed expectation which may often be seen to predispose men to a sort of restless silence, on the known eve of an exciting event. And, through the whole of it, no incident or circumstance transpired affecting the great interest of the occasion, till about noon; when the news spread that the anxiously-awaited party from the upper lakes were approaching. As they came up to the tavern, the now excited crowd quickly closed around them, and eagerly listened to their report. Of Claud Elwood, whom they had unknowingly passed and repassed, on their way up and down the lakes, while he was lying helpless in the secluded retreat to which his fair and devoted preserver had conveyed him, they had heard nothing, seen nothing, and discovered no clues by which his locality or fate could be traced or conjectured. But they had visited, and carefully examined, the place pointed out by Moose-killer as the one where Mark Elwood was supposed to have been slain; and, although they had failed to find the body on the land, or in the lake, with the best means they could command for dragging it, and although time had measurably effaced the traces by which the sagacious Indian had judged of the suspected deed, yet every appearance went to confirm the strict accuracy of his previous account. And, in addition, they at last found, slightly imbedded in the bark of a tree, in the range of the path, and a short distance to the south of the spot, a rifle bullet, which had evidently been, before striking the tree, smeared with a bloody substance, and also slightly flattened, as it might naturally have been, in striking a bone, on its way through a man's body. This seemed to establish, as a fact, the commission of a murder; but on whom committed was still left a debatable question. The movers of the prosecution had hoped, through this mission up the lakes, to obtain evidence which would conclusively establish the guilt of the prisoner. But, to effect this, and thus insure his conviction, something more conclusive was still obviously wanting. And it was then that the indefatigable hunter made, as the reader has already been apprised, his last rapid but fruitless journey to the chief's residence, in the hope that his mysteriously absent daughter might have returned with discoveries that would complete the chain of evidence. He having come back, however, without accomplishing any part of his object, and the prisoner's counsel having arrived, and, after a consultation with his client, become strangely clamorous to proceed at once to the examination, they finally concluded to go into the hearing with the presumptive evidence in possession, and, backing it with the showing of Gaut's previously suspicious character, for which they were now well prepared, call themselves willing to abide the result. All this being now settled, the court was declared open, and the counsel for the prosecution was requested to proceed with the case.

After the attorney for the prosecution had read the papers on which it was founded, and made a statement of what was expected to be proved in its support, the witnesses in that behalf were called and sworn. The first testimony introduced was that of Codman and others, to show the deep malice and implied threats of revenge which the prisoner had so clearly exhibited towards the supposed murdered man, in the prosecution of which the latter was a principal mover, the winter before. But this evidence, when sifted by the long and severe cross-examination that followed, and found to consist, instead of definite words, almost wholly of menacing looks and other silent demonstrations of rage, which are ever extremely difficult to bring out in words with their original effect, amounted to so little that the prisoner's counsel attempted to turn it into ridicule with considerable show of success. Testimony in relation to the canoe of the Elwoods, recently found washed up among the rapids, which was next introduced, was found, when tested in the same way, in despite of the opinions of the practical boatmen who were the witnesses, to be almost equally inconclusive of the prisoner's guilt; so much so, indeed, that his counsel seemed greatly inclined to appropriate it, as showing the probable manner in which the Elwoods, if they were not still both alive, had come to their end.

By this time,—as the court of inquiry was not opened till nearly sunset, and as the examinations, cross-examinations, and preliminary speeches of the opposing counsel, on disputed points of evidence, had been drawn out to seemingly almost interminable lengths,—by this time, it was nearly midnight; and the prosecuting party now proposed an adjournment till morning. But this was strenuously opposed by Gaut's lawyer, who, affecting to believe that the whole affair was a malicious prosecution growing out of the suit last winter, and got up by certain men who had banded together to revenge their defeat on that occasion, and ruin his client, boldly demanded that the prisoner should be discharged, or his conspiring enemies be compelled to proceed at once with "their sham prosecution," as he put on the face to call it.

This stand, which was obviously instigated by the prisoner himself, who narrowly watched the proceedings, and, from time to time, was seen whispering in the ear of his counsel, produced the desired effect: the motion was overruled, and the counsel for the prosecution told to go on with his evidence.

Moose-killer was then called on to the witnesses' stand, when, for the first time, Gaut exhibited evident feigns of uneasiness, and whispered something in the ear of his counsel, who thereupon rose and went into a labored argument against the admissibility of the evidence of an Indian, who was a pagan, and knew nothing about the God whose invocation constituted the sacred effect of the oath he had taken. But, on the questioning of the court, Moose-killer declared his full belief in the white Christian's God and Bible, and this objection was overruled, and the witness requested to proceed with his story.

The demure Indian, unmoved by the burning and vengeful eye of Gaut, which was kept constantly riveted upon him, then succinctly but clearly related all the facts, of which the reader has been apprised in the preceeding pages, in relation to the atrocious deed under investigation. And at the conclusion of his story he produced the bullet found imbedded in the tree, called attention to its smeared and flattened appearance, and then asked for the prisoner's rifle, to see whether it would fit in the bore. The rifle in question was then brought into court, the bullet applied to the muzzle, and pronounced an exact fit! A shout of exultation burst from the crowd, and in a tone so significant of the public feeling, and of their unanimous opinion on this point, that for a moment both the prisoner and his counsel were completely disconcerted. But, soon rallying, the latter started to his feet, and, having summoned back to its place his usual quantum of brass, demanded "the privilege of just looking at that rifle they were all making such a fuss about." It was accordingly handed to him; when, after noticing the size of the bore, which was a common one, and then glancing at some other rifles held in the hands of different spectators, he confidently requested that the first half-dozen rifles to be found among the crowd should be brought on to the stand. Five of the designated number were soon gathered and brought forward; and it was found, in the comparison, that three of them were of the same bore as that of Gaut, and that the ball in question would fit one as well as another.

"There! what has become of your bullet evidence now?" sneeringly exclaimed the exulting attorney. "Wondrous conclusive, a'n't it? But, as weak as the whole story is, I will make it still weaker. It is my turn with you now, my foxy red friend," he added, settling back in his seat to commence his cross-examination.

His vaunted cross-examination, however, resulted in giving him no advantage. The Indian could not be made, in the whole hour the brow-beating inquisitor devoted to him, either to cross himself or vary a single statement of his direct testimony, and he was petulantly ordered to leave the stand.

"Not done talk yet," said Moose-killer, lingering, and glancing inquiringly to the court and the counsel for the prosecution. "More story me tell yet."

Gaut's lawyer looked up doubtfully to the witness; but, thinking he must have told all he could to implicate the prisoner, and that any thing now added might show discrepancies, of which some advantage could be taken, remained silent, and, for once, interposed no objection to letting the Indian take his own course; when the latter, on receiving an encouraging intimation to speak from the other attorney, proceeded, in his peculiarly broken but graphic manner, to make in substance the following extraordinary revelation:

About ten years ago (he said), there came, from what part nobody knew, a strange, questionable personage, into the neighborhood of a few families of St. Francois Indians, encamping for the hunting season around the headwater lakes of the Long River, as he termed the Connecticut, and went to trapping for sable and beaver. But he soon fell into difficulties with the Indians, who believed he robbed their traps; and with one family in particular he had a fierce and bitter altercation. This family had a small child, that began to ramble from the wigwam out into the woods, and that, one night, failed to come home. They suspected who had got it, and next day followed the trail to the man's camp; when they soon found where the child had been butchered, cut up, and used to bait his sable-traps! But the monster, becoming alarmed, had fled, and never afterwards could be found.

With this, Moose-killer, who had evidently put his story in this shape to avoid interruption, suddenly paused, and then, with one hand raised imploringly towards the court and the other stretched out menacingly towards the prisoner, wildly exclaimed:

"O, that was *my* child! and this was the man who murdered it!"

A thrill of horror ran through the crowd as the witness came to the conclusion of his revolting story. And so completely were all taken by surprise by the startling, and as most of them believed truthful, revelation, and so great was the sensation produced by the appalling atrocities it disclosed, that the proceedings of the court were for some moments brought to a dead stand. But soon the shrill, harsh voice of Gaut's lawyer was heard rising above the buzz of the excited crowd, and bursting in a storm of denunciation and abuse on the witness, and all those who had a hand in bringing him forward, to thrust in, against all rule, such a story,—which, if true, had no more to do with the prosecution now in progress than the first chapter of the Alcoran. But it was not true. It was a monstrous fabrication. It represented as a fact what never occurred in all Christendom. It was stamped with falsehood on the face of it; and not only spoke for itself as such, but was a virtual self-impeachment of the witness, whose whole testimony the court should now throw to the winds. And so, for the next half-hour, he went on, ranting and raving, till the court, interposing, assured him that the witness' last story would not be treated as testimony in the case; when he became pacified, and took his seat.

The counsel on the other side, who, during his opponent's explosive display of rhetorical gas and brimstone, had been holding an earnest consultation with Phillips (now also at hand with a disclosure which had been reserved for the present moment), then calmly rose, and said he had a statement to make, which he stood ready to substantiate, and to which he respectfully asked the attention of the court, as a matter that should be taken into the account in considering the prisoner's guilt in the present case, it being one of the many offences that appeared to have marked his career of almost unvarying crime and iniquity. He was well aware of the *general* rule of evidence, which excludes matters not directly connected with the point at issue; but there *were* cases in which that rule often had, and necessarily ever must be, materially varied,—as in the *crim. con.* cases reported in the books, where previous like acts were admitted, to show the probability of the commission of the one charged, and also in cases like the present, resting, as he admitted it thus far did, on presumptive evidence. In this view, notwithstanding all that had been said or intimated, he believed the concluding testimony of the last witness proper to be considered in balancing the presumptions of the prisoner's guilt or innocence. And especially relevant did he deem the statement, and the introduction of the evidence he had at hand to substantiate it, which he had now risen to offer. But, even were it otherwise, it would soon be seen that the step he was about to take would be particularly suitable to be taken while the court and the officers of justice were together, and the prisoner under their control. With these preliminary remarks, he would now proceed with the statement he had proposed.

"This man," continued the attorney (whom we will now report in the first person), "the man who stands here charged, and, in the minds of nine out of ten of all present, I fearlessly affirm, *justly* charged, with a murder, to the deliberate atrocity of which scarce a parallel can be found in the world's black catalogue of crime,—this man, I say, is a felon-refugee from British justice.

"Many years ago,—as some here present may know, as a matter of history,—a secret and somewhat extended conspiracy to subvert the government of Lower Canada was seasonably discovered and crushed at Quebec, which was its principal seat, and which, according to the plan of the conspirators, was to be the first object of assault and seizure. This was to be effected by the contemporaneous rising of a strong force within the city, headed by a bold adventurer, a bankrupt merchant from Rhode Island, and of an army of raftsmen, collected from the rivers, without, led on by a reckless and daring, half-Scotch, half-Indian Canadian, who had acquired great influence over that restless and ruffian class of men. The former had been in the province in the year before, and, from witnessing the popular disaffection then rampant from the enforcement of an odious act of their Parliament to compel the building of roads, had, with the instigation of such desperate fellows as the latter, his Canadian accomplice, conceived this plot, and had now come on, with a small band of recruits, to carry it into execution; when, as all was nearly ripe for the outbreak, the whole plot was discovered. The poor Yankee leader was seized, tried for high treason, condemned to death, and strung up by the neck from the walls of Quebec. [Footnote: See Christie's History of Lower Canada] But the more wary and fortunate Canadian leader, though tenfold more guilty, escaped into the wilderness, this side of the British line; lingered a year or two in this region, trapping and robbing the Indians; then took to smuggling; engaged in the service of the man whose murder we are now investigating, followed him to the city, nearly ruined him there, and then dogged him to this settlement to complete his destruction."

"Who do you mean?" thundered Gaut Gurley.

"Ask your own conscience," replied the attorney, fearlessly confronting the prisoner.

"'Tis false as hell!" rejoined Gaut, with a countenance convulsed with rage.

"No, you mistake,—it is as true as hell," promptly retorted the other; "or, rather, as true as there is one for such wretches as you. Mr. Phillips," he added, turning to the hunter, who stood a little in the background, with his rifle poised on his left arm, with an air of carelessness, but, as a close inspection would have shown, so grasped by his right hand, held down out of sight, as to enable him to bring it to an instant aim,—"Mr. Phillips, were you in the habit of going to Quebec, fall and spring, to dispose of your peltries, about the time of this plotted insurrection?"

"I was."

"Did you ever have the Canada leader I have spoken of pointed out to you, previous to the outbreak?"

"Often, on going down the Chaudiere river, often; why, I knew him by sight as well as the devil knows his hogs!"

"Did you afterwards see and identify him in this region?"

"I did."

"Is not, then, all I have stated true; and is not the prisoner, here, the man?"

"All as true as the Gospel of St. Mark; and that *is* the man, the very man; under the oath of God, I swear it!"

During this brief but terribly pointed dialogue, Gaut Gurley,—whose handcuffs, on his complaint that they galled his wrists, had been removed after he came into court,—sat watching Phillips with that same singularly sinister expression which we have, on one or two previous occasions, tried to describe him as exhibiting. It was a certain indescribable, whitish, lurid light, flashing and quivering over his countenance, that made the beholder involuntarily recoil. And, as the last words were uttered, his hand was seen covertly stealing up under the lapel of his coat; but it was instantly arrested and dropped, at the sharp click of the cocking of the hunter's rifle, which was also seen stealing up to his shoulder.

"Nonsense!" half audibly said the sheriff, to something which, during the bustle and sensation following these manifestations, the hunter had been whispering in his ear; "nonsense! I searched him myself, and *know* there is nothing of the kind about him."

"I am not so sure about that," responded the hunter, edging along through the crowd, with his eye still on the prisoner, and soon disappearing out of the door.

This little judicial interlude in the remarks of the attorney being over, he resumed:

"My statement having been thus corroborated, and, as I am most happy to find, without any of the expected interruptions, it now only remains for me to say, that this indefatigable Mr. Phillips, becoming perfectly convinced that the prisoner was a man of whom it was a patriotic duty to rid the settlement, has, within the last two months, made a journey into Canada; obtained a written official request from the governor-general, addressed to the governor of New Hampshire, for the delivery of Gaut Gurley, at the time when, on notice, the proper officers would be in waiting to receive him; that our governor has responded by issuing his warrant; which," he continued, drawing out a document, "I now, in this presence, deliver to the sheriff, to be served, but only served, in case we fail—as I do not at all anticipate—to secure the commitment and final conviction of the prisoner, on the flagitious offence now under investigation, and loudly demanding expiation under our own violated laws, in preference to delivering him up for the punishment of other and less crying felonies."

The prisoner and his counsel, on this new and unexpected development, held an earnest whispered consultation. The latter had supposed, till almost the last moment, that his opponent was intending only to bring in another piece of what he deemed wholly irrelevant testimony, in the shape of another gone-by transaction; and he was preparing another storm of wrath for the judicial outrage. But, when he found that the statement was a preliminary to a different and more alarming movement, and especially when he saw placed in the sheriff's hands a warrant for delivering up his client to the British, to be tried for a former felony, from the punishment of which, he feared, from what he had just heard, there would be no escape, he was sadly nonplussed, and knew not which way to turn himself. And it was not until Gaut, who, though thus suddenly brought into a dilemma which he was little expecting, was yet at no loss to decide on his course,—that of making every possible effort to escape the more immediate pending danger, and then of trusting to chance for eluding the more remote one just brought to view,—it was not till Gaut, with assurances of the last being but a miserable, trumped-up affair, had pushed and goaded him up to action, that the dumbfounded attorney recovered his old confidence. He then straightened back in his seat, and, with the air of one who has meekly borne some imposition, or breach of privilege, till it can be borne no longer, turned gruffly to his opponent, and said:

"Well, sir, having dragged every thing into this case except what legitimately belongs to it, I want to know if you are through, *now?* We, on our side, have no need of introducing testimony to meet any thing you have yet been able to show. Why, you have not even established the first essential fact to be settled in prosecutions for homicide. You have arraigned my client for killing a man, and yet have shown nobody killed! No, *we* shall introduce no witnesses till the body of the alleged murdered man is produced; for, till then, no court on earth—But I am not making a speech, and will not anticipate. All I intended was, to ask, as I do again, are you through with your evidence *now?*"

The attorney for the prosecution then admitted—rather prematurely, as it was soon seen—that he thought of nothing more which he wished to introduce.

"Go on with your opening speech, then," resumed the former.

"No," said the other, "I waive my privilege of the opening and close, and will only claim the closing speech."

"O, very well, sir," said Gaut's lawyer, throwing a surprised and suspicious look around, as if to see whether some trap was not involved in this unexpected waiver of the usually claimed privilege. "Very well; don't blame you; shouldn't think you could find honest materials even for one speech."

The hard-faced attorney, who was reputed one of the best of what are sometimes termed *devil's lawyers,* in all that part of the country, then consequentially gathered up his minutes of the testimony, glanced over them, and, clearing his throat, commenced his great final speech, which was to annihilate his opponent, and quash the whole proceedings of the prosecution. But he had scarcely spoken ten words, before a tremendous shout, rising somewhere in the direction of the bridge,—to which their attention had been before called, when a part of it had been swept away during the first hours of the night,—broke and reverberated into the room, bringing him to an instant stand. Feeling that something extraordinary had occurred, the startled court, parties and spectators, alike paused, and eagerly listened for something further to explain the sudden outbreak. But, for several minutes, all was still, or hushed down to the low hum of mingling voices, and not a distinct, intelligible sound reached their expectant senses. Soon, however, the noise of trampling feet and the rush of crowds was heard, and perceived to be rapidly approaching the door of the court-room. And the next moment the clear, loud voice of the now evidently excited hunter was heard exultantly ringing out the announcement:

"A witness, a new witness! A witness that saw the very deed!"

This sudden and exciting announcement of an occurrence which had been hoped for, in some shape, on one side, and feared on the other, but, at this late hour of the night, little expected by either, at once threw all within the crowded courtroom into bustle and commotion. Both parties to the prosecution were consequently taken by surprise; and both, though neither of them were yet apprised of the character of the witness, were aroused and agitated by the significant announcement. But, of all present, none seemed so much stirred as the obdurate prisoner, who had, thus far in the examination, scarcely once wholly lost his usual look of bold assurance, but who now was seen casting rapid, uneasy, and evidently troubled glances towards the door; doubtless expecting, each moment, to see the fear which had haunted him from the first—that Claud Elwood would turn up alive, and appear in court against him—realized in the person of the new witness. His lawyer also, appeared to be seized with similar apprehensions; and, the next moment, he was heard loudly demanding the attention of the court. He objected, he *pointedly* objected, he *protested*, in advance, against the admission of further testimony. He had borne *every thing* during the hearing, but could not bear *this*. The pleas were closed, and the case concluded against the introduction of new evidence; and that, too, by the express notice and agreement of the counsel for the prosecution. And now to open it would be in glaring violation of all rule, all law, and all precedent. In short, it would be an outrage too gross to be tolerated anywhere but in a land of despotism. And, if the court would not at once decide to exclude the threatened testimony, he must be heard at length on the subject.

But the court declining so to decide, and intimating that they were willing to hear an argument on the point, of any reasonable length, he spread himself for the wordy onset. The sheriff—who, in the mean time, had started for the door to make an opening in the crowd for the expected entrance,—seeing that a long speech was in prospect, now went out, conducted the proffered witness, in waiting near by, to another room in the house to remain there till called; and then returned, and, in a low tone, made some communication to the court.

The pertinacious lawyer then went on with his heated protest, as it might be called far more properly than an argument, to the length of nearly an hour. The calm, manly, and cogent reply of his opponent occupied far less time, but obtained far more favor with the sitting magistrates; who, after a short consultation among themselves, unanimously decided to hear the proposed evidence, and thereupon ordered the sheriff to conduct the witness at once into court.

A breathless silence now ensued in the court-room, and every eye was involuntarily turned towards the door. In a few minutes the sheriff closely followed, by two females, made his appearance and cleared his way up to the stand that had been occupied by the witnesses. No names had been announced, and both the ladies were veiled, so that their faces could not be seen in the dusky apartment, lighted only by two dim candles, made dimmer, seemingly, by the morning twilight, then beginning to steal through the windows, and to produce that dismal and almost sickening hue peculiar to the equal mingling of the natural light of day with the artificial light of lamp or taper. And it was not consequently known, except to one or two individuals, who they were; but enough was seen, in the enlarged form and sober tread of the one, and in the rounded, trim figure and elastic step of the other, to show the former to be a middle-aged matron, and the latter a youthful maiden. Each was garbed in rich black silk, to which were added, in the one case, some of the usual emblems of mourning, and in the other, a few simple, tastily contrasted, light trimmings.

"What are these ladies' names? or rather, first, I will ask, which of them is the witness?" said the leading magistrate.

"I am, I suppose," said the maiden, in tones as soft and tremulous as the lightly-touched chord of some musical instrument, as she threw back her veil, and disclosed a beauty of features and sweetness of countenance that at once raised a buzz of admiration through the room.

"Your name, young lady?"

"Fluella, sir; and this lady at my side is Mrs. Mark Elwood, who comes only as my friend."

"You understand the usages of courts, I conclude; and, if so, will now receive the oath, and go on to tell what you know relative to the crime for which, you have doubtless heard, the prisoner here is arraigned."

At once raising her hand, she was sworn, and proceeded directly to state that part of the transaction she had witnessed on the lake, which the hunter, in the conversation she found means to have with him while waiting to be taken into court, had advised her was all that would be important as evidence in the case.

Gaut Gurley, the alarmed prisoner, who at first had appeared greatly relieved on finding that the announced witness was not the reanimated young Elwood, as he had feared, now seemed utterly at fault to conjecture what either of these women could know of his crime. But the moment the maiden, whom he had seen the previous year, and regarded with jealous dislike, as the possible rival of his daughter, revealed herself to his view, his looks grew dark and suspicious; and when she commenced by mentioning, as she did at the outset, that she was on a boat excursion along the western shore of the Maguntic, on the well-remembered day when he consummated his long cherished atrocity, he seemed to comprehend the drift of what was coming, and his eyes fastened on her with the livid glare of a tiger; while those demoniac flashes, before noted as the usual percursor of hellish intent with him, began to burn up and play over his contracting countenance.

But these suspicious indications had escaped the notice of all,—even of the watchful hunter, whose looks, with those of the rest, were for the moment hanging, with intense interest, on the speaking lips of the fair witness. And she proceeded uninterrupted, till, having described the position in the thicket on shore, in which she was standing, as Mark Elwood, followed by Gaut Gurley, both of whom she recognized, came along, she, nerving herself for the task, raised her voice, and said:

"I distinctly saw Mr. Elwood fall, convulsed in death,—heard the fatal shot, and instantly traced it to Gaut, before he had taken his smoking rifle from his shoulder,—this same man who now—"

When, as she was uttering the last words, and turning to the prisoner, she stopped short, recoiled, and uttered a loud shriek of terror. And, the next instant, the deafening report of a pistol burst from the corner where the prisoner was sitting, filling the room with smoke, and bringing every man to his feet, in the amazement and alarm that seized all at the sudden outbreak.

There was a dead pause for a moment; and then was heard the sudden rush of men, the sharp, brief struggle, and the heavy fall of the grappled prisoner, as he was borne overpowered to the floor.

"Thank God!" exclaimed the hunter, the first to reach the bewildered maiden, and ascertain what had befell from this fiendish attempt to take her life simply because she was instrumental in bringing a wretch to justice,— "thank God, she is unhurt! The bullet has only cut the dress on her side, and passed into the wall beyond."

"Order in court!" sternly cried the head magistrate. "It is enough! Mr. Phillips, conduct these ladies to some more suitable apartment. We wish for no more proof. The prisoner's guilt is already piled mountain-high. We commit him to your hands, Mr. Sheriff. Within one hour, let him be on his way to Lancaster jail, there to await his final trial and doom, for one of the foulest murders that ever blasted the character of human kind!"

We will not attempt to describe, in detail, the lively and bustling scene, which, for the next hour or two, now ensued in and around the tavern, that had lately been the unaccustomed theatre of so many new and startling developments. The running to and fro of the excited and jubilant throng of men, women, and children, who, in their anxiety to witness and know the result of the trial, had passed the whole night in the place,—the partaking of the hastily snatched breakfast, in the tavern, by some, or on logs or bunches of shingles in the yard, by others, from provisions brought along with them, from home,—the hurried harnessing of horses and running out of wagons, preparatory to the departure of those here with the usual vehicles of travel,— the resounding blows and lumbering sounds of the score of lusty men who had volunteered to replace and repair the bridge from the old materials luckily thrown on the bank a short distance down the stream, so as to permit the departing teams, going in that direction, to pass safely over,—and, lastly, the bringing out, the placing on his bed of straw in the bottom of a wagon, and the moving off of the caged lion, with his cavalcade of guards before and behind,—the fiercely exultant hurrahing of the execrating crowd, as he disappeared up the road to the west, together with the crowning, extra loud and triumphant *kuk-kuk-ke-o-ho!* of Comical Codman, who had mounted a tall stump for the purpose, and made the preliminary declaration that, if he was *ever* to have another crow, it should be now, on seeing the Devil's unaccountable and first cousin, to say the least, in relationship, so handsomely cornered, and, at last so securely put in limbo,—these, all these combined to form a scene as stirring to the view, as it was replete with moral picturesque to the mind. But we must content ourself with this meagre outline; another and a different, quickly succeeding scene in the shifting panorama, now demands our attention.

Among the crowd who had arranged themselves in rows, to witness the departure of the court officials and the prisoner, were the two now inseparable friends, Mrs. Elwood and Fluella; who, on turning from the spectacle, had strolled, arm-in-arm, to a green, shaded grass-plot at the farther end of the tavern building, and were now, with pensive but interested looks, bending over the garden fence, and inspecting a small parterre of budding flowers, which female taste had, even in a place so lately redeemed from the forest as this, found means to introduce. They were lingering here, while others were departing, for the arrival of expected friends, though evidently not conscious of their very near approach. But even then, as they stood listlessly gazing over upon the mute objects of their interest, those friends were coming across the bridge, in the singularly contrasted forms of an aged man, walking without any staff, and with a firm elastic tread, and quite a youngerly one, walking *with* a cane, and with careful steps and a restrained gait, betokening some lingering soreness of body or limb. On reaching the nearest part of the tavern-yard, the young man gazed eagerly round among the still numerous crowd, when, his eye falling on those of whom he seemed to be in search, he turned to his companion and said:

"There they are, Chief, I will go forward and take them by surprise."

The next moment he was standing closely behind the unconscious objects of his attention; when, with a smiling lip but silent tongue, he gently laid a hand on a shoulder of each.

"Claud!" burst from the lips of the surprised and reddening maiden, the first to turn to the welcome intruder.

"Claud! Claud!" exclaimed the agitated matron, as she also turned, in grateful surprise, to greet, for the first time since his return, her heart's idol. "My son! my son!" she continued, with gathering emotion, "are you indeed restored alive to my arms, and, but for you, my now doubly desolate home? Thank Heaven! O thank Heaven! for the happy, happy restoration!"

"That is right, dear mother!" at length responded the visibly touched young man, gently disengaging himself from the long maternal embrace; "that is all right. But," he added, turning to the maiden, whose sympathetic tears were coursing down her fair cheeks, "if you would thank any *earthly* being for the preservation of my life, it should be this good and lovely girl at your side."

"I know it," said the mother, after a thoughtful pause, "I know it; and, Claud, I would that she were *indeed* my daughter."

There was an embarrassing pause. But the embarrassment was not perceived and felt by these two young persons alone. Another, unknown to them, had silently witnessed the whole interview from an open, loosely-curtained window of the chamber above; and perceived, and felt, and appreciated, all that had transpired, in word and look, no less keenly than the young couple, whose beating hearts, only, were measuring the moments of their silent perplexity. That other was Gaut Gurley's lovely and luckless but strong-hearted daughter. Having instinctively read her father's guilt, she had come to his trial with a sinking heart; shut herself up alone in this small chamber; so arranged the screening curtains that she could sit by the open window unseen, and kept her post through that long night of her silent woe, hearing all that was said by the crowd below, and, through their comments, becoming apprised of all that was going on in the court-room, in the order it transpired. She had known of Fluella's arrival,—her perilous passage over the river,—of the report she then made to the hunter of her discoveries,—of her bringing back the wounded Claud in safety,—of the dastardly attempt of the prisoner to take that heroic girl's life,—of his sentence, and, finally, of his departure for prison, amidst the execrations of a justly indignant people. She had known all this, and felt it, to the inmost core of her rent heart, with the twofold anguish of a broken-hearted lover and a fate-smitten daughter. She had wrestled terribly with her own heart, and she had conquered. She had determined her destiny; and now, on witnessing the last part of the tender scene enacting under her window, she suddenly formed the high resolve of crowning her self-immolation by a public sacrifice.

Accordingly she hastily rose from her seat, and, without thought or care of toilet, descended rapidly to the yard, and, with hurrying step and looks indicative of settled purpose, moved directly towards the deeply surprised actors in the little scene, of which she had thus been made the involuntary witness.

"No ceremony!" she said, in tones of unnatural calmness, with a forbidding gesture to Claud, who, while Fluella was instinctively shrinking to the side of the more unmoved but still evidently disturbed Mrs. Elwood, had advanced a step for a respectful greeting. "No ceremony—it is needless; and no fears, fair girl, and anxious mother—they are without cause. I come not to mar, but to make, happiness. Claud Elwood, my heart once opened and turned to you, as the sunflower to its god; and our paths of love met, and, for a while, ran on pleasantly together as one. But, even then, something whispered me they would soon again diverge, and lead off to separate destinies. The boded divergence, as I feared, began with the fatal family feud of last winter, and has now resulted, as I still more feared, in plunging us, respectively, in degradation and sorrow, and also in placing our destinies as wide as the poles asunder. Claud, Claud Elwood,—can you love this beautiful girl at your side? You speak not. I *know* that you can. I relinquish, then, whatever I may have possessed of your heart, to her, if *she* wills. And why should she not? Why reject one whose life she would peril her own to save? She will not. Be you two, then, one; and may all the earthly happiness *I* once dreamed of, with none of the bitter alloy it has been my lot to experience, be henceforth yours. You will know me no more. With to-morrow's sun, I travel to a distant cloister, where the world, with its tantalizing loves and dazzling ambitions, will be nothing more to me forever. Farewell, Claud! farewell, gentle, heroic maiden! farewell, afflicted, happy mother! If the prayers of Avis Gurley have virtue, their first incense shall rise for the healing of all the heart-wounds one of her family has inflicted."

As the fair speaker ceased, and turned away from this doubtless unspeakably painful performance of what she deemed her last worldly duty, as well as an acceptable opening act in the life of penance to which she had resolved now to devote herself, an audible murmur of applause ran through the throng, who, in spite of their wish not to appear intrusive, had paused at a little distance, to listen to and witness the unexpected and singular scene. Among the voices which had been thus more distinctly raised was that of a stranger, who, having arrived a few minutes before, given his horse to the waiter, shook hands with the hunter and the chief, to whom he appeared well known, had joined the crowd to see what was going on, and who had been particularly emphatic in the open expression of his admiration. The remembered tones of his voice, though attracting no attention from others, instantly reached the quick ears of one of the more silent actors of the little scene we have been describing. She threw a quick, eager glance around her; and, having soon singled out from the now scattering crowd, the person of whom her sparkling eye seemed in search, she flew forward towards him, with the joyful cry:

"My father! my white father! I am glad, O, so glad you have come!" and she eagerly grasped his outstretched hand, shook it, kissed him, and, being now relieved from the embarrassment she had keenly felt in the position in which she had just been so unexpectedly placed, appeared to be all joy and animation.

"Come, come, Fluella, don't shake my arm off, nor bother me now with questions," laughingly said the gentleman, thus affectionately beset, as he pulled the joyous girl along towards the spot where the wondering Mrs. Elwood and her son were standing. "You must not quite monopolize me; here are others who may wish to see me."

"Arthur!" exclaimed Mrs. Elwood, with a look of astonishment, after once or twice parting her lips to speak, and then pausing, as if in doubt, as the other was coming up with his face too much averted to be fairly seen by her; "it is—it is—Arthur Elwood!"

"Yes, you are right, sister Alice," responded the hard-visaged little man thus addressed, extending his hand. "It is the same odd stick of an old bachelor that he always was. But who is this?" he added, with an inclination of the head towards Claud. "Your son, I suppose?"

The formal introduction to each other of the (till then) personally unacquainted uncle and nephew; the full developing to the astonished mother and son of the fact, already inferred from what they had just witnessed, that this, their eccentric kinsman, was no other than the foster-father of Fluella,—that he was the owner of large tracts of the most valuable wild lands around these lakes, the oversight of which, together with the unexpected tutelary care of the Elwood family since their removal to the settlement, he had intrusted to the prudent and faithful Phillips,—and, finally, the melancholy mingling of sorrows for the untimely death of the fated brother, husband, and father of these deeply-sympathizing co-relatives, now, like chasing lights and shadows from alternating sunshine and cloud on a landscape, followed in rapid succession, in unfolding to the mournfully happy circle their mutual positions and bonds of common interest.

"Evil has its antidotes," remarked Arthur Elwood, as the conversation on these subjects began to flag and give room for other thoughts growing out of the association; "evil has its antidotes, and sorrow its alleviating joys. And especially shall we realize this, if the suggestions of that self-sacrificing girl, who has just addressed you so feelingly, be now followed. What say you, Claud?"

"They will be," promptly responded the young man, at once comprehending all which the significant question involved; "they will be, on my part, uncle Arthur, joyfully,—proudly."

"And you, Fluella?" persisted the saucy querist, turning to the blushing girl.

"He has not asked me yet," she quickly replied, with a look in which maiden pride, archness, and unuttered happiness, were charmingly blended. "If he should, and *you* should command me"—

"Command? *command!* Now, that is a good one, Fluella," returned the laughing foster-father. "Well, well, a woman will be a woman still, any way you can fix it. All right, however, I presume. But, chief," he added, turning to the natural father, who stood with the hunter a little in the background, "what has been going on here cannot have escaped your keen observation; and you ought to have a voice in this matter. What do *you* say?"

"The chief," replied the other, with his usual dignity, "the chief has had one staff, one light of his lodge; he will now have two. Wenongonet is content."

"It is settled, then," rejoined the former, whose usually passionless countenance was now beaming with pleasure; "all right, all round. Now, sister Alice, let us all adjourn to your house, where you and Fluella, from some of those splendid lake trout which I and Mr. Phillips, who, as well as the chief, must be of the party, will first go out and catch for you,—you and Fluella, I say, must cook us up a nice family dinner, over which we will discuss matters at large, and have a good time generally."

In a few minutes more the happy group were on their way to the Elwood cottage.

The principal interest of our story is at an end; and with it, also, the story itself should speedily terminate. A few words more, however, seem necessary, to anticipate the inquiries which will very naturally arise in the mind of the reader, respecting what might be expected soon to follow the *eclaircissement* of the few last pages; and, accordingly, as far as can be done without marring the unity of time, we will proceed, briefly, to answer the inquiries thus arising.

The body of the fated Mark Elwood, perforated through the breast by the bullet of his cold-blooded murderer, having broken from the sinking weights attached to it, and risen to the surface of the lake, was found in about a fortnight, brought home, and buried on his farm.

Not far from the same time the faithful hunter received, from the hands of a gentleman passing through the settlement, a deed of gift of three hundred acres of valuable timber-land, adjoining his own little patch of a lot, all duly drawn, signed, and executed by Arthur Elwood; who, after a pleasant sojourn of a week at the Elwood cottage, apprising its inmates of what he had in store for them, in the line of property, had departed for his home, a happier man than he had been, since, for secret griefs, he had dissolved partnership with his brother Mark, and left the little interior village where the pair first made their humble beginning in life.

Codman, the trapper, continued to trap it still, and, as all the settlers within a circuit of many miles around them were often unmistakably made aware, to crow as usual on all extra occasions.

Tomah, the college-learned Indian, immediately left, with the escort of the prisoner, and, kept away by the force of some associations connected with the settlement as disagreeable to him as they were conjecturable to others, was never again seen in the settlement; against which, on leaving, he seemed to have kicked off the dust of his feet behind him.

Carvil, the cultivated amateur hunter, had also immediately departed, with the court party, on his way to his pleasant home in the Green Mountains; not wholly to relinquish, however, his yearly sojourns in the forests, to regain health impaired for the want of a more full supply of his coveted, life-giving oxygen.

And, lastly, Gaut Gurley, whose infernal scheming and revolting atrocities have been so inseparably interwoven with the main incidents of our story, broke jail, on the night preceding the day set for his final trial, by digging through the thick stone wall of his prison, with implements evidently furnished from without, leaving bloody traces of his difficult egress through the hardly sufficient hole he had effected for the purpose; and, though instant search was everywhere made for him, he was not, to the sad disappointment of the thousands intending to be in at the hanging, anywhere to be found or heard of in the country. And the mystery of his retreat, and the still unexplained mystery of his strange and ruinous influence over the man whom he at last so flagitiously murdered, were not cleared up until years afterwards.

SEQUEL.

It was a terrible storm. The wind, with all the awful accompaniments of rain, hail, rattling thunders, and fiercely glaring lightnings, had burst down upon the liquid plains of the startled deep, in all the fury of a tropical tornado. The black heavens were in terrific commotion above; and the smitten and resilient waters, as if to escape the impending wrath of the aroused sister elements, were fleeing in galloping mountains athwart the surface of the boiling ocean, beneath.

Could aught human, or aught of human construction, be here, now, and survive? It would seem an utter impossibility; and yet it was so. Amidst all this deafening din of battling elements, that were filling the heavens with their uproar and lashing the darkened ocean into wild fury and commotion, a staunch-built West India merchant-ship was seen, now madly plunging into the troughs of the sea, and now quivering like a feather on the towering waves, or scudding through the flying spray with fearful velocity before the howling blast.

On her flush deck, and lashed to the helm, with the breaking waves dashing around his feet, and the water dripping from the close cap and tightly-buttoned pea-jacket in which he was garbed, stood her gallant master, in the performance of a duty which he, true to his responsibility, would intrust to no other, in such an hour as this,—that of guiding his storm-tossed bark among the frightful billows that were threatening every instant, to engulf her. Thus swiftly onward drove the seemingly devoted ship, strained, shivering, and groaning beneath the terrible power of the gale, like an over-ridden steed, as she dashed, yet unharmed, through the mist and spray and constantly-breaking white caps of the wildly-rolling deep; thus onward sped she, for the full space of two hours, when the wind gradually lulled, and with it the deafening uproar subsided. Presently a young, well-dressed gentleman made his appearance on deck, amidships, and, having noted a while the now evident subsidence of the tempest, slowly and carefully, from one grasped rope to another, made his way to the side of the captain, at the wheel.

"A frightful blow, Mr. Elwood," said the latter; "for the twenty years I have been a seaman, I have never seen the like."

"It certainly has exceeded all my conceptions of a sea-storm," said the other. "But do you know where we are, and where driving at this tremendous speed?"

"Yes, I think I do, both. When we were struck by the gale, which I saw was going to be a terrible norther, and saw it, too, very luckily, at a distance that enabled me to become well prepared for it, look at my reckoning, and make all my calculations,—when we were struck, we were three hundred and fifty miles out of Havana, north'ard, and about forty from the American coast. I at once put the ship before the wind, and set her course southeast, which, being perfectly familiar with these seas, I knew would give her a safe run, and, in about sixty miles, carry her by the southern point of the Little Bahama Bank, where, rounding this great breakwater against northers, we should be in a comparatively smooth sea, that would admit of either laying to or anchoring. It is now over two hours since we started on this fearful race, which has kept my heart in my mouth the whole time; and I am expecting, every minute, to get sight of that rocky headland."

"But that," rejoined Elwood (for the gentleman was no other than Claud Elwood, as the reader has doubtless already inferred), "that will bring us, according to the late rumor, into one of the principal haunts of the pirates, will it not?"

"Yes, partly, perhaps," replied the captain; "but I hear that Commodore Porter has arrived, with the American squadron, in these seas, to break up these pests, and I presume *has* done it, or frightened them away, so that we sha'n't be molested. At any rate, I saw no safer course to outlive such a tempest. You are the owner of ship and cargo, to be sure; but you put on me the responsibility of her safety."

"Certainly," rejoined the other, "for my guidance would be a poor one; and, instead of any disposition to criticise your course, Captain Golding, I feel but too grateful, with the life of a beloved wife at stake, to say nothing of my own, and so much property, that your skill has enabled us to outride the storm—now nearly over, I think—so unexpectedly well. But what is that, a little to the left of the ship's course, in the distance ahead?"

"Ah, that is it!" cheerily exclaimed the captain, casting an eager look in the indicated direction. "Why, how like a race-horse the ship must be driving ahead! I looked not ten minutes ago, and nothing was to be seen; and now there is the headland, in full view, but two or three leagues distant! And stay,—what is that dark object around and a little beyond the point? A ship? Yes, it grows distinct now,—a large, black ship. That, sir, is an American frigate. Hurra to you, Elwood! We will now soon be safe, and in safe company."

It was about sunset. The merchantman, having passed the protecting promontory, and swept around the tall ship of war, had gained an offing, about a half mile beyond, under the lee of a thickly-wooded, long, narrow island; and was now lying snugly at anchor, riding out the heavy ground-swell occasioned by the abated storm; while all on board, unsuspicious of molestation, were making preparations to turn in for the night.

"A sail to the leeward!" shouted a sailor, just sent aloft to make some alteration in the rigging.

The word was passed below; and the captain, mates, and Elwood, were instantly on deck, and on the lookout. They at once descried a large black schooner, creeping out from behind the farther end of the island against which they were anchored, about a mile distant, and tacking and beating her way towards them. She carried no colors by which her character could be determined; but the very absence of all such insignia, together with the sinister appearance of her long, low sides, which exhibited the aspect of masked port-holes, and also the peculiar stir of her evidently large and strange-looking crew, at once marked her as an object of suspicion.

"Elwood, your fears were prophetic," said the captain, lowering his glass from a long, intent observation. "That craft is a pirate, with scarce a shadow of doubt. But don't the mad creature see the frigate, and the frigate her?"

With this, they all turned towards the ship of war; but she was no longer visible. A narrow vein of land fog, put in motion by some local current in shore, had been wafted out on to the water, and completely enshrouded her from their view.

"I see it all," exclaimed Elwood. "That pirate has been lying, all the afternoon, concealed behind this island; and his spies, sent into the woods on the island, and to this end of it, probably, saw both our ship and the frigate take their positions, and this intervening fog coming on, and reported all to their master; who at once conceived the bold design which he has now started out to execute,—that of snatching us, as its prize, from under the very guns of the frigate!"

A brief, earnest consultation was then held; when, knowing the uselessness of trying to signalize the frigate, they first thought to weigh anchor and try to escape to her protection; but a little reflection told them the enemy would be down upon them before this could be effected, and they would be taken, unprepared for defence. The only other alternative left them was, therefore, quickly adopted; and, in pursuance, the second mate and two seamen were lowered in the life-boat, with orders to keep the ship between themselves and the schooner till they got into the screening fog, and then make their way, with all speed, to the frigate, to invoke her aid and protection; while all the rest should arm themselves with the muskets, swords, and pistols on board, and, if possible, hold the enemy at bay till succor arrived. And scarcely had these hasty preparations been made, before the piratical schooner, which had made a wide tack outward to catch the wind, came swiftly sweeping round to their side, like a towering falcon on his prey. But, by some miscalculation of her helmsman, she went twenty yards wide of them—not, however, without betraying the full extent of her bloody purposes; for as, under the impulse of a speed she found herself unable instantly to check, she swept by on the long, rolling billows, a score or two of desperate ruffians, headed by their burly and still more fierce-looking captain, stood on her deck, armed to the teeth, and holding their hooks and hawsers, ready to grapple and board their intended prey. But, still forbearing to unmask their batteries or fire a gun, lest they should thus bring down the frigate upon them, her grim and silent crew sprang to their posts, to tack ship and come round again, with the narrowest sweep, to repair their former mischance. And, with surprising quickness, their well-worked craft was again, and this time with no uncertain guidance, shooting alongside of the devoted merchantman. Still the crew of the latter quailed not; but, well knowing there was no longer any hope of escaping a struggle in which death or victory were the only alternatives, stood, with knitted brows and fire-arms cocked and levelled, silently awaiting the onset. It came. With the shock of the partial collision as the assailing craft raked along the sides of their ship, and the sudden jerk as she was brought up by the quickly-thrown grapples, the pirate captain, with a fierce shout of defiance, cleared, at a single bound, the intervening rails, and landed, with brandished sword, upon their fore-deck. A dozen more, with a wild yell, were in the act of following, when they were met by a full volley from the guns of the defenders, poured into their very faces. There was a pause,—a lurch,—a crack of breaking fixtures; and the next moment the schooner, torn away from her fastenings by the force of a monstrous upheaving wave, and thrown around at right angles to the unharmed prey so nearly within her clutches, was seen rolling and reeling on the top of a billow, fifty yards distant. At that instant, twenty jets of blinding flame fiercely burst from the edge of the fog-cloud, almost within pistol-shot to the windward, and, with the startling flash, rent sky and ocean leaped as with the concussion of a closely-breaking volley of linked thunder-peals. There was another and still more awful pause; when, through the cloud of sulphurous smoke that was rolling over them, the astounded defenders heard the gurgling rush, as of waters breaking into newly opened chasms, in the direction of the enemy; and they comprehended all. The frigate, unperceived by the eager pirates, had dropped down, rounded to, and sent a whole broadside directly into the uprolled hull of the devoted craft, which had been reduced to a sinking wreck by that one tremendously heavy discharge of terrible missiles. Within two minutes the lifting smoke disclosed her, reeling and lurching for the final plunge. Within one more, she rose upright, like some mortally-smitten giant, quivered an instant, and, with all her grim and hideously-screeching crew, went down, stern foremost, amid the parting waves of the boiling deep.

These startling scenes had transpired so rapidly that the amazed crew of the merchantman had taken no thought of the pirate captain whom they had seen leaping on their deck; but they now turned to look for him, and, whether dead or alive, to take charge of him, to crown the fortunate result of this fearful encounter. There he stood at bay, with back turned to the foremast, facing his virtual captors, with a brandished sword in one hand and a pistol in the other, as if daring them to approach or fire on him. But they were spared the necessity of attempting either. A boat's crew of armed men from the frigate were already mounting the deck, to claim whoever of the pirates they found alive, as their trophies. The formidable desperado was pointed out to them; when, firing a volley over his head, to confuse without killing him, they rushed forward in the smoke, disarmed, bound, and dragged him along, to pass him down to their boat. As he was being urged across the deck, his eyes met those of Elwood. The recognition was mutual. It was Gaut Gurley!

It was morning, and the bright sun was looking down upon an ocean as calm and peaceful as if its passive bosom had never been disturbed by the ensanguined tumults of warring men, or the commotions of battling elements.

A youthful couple were standing by the rail, on the deck of the still anchored merchantman, and glancing up admiringly at the towering masts of the ship-of-war, which had also anchored for the night on the very spot from which she had dealt such destruction to the pirates, whose awful fate and the connected circumstances had been with them the topic of conversation.

"This has been such a fearful ordeal to you, dear Fluella," said the young man, smilingly, "that I shall probably never be able again to induce you to leave home to cross the ocean, either for health or pleasure, shall I?"

"For pleasure, no, my dear husband," affectionately responded the other; "no, with my happy New England home, never, for pleasure, Claud."

"But this was for *health*," rejoined Elwood. "I have never told you how much I was concerned about you last summer, or that your physician warned me, as cold weather approached, he could not answer for your life through another winter at the North. It was this only that led me to urge you to accompany me to Cuba, to remain there till I came back for you in the spring, as I have now done. And, to say nothing of the gains which my two trips will add to the estate of which I am heir in expectation,—or rather, as my good uncle will have it, in possession with him,—to say nothing of this, I shall always be thankful for your coming, for it has so evidently restored you, I had almost said, to more of health and beauty than I have seen you exhibiting for the whole two and a half happy years of our married life."

"Thank you, Claud, for the beautiful part of it," said the happy wife, snapping her handkerchief in his face, with an air of mock resentment; "but I am thinking of home. When shall we reach there?"

"Well, let us calculate," replied the husband, beginning to catch the affectionate animation of the other: "this is the 22d of April; and I think I can promise you the enjoyment of a May-day in New England."

"I hold you to that, sir," playfully rejoined the wife, "for I wish to be preparing for our summer residence at your cottage on my native lakes. My illness deprived me of that pleasure last summer, you know, husband mine."

"Yes," said he, with kindling enthusiasm, "we will go, Fluella. I want to see the good old chief; I want to enjoy the visit I have promised me from my friend Carvil; I want to hear Phillips discourse on woodcraft, and Chanticleer Codman wake the echoes of the lakes by his marvellous crowing. Yes, yes, we will go, and make uncle and mother go with us, this time."

"Uncle and mother!" cried Fluella, laughingly; "how odd that is getting to sound, Suppose I call your mother aunt? Have they not now been married long enough to be both entitled to the more endearing names of father and mother? and are they not happy enough and good enough to merit the dearest names?"

"Yes," answered Elwood, "I will correct the habit, if you really wish it. Yes, yes; the once-styled crusty old bachelor, Arthur Elwood, and my mother, are indeed a happy couple. Did you ever know a happier?"

"Yes, one," replied the hesitating, blushing wife, drawing down her husband's head, and slyly imprinting a kiss on his cheek.

The conversation between the happy pair was here interrupted by the appearance of a boat putting off from the frigate, under the charge of a midshipman; who, having come on board and inquired out Elwood, now approached and presented him a letter, saying, as he departed, it was from the pirate prisoner, and would doubtless require no answer.

The greatly surprised young man tore open the letter, and, in company with his wife, read, with mingled emotions of pain and indignation, the following singular but characteristic compound of malicious vaunt and shameless confession:

"To CLAUD ELWOOD:—My career is ended, at last. Well, I have the satisfaction of knowing that I have been nobody's fool nor nobody's tool. Early perceiving that nine out of ten were only the stupid instruments of the tenth man, the world over, I resolved to go into the system, and did, and improved on it so as to make *nineteen* out of *twenty* tools to *me*,—that is all. I have no great fault to find with men generally, though I always despised the whole herd; for I knew that, if they used me well, it was only because they dared not do otherwise. I don't write this, however, to preach upon that, but to let you know another thing, to chew upon.

"You call me a murderer; and I want to tell you that *you* are the *son* of a murderer, and therefore stand on a par with my family, even at that. Your father, when we used to operate together in smuggling, being once hard chased, on an out-of-the-way road, by one of the custom-house crew, knocked him down with a club, and finished with the blow, to save a thousand dollars' worth of silk. But I sacredly kept his secret; yes, even to this day, besides making one good fortune for him, and being on the point of making him another. And yet he betrayed and turned against me. Yes, in that affair about the missing peltries, he betrayed me, out and out, and spoilt every thing. That was his unpardonable sin, with me. I resolved he should die for it; and he *did*. I didn't want to kill you, but couldn't suffer you to become a witness. No, I never had any thing against you, except for allowing matters to take the turn that drove my daughter to anticipate you in breaking off the match. But it was just as well, as it turned out. Avis, in the position of *lady abbess* of a convent in one of your eastern cities, which it is settled she will have, will stand quite as high, I guess, as in the position of lady Elwood.

"I have done, now, except to ask one favor,—the only one I will ever ask of *any* man,—and that is, that you won't publish my name, and couple it with the unlucky miss-go of last night; so that my wife and daughter, who know I am in this region, but not my business, may never learn that the captain of the *Black Rover* and I are one. As my brave boys are all gone down, and as *I* shall have no trial to bring it out, it rests with you to say whether it is ever to be known or not; for, as I have said, I have no notion of being either tried or hung, any more than I had at the North. GAUT."

On finishing this singular and remorseless missive, with its strange, painful, but as he feared too true disclosure of the secret of that fatal influence which had proved the ruin and final destruction of his father, Claud Elwood was too much troubled and overcome to utter a word of comment; and, with his pained and shuddering wife, he stood mute and thoughtful, until aroused by the stir on board, in preparations for weighing anchor, and the cheering announcement of the captain that a favoring breeze was springing up, and that within twenty minutes they would be, under the fairest of auspices, on their rejoicing way to their own beloved New England.

But the cheering thought was not to be enjoyed without the drawback of being compelled to witness one more and a concluding horror.

As Elwood and his beautiful companion were on the point of retiring from deck, their attention was suddenly arrested by a light, crashing sound, high up the tall side of the frigate. They looked, and caught sight of broken pieces of board or panelling flying out, as if beat or kicked from what appeared to have been a closed port-hole. Presently the body of a man, whom they at once recognized, was protruded through the ample aperture he had evidently thus effected, till he brought himself to a balance on the outer edge. Then came the sharp cry from some one of the frigate's officers:

"Look out, there, for the pirate prisoner!"

There was at once a lively stir on board, but too late. The next moment the heavily-manacled object of the alarm descended, like a swiftly-falling weight, to the water; and, with a dull plunge, the recoiling waves rolled back, forever closing over the *traitor*, the *robber*, the *murderer*, and the *pirate*, GAUT GURLEY!

Milton Keynes UK
Ingram Content Group UK Ltd.
UKHW040044180324
439604UK00006B/973